# DARK LIBERTY

## DON'T ASK, DON'T TELL

### JONATHAN WITTE

Dark Liberty: Don't Ask, Don't Tell
Copyright © 2020 Jonathan Witte

ISBN: 978-1-09830-237-5

## Dedication

To Dorothy Hajdys who raised her son Allen Schindler, a wonderful young man with a huge heart, to my parents and wife who were patient with me and putting up with my issues and helping me through the world, to my children to be proud with who you are (you all have a place in the world), to my shipmates; Szerlag, Knight, J.R., Martinez and Marion who supported me and protected me through the incident…

And to Allen Schindler, my shipmate and one of my shipmates who I served with on the USS Belleau Wood who shared his personal life and stories with me two days before he was murdered. You have saved and paved many wonderful lives after you were taken away from this world. Without you, there would not have been many brave men and women that served openly in our military. You are not a victim to some – you are a hero to many…which unfortunately you paid with your life.

# NOTE FROM THE AUTHOR

Since 1992, my life has been affected by witnessing the horrendous, brutal murder of Allen R. Schindler which has left me continually running away from a nightmarish memory and feelings. It wasn't until 2018 when I was approached by a team of producers recreating the murder for the television show "Deadliest Decades:1990s, Don't Ask, Don't Tell" asking more, undisclosed details about the murder. Though it was extremely difficult to bring these feelings back let alone explain them, I was able to tell my side of the story which has been kept secret for decades.

Several of these producers suggested that I write a book explaining more of the details around the murder given that the story would require more time to explain than one hour of the television series. This book hopefully will provide more details and understanding of why Allen Schindler was murdered.

In 1997, the Lifetime Network created a television movie called "Any Mother's Son" depicting Allen Schindler's mother, Dorothy Hajdys story dealing with her son's death. Although the movie did articulate Dorothy's side of the story and her feelings on how the Navy dealt with Allen Schindler's brutal murder, it lacked the information and details of what happened around the murder.

The Navy was less forthcoming explaining the reasons and situations which led up to the murder, the murder itself and afterwards. This reason was because no one knew – only I knew. I never told anyone about the events except for the NCIS (Naval Criminal Investigation Service) and during the trial of "U.S. versus Terry Helvey" as that would have been extremely difficult to revisit the feeling and the memories of what happened around the time of the murder.

As for the media, they only jumped to conclusions about the details of the murder which were not true or accurate, as their stories were told. They were more interested in the murder and reason itself however, there was much more to that than anyone knew. Only a few of my shipmates and I knew everything that happened before, during and after the murder which I felt the media didn't write, nor did the military. Shipmates who knew Allen Schindler fabricated the story that threw off the investigation and negotiations to prosecute the murderer provided less sentences for accessory to the murderer and more time served in prison for the ones who tried to provide more evidence to further prosecute the murderer.

Not only was it difficult to explain but I lacked the information until I received it in 2018 (26 years after the murder) of the actual NCIS report which shares testimonies from the murderer, Allen Schindler's diary and other witnesses. With this report, I was able to piece the story together to make sense of it all.

I have reached out to Allen Schindler's sister and mother to ask if they could share more insight to him and provided this manuscript for them to read before I published it. They declined however, acceptable with me writing this book and I have done it with full respect to their wishes and was given permission to publish my story around this incident. We will never-ever share Allen's autopsy photographs so please never ask us for these out of the respect for the family and Allen.

With the Investigation Discovery channel was going to air the "Deadliest Decades 1990s" series named "Don't Ask, Don't Tell" in only five months (January 2019), it only gave me a short time to recollect memories, conversations and situations back in 1992 and write a book about it. It would also provide more information which the public lacks hoping to close the book on these chapters.

On another note, I would like to provide a warning to those who are unfamiliar with military life, especially before political correctness became mainstream. The life of a sailor back in the 1990s was not something to write home about and we mostly kept stories of our travels and adventures to ourselves. Such stories can be too strange, violent, inappropriate and sometimes too personal. A lot of what is written in this book may not be suitable for the general public (especially for children) as the contents are sexual in nature (at times extreme) and the language is that of what you may think how sailors talk. If you have heard "curse like a sailor", it is spot-on and valid. The editor/proofreader and I have frequently discussed and debated to either include or exclude graphic details (in sexual, language and situations). There is a fair balance as we want the reader to enjoy this story as well as it being as honest and clear as possible to share the journey.

Though the book is based around the brutal murder of Allen Schindler, I have included my own personal journey leading up to, during and after the murder to provide a setting of an average young man entering the world with innocence and how it affected me during and after the murder. My story sets the stage and perspective on how I saw the world. Upon entering the US Navy, the indoctrination into the military life was unusual, barbaric and exciting. Some of which gave subtle hints about what was going to change many lives forever.

Some names have been changed to conceal their identities however the contents of this book are true based on my first-hand experience and documentation obtained under the FOIA (Freedom Of Information Act).

I hope that you will gain more of a clear understanding of the true events around the brutal murder conspiracy of Allen R Schindler. Writing this book has helped me answer questions that I have been searching for years. It helped me understand the reasons why the "Don't Ask, Don't Tell" policy was put in place, how our culture has changed to be more accepting of others and learn more details about the murder as I hope it will for you.

This is a true crime story, which I witness first-hand and finally share this with you…

# ACKNOWLEDGMENTS

Thank you to the producers and staff at Lion TV and Investigation Discovery Channel for supporting me in writing this book. Thank you to Michael Petrelis for providing information and ongoing determination in seeking justice for Allen Schindler since 1992.

Chip Brown, thank you for getting the details out into the public eye.

Thank you T. Young for confronting me to seek help from the Veterans Hospital. I wouldn't have gone that route if it wasn't for your kind guidance.

Thank you, Dorothy Hajdys for being strong. Your strength is fierce. Only you could have taken on the military, confronting them for the sake of love for your son.

A HUGE 'thank you' to my mother and father for proofreading, editing and advising me for making this book possible.

# NOTABLE PEOPLE

**THE VICTIM**

ALLEN R. SCHINDLER – 22 years old, murder victim, son of Dorothy Hajdys, Petty Officer Third-Class (Rank E4) shipmate stationed aboard the USS Belleau Wood

DOROTHY HAJDYS – Mother of Allen Schindler

**KEY WITNESS**

JONATHAN WITTE – 19 years old, Culinary Specialist (Rank E3) and author of "Dark Liberty"

**THE ACCUSED**

TERRY M. HELVEY – Murderer of Allen Schindler, 20 years old, Airman Apprentice (Rank E3), shipmate stationed aboard the USS Belleau Wood, V4 Supply Division

CHARLES E. VINS – Accessory to the murder of Allen Schindler, 20-years old, friend of Terry Helvey, Airman Apprentice (Rank E3), shipmate stationed aboard the USS Belleau Wood

**SHIPMATES and FRIENDS OF JONATHAN WITTE**

B. SZERLAG – Ship Serviceman (Rank E2)

W. KNIGHT – (name intentional changed) Ship Serviceman (Rank E3)

J. R. – Data Technician (Rank E3)

A. MARION – Culinary Specialist (Rank E3)

F. MARTINEZ (name intentionally changed) – Culinary Specialist (Rank E4)

## THE "FABULOUS FIVE"

K. SIMS – 20 years old, Gunners Mate (Rank E4)

R. EASTMAN – 21 years old, unknown (Rank E3)

C. MALCOLM – 20 years old, unknown (Rank E3)

ALLEN SCHINDLER – 22 years old, Radioman (Rank E4)

(Other member unknown)

## SHORE PATROLMEN

APTIMES – Chief Petty Officer (Rank E7)

K. PARSONS – Boiler Technician (Rank E4)

M. JOHNSON – Operations Specialist (Rank E4)

## OFFICERS COMMANDING USS BELLEAU WOOD

D. BRADT – Captain of the USS Belleau Wood

R. FRANKLIN – (name intentionally changed) Executive Officer of the USS Belleau Wood

## OFFICERS for JAG (JUDGE ADVOCATE GENERAL)

S. MAGGIO (Name intentionally changed) – Prosecuting Attorney, Marine Captain

B. WILSON (Name intentionally changed) – Defense Attorney, Air Force Major

J. SMITH – Defense Attorney, Navy Lieutenant

S. YOUNG – Psychiatrist, Lieutenant Commander

## NCIS AGENTS (formally NIS)

D. W.– NIS Special Agent (name withheld)

K. P. – NIS Special Agent (name withheld)

# LIST OF EVENTS BY DATE

**JAN 00 1991**

Allen Schindler is transferred to the USS Midway

**DEC 00 1991**

Allen Schindler is transferred to the USS Belleau Wood as Jonathan
Witte joins the Navy

**MAY 00 1992**

Jonathan Witte reports to the USS Belleau Wood

**SEP 10 1992**

USS Belleau Wood arrives in Pearl Harbor, Hawaii

**SEP 11 1992**

Hurricane Iniki abruptly changes course from heading west to north
towards the Kaua'I Island in Hawaii

**SEPT 12 1992**

Humanitarian aid is provided to the island of Kaua'i by the crew of
the USS Belleau Wood

**SEP 22 1992**

Allen Schindler relays "2-Q-T-2-B-S-T-R-8" on secured airwaves to
the Pacific Fleet

**SEP 24 1992**

Schindler attends an opened Captain's Mast in front of 15 other sailors. He is Also given a 30-day ship restriction and advised to attend AA Meetings

**OCT 25 1992**

Rumors of Allen Schindler being gay are spreading

**SEP 30 1992**

USS Belleau Wood arrives in Sasebo, Japan as its home.

**OCT 09 1992**

Largest brawl on Sasebo Naval Base spills out into Sasebo

**OCT 24 1992**

Allen Schindler finally gets off the 30-day ship restriction and visits friends in Sasebo

**OCT 25 1992**

Allen Schindler and Jonathan Witte meet in Sailor Town and drink at a bar called "Snack Shipmates" and talk for a few hours about his life on the Belleau Wood.

**OCT 26 1992**

Rumors spread that Allen Schindler and I are boyfriends

**OCT 27 1992**

23:47 Allen Schindler is murdered.

00:43 We lose Allen Schindler's pulse on Albuquerque Bridge in Nimitz Park

00:09 Sasebo Medical Hospital pronounces Allen Schindler dead as precise time of death was difficult to determine.

Jonathan Witte Meets Captain Bradt and XO Franklin to discuss the murder

Jonathan Witte cleans out Allen Schindler's locker containing green journal

**OCT 28 1992**

USS Belleau Wood departs Sasebo for the Philippines

Both Terry Helvey and Charles Vins are apprehended on the USS Belleau Wood and provide their testimonies to NCIS

**NOV 02 1992**

NCIS agents conduct a "Command Authorized Search" to retrieve Schindler's diary

**NOV 05 1992**

Allen Schindler's body is returned home. His mother

**NOV 19 1992**

USS Belleau Wood arrives in Olongapo, Philippines

**NOV 23 1992**

Charles Vins signs testimony against Helvey and is given in exchange for only 78 days in jail

**NOV 24 1992**

Left Olongapo, Philippines, Closed Subic Bay

**DEC 15 1992**

Arrived in White Beach, Okinawa, Japan

**DEC 17 1992**

Left White Beach, Okinawa, Japan for Sasebo (homeport)

**DEC 19 1992**

Arrived back in Sasebo, Japan (homeport)

**DEC 28 1992**

JAG officers find Jonathan Witte and prepare for his undetected
extraction From the USS Belleau Wood and to the Pacific Fleet
Headquarters in Yokosuka Naval Base

**JAN 04 1993**

USS Belleau Wood leaves homeport for Okinawa

**JAN 07 1993**

10:00 USS Belleau Wood Arrives in White Beach Okinawa, Japan

12:00 Jonathan Witte is escorted off of USS Belleau Wood

14:00 USS Belleau Wood Departs in Okinawa, Japan for Pacific tour

**JAN 08 1993**

Jonathan Witte arrives in Yokosuka, Japan, Pacific Fleet Headquarters

**FEB 09 1993**

Charles Vins released from prison and proceeds in being discharged
from Navy

**FEB 21 1993**

Jonathan Witte meets with prosecuting attorneys as the key witness

**MAR 00 1993**

US vs Terry Helvey General Court Martial Trial begin

**MAY 21-27 1993**

Jonathan Witte testifies as the key witness to the murder

US vs Terry Helvey General Court Martial Trial ends and is found
   guilty for the assault and murder of Allen Schindler

**JUN 01 2002**

Each year, Terry Helvey is eligible for parole/clemency

# TABLE OF CONTENTS

# Part 2: The New And Untamed Worlds

# Part 3: How Soon Is Now?

## Part 4: The Contrast In Colorful Humans

## PART 1

# GROWING UP THE SAME

"Boys Be Ambitious"
—William S. Clark (1877)

"SH*T!", I yelled as I just saw 10 seconds of a nightmare. One guy was singing with every beat of his made-up song, he uses his 200-plus body weight and stomps on the torso portion of a body which lays motionless. With each of the several stomps, I see blood gushing out from the laying body's head. Had I just stepped into a movie scene? Was I imagining this? I see another figure stepping away from the action and hide away. As I got closer while trying to grasp what I was watching, the body on the ground and the details of the assailant becomes more clear: someone is being brutally murdered! Knowing that the victim has no way of protecting himself from more stomps to come, my body becomes cold as the night. If it were just a typical fight which I have seen plenty of in high school and the Navy, I would have jumped in and stopped them. But there were two people doing serious harm from the abundance of blood that kissed the walls and fish-eyed window bricks that separated us. I needed help!

I start running away from a public restroom in Nimitz Park, which is located less than a mile away from the Command Fleet Naval Base in Sasebo, Japan.

I had never ran that fast in my life. I remembered seeing three Shore Patrolmen when my senior, PO3 Martinez and I walked into the park after Albuquerque Bridge that chilly night on October 27, 1992 at 23:47 (11:47 PM).

"Someone's getting f**ked up!", I yelled at the Shore Patrolmen as I ran back to them who then immediately flicked their newly-lit cigarettes in three opposite directions away from their preparations to jump into action from where they were sitting on the back of a park bench with their feet on the seat and ran after me to where Schindler was being badly beaten.

As we ran back towards the public bathroom, we were not prepared for what horror that was going to be presented to us…the sight, the sounds and the smell. Nor was I prepared to endure the political effects that led up to, during and after the brutal murder of Radioman Allen Richard Schindler…

# CHAPTER 1

# A SKEWED JOURNEY TO MANHOOD

## 1983

### Breakfast In America

"Crunch…crunch…crunch…slurp…crunch…" Rice Crispies, Capt. Crunch, Sugar Pops, Lucky Charms… The part of our American breakfast. The reading of the cereal box, digging for the plastic toy at the bottom and the silly yet cleaver jokes on the back…

My parents, ex-hippies, cleaning up the house and jamming out to Manfred Mann's Earth Band's "Blinded By The Light" on a late Saturday morning.

A typical breakfast event as I watch a He-man and then Teenage-Mutant-Ninja Turtle cartoons on a Saturday morning, just as any other typical kid growing up in the 1970's. Of course, moms would have made an egg or two served with orange-juice, but at the age from four to eight (or even in their adult age), we preferred our breakfast cereal. It's what made the majority of American kids happy!

From Elementary to junior high school, I played with Star Wars action figures…Or Barbie Dolls…they're the same, just different genders. The both had the same functions and goals – to control, save the world, be a hero and have friends!

To others, they had different purposes in life. We began discovering ourselves with these action figures and dolls. We find friends at school or in the neighborhood that had similar toys, ambitions and purposes, goals in life. They so coincidently happened that if you played with Star Wars action figures, you sided with the boys, you rode your bikes in gangs, you played battles, got dirty, got hurt and went to the side of a neighbor's house you barely knew to drink water from their outside faucet.

Those who played with miniature dolls, dresses and makeup were typically girls who gossiped, always stayed clean, read teen-boy magazines and took up the phone lines talking about whatever the hell girls talked about.. feelings? Rainbows? Whatever...

But they wouldn't be invited to hang with the bicycle gang and jump small creeks and ditches and sometimes our naïve friend who would do anything to be part of the gang...

Video games? What the hell is that!? Online? The internet!? Why the hell stay glued to a device when there are friends, bikes and creeks to jump? The 1980s were all filled with being outside with friends, interacting with others, getting into kid-troubles, running through an old man's yard just to hear him bitch and yell at to us for crossing his yard... That was the great life and so many great memories during those years. We made so many friends, fresh air and ate so many popsicles. Life was very simple and easy to live through for the majority of us. But there were some that didn't have such a wonderful life growing up. I knew a few but have no idea where they ended up. Regardless what kind of crazy sh*t happened at everyone's home, we ALL played outside...And these days we thought it would last forever!

"Faggot!", one could hear quite often in the high school hallways when one guy bumped into another. "F**king queer", you'd hear the other say to maintain the balance of the ever-tilting and escalating hormones of young teenagers. Back in these late 1980s to early 1990s, "Political Correctness" did not exist either in the Webster's Dictionary nor in the American culture so everyone was calling anyone a faggot, queer, gay, retard anything to insult the other. It was such the norm that during these times that when you'd watch an actor make fun of someone who acted gay followed by the canned-laughter.

It was normal during the 1980s to make fun of those who were different from those who rode bicycles and jumped creeks. Gays would be the guys who would play with the dolls – not ride in our gang. Homosexuality was described as a disability by the DSM-III (Diagnostic and Statistical Manual, 3rd version) before it was removed in 1987, so anyone who was homosexual wasn't invited to hang with us...too much of a risk.

And though homosexuality was dismissed by the APA (American Psychiatric Association) in 1987, it was still imbedded into the American culture. There was no the Internet or social media apps to tell all of Americans "that those who were homosexual are just like anyone else".

As far as our bicycle gangs go, homosexuals were not allowed to play with us. They were just 'too strange'. We couldn't relate to them. And the television shows were still making fun of homosexuals. God forbid making it a law, instructing public education, workplaces, TV networks, movies, billboards to make it a legal requirement to allow those who are homosexual to come out and make it a law to accept gays in our culture..."And to allow by law a gay guy to ride in our bicycle gang!? How the heck can we relate to a gay guy!?", the majority of our culture would comment back in the 1980s. But really, what are the chances that there was a gay guy in our bicycle gang? There were only 6 of us ....

A pretty strong chance that one of our friends was a 'homosexual sleeper' hoping to penetrate our cool, neighborhood bicycle gang, according to Statista, a website which collects statistical data and information on various topics, mentions that "Two in 100 American men identify as homosexual, with another four percent of Americans identifying as bisexual". [1]

How could we tell if one of our bicycle gang members are gay? I suppose not in our gang cause we would know simply by looking at them. Were they wearing pink clothing? Walked funny? Wore makeup? Nope, not in our gang. So that means that this 'pink clothes-wearing, walking funny, makeup wearing faggot' must be in another neighborhood bicycle gang.

According to the statistics provided above, there could be a strong chance that 1 or 2 of our members were gay. But there was no way to tell since our belief of what a homosexual would look like wasn't correct.

We never knew if and which one of our members were homosexual or bisexual. We simply carried on with our adventures jumping over creeks, getting dirty, talking about the size of some other girl's breasts, or do our homework. The topic never came up in our discussions. But if one of us acted unlike the other, we would call them a 'faggot' which would result in a cursing battle or challenge. "Jump

---

1    U.S. Homosexuality – Statistics & Facts (https://www.statista.com/topics/1249/homosexuality/)

over that ditch filled with piss and sh*t", one would challenge. The other would decline which promoted the other members to call them a 'pussy' or 'queer'. Otherwise, we would just do what other boys did back in the 1980s.

We did have a homosexual guy in our Irving, Texas school named "Gary". He was clearly very queer and was damn proud of it. So proud that he wore a skirt to school, held his books to his chest as girls did and walked with a woman-like groove as to him wanting to be noticed and liked. We called him "Gary the Fairy". But you wouldn't say this to his face. He was pretty big and strong. He was also was protected and well-liked by the most popular girls in the school. So if anyone was to harass or harm him, you would get your ass kicked and then your reputation would become tainted. So we only watched him happily skip through the high school only to entertain us between our boring classes.

Returning to the statistics – 4-5 in 100 men consider themselves as homosexual and in my high school of 2000 students...there were around 60-80 or even a perfect number of 100 homosexuals that were in hiding or have yet to know or understand their gender identity. Let's confirm that all of us at that age in high school, we didn't know who we were, were becoming or will become.

## We Are All The Same

We are all the same as we grow from a small child to a teenager. We all have the same school, watch the same cartoons, eat the same cereal, and we love our families...As I have mentioned before, we all come from some type of imperfect family. Some families are really dysfunctional in some way but in reality and when we were outside playing with our friends, we were all the same.

High school was quite challenging for me. Any research needed for projects required a bus trip to the library. Repetitive math work was naturally complex. I ended up hanging with a different crowd. Though I wanted to be with the cool and popular kids, my poor school grades, teenage acne and not having my own job or car held me back from achieving. I felt trapped. The vicious circle of doing hard work to the best of my ability rewarded me with a boring high school time with other under-achievers, bad grades and nothing to look forward to. My grades continued to fall. When my parents had found out the scores on my report card, I was grounded…I was continually grounded. And I had 2 more years of this vicious circle to go.

In my junior year in a high school English class, my vicious circle became even worse. My English class had no windows, it was cold, after lunch and the teacher liked to keep the room even darker which allowed a lot of us to take advantage of the moment to take quick naps. The only attentive one was a guy who later became my best friend named "Michael". This guy "Michael" seemed to be having fun! As everyone was napping or actually 'taking notes', Michael would suddenly jump up from his seat and aggressively sniff the air. Everyone would laugh at him and his expression not only from others, seemed very happy. I wanted that expression and feeling.

We quickly became friends and from this point my life seemed more lively and exciting. However, I was headed in the opposite and most dangerous direction in which I still regret to this day.

Michael was the best friend that I have ever had…during that time. Others in school would pick fights and sometimes with me.

Though I lost a few, I stood up for myself and if I needed help, my new best friend was there to watch my back.

## Hajimemashite
### Sometime during the school year of 1989

Towards the middle of this year, I met a girl from Japan named "Yukiko" who was on some type of foreign exchange student program. I met her as I was looking for my elder sister who was sharing the same class.

"Have you seen my sister, Amber?", I nervously asked since she was one of the most sexiest girls I have seen in my isolated city of Irving. "I'm sorry, I do not know who Amber is", she replied in a strong Japanese accent.

The only thing that was in my head besides seeing an image of her naked and smiling, was "let me walk you home this aftern...."

Expecting her refusal since we had just met, "Walk me home", Yukiko replied before I could even finish my request.

That afternoon, I walked her home. On the 3rd time walking her home, I planted a kiss on her lips like a virgin would who is eager, fast and sloppy. "Slow down...", Yukiko said in a very quiet, soothing, feminine, Japanese-accented voice. It was the first normal yet passionate kiss I had. So we know what this means...yup, I'm in love... yeah, right..."Head Over Heels" by Tears for Fears was strongly playing in my head.

Almost every day after school, I would go to her house within walking distance from school and have Japanese snacks that consisted of sweetened rice cakes filled with sweet beans, perfectly sweetened candy and very spicy wasabi beans which her mother served and from then, Yukiko and I would go up into her room and do other things besides homework. It was a daily activity in which brought happiness. It cut into my boring, never-rewarding life and during these adolescent times. I thought I hit the jackpot!

Yukiko and I formed a more serious relationship and we became a couple. It's almost impossible to have a relationship without a car, which I did not have…but Yukiko had a car! It was an amazing opportunity! A great cycle: finish school, walk Yukiko home, get served a snack, make out and then go home right before my parents got home. I was living the dream of a 15-year old adolescent.

All of my years up to my 15th age, I didn't feel like a man. Yukiko however, was like my teacher. Her being 3 years my senior, I looked up to her. To add to my "turning into a man", she advised that I smoked for 2 reasons; 1. She liked the taste of cigarettes when we kissed and 2. She thought I looked like a man when I smoked. Damn-it, she opened the doors to my cigarette addiction for years. But during that time, I felt I was free, happy, respected, smart and paving a great future for my life! "I am man", I felt to myself from this point on. How embarrassing it appears in hindsight.

She also shared photographs of herself with friends in Japan, front of her house, schoolmates in her high school, several vacation trips she took at various places across Japan. I was fascinated with how Japan looked. Besides seeing a few pictures in a National Geographic magazine, the photos which Yukiko shared enticed me to learn more about Japan.

As Yukiko had a car, she asked me to drive her to the local Japanese store in Carrollton, Texas. There was one just down the street from her place in Irving, but we ventured out further as I wanted to learn about Japan as much as I could…even if it was just a small store.

Yukiko and I continued on with our relationship visiting Japanese grocery stores, the Galleria Mall in just north of Dallas and finding secluded places to make out. It was a new and adventurous life which I wanted to continue however, it was soon coming to an end.

The weeks and months followed into the last week of our Junior year at high school. No one was having an end-of-the-year school party…or no one invited me. I didn't seem too popular back in the school.

"The hell with them", I told Michael who then replied, "dude, I'm having a party at my place". I thought it would be some stupid lame-ass party with potato chips, coke and cake…I didn't feel up to it anyways so I replied, "Na, I'm good…I'll just go home and watch a Silver Spoons episode and…"

"Dude…" interrupted Michael, "I have beer and my mom does care…I also can get some pot. My other friends will be there. We will have a great time!", he ended with a true smile. There weren't any other parties anyways and I surely didn't want to go home except to watch television. And a party was something that was better than going home to.

Finally came the last day of my junior year of high school. We had our last examination and quite honestly, I did horribly on the majority of my classes. I didn't care at that time since there was going to be a party!

Since my girlfriend Yukiko was a senior, she graduated earlier and went back to Japan to visit her family. She left her car in my care while she was overseas even though I had yet to get my driver's license.

I drove that car as if it was mine. I stopped taking the school bus and was even more of a man driving my own...er...my girlfriend's car.

I couldn't let my friend Michael take the bus to his house so we both took Yukiko's car to Michael's house party.

There had to have been 20 or more people at the party. A lot of these people were from another school in which Michael had been kicked out from for bad behavior. Everyone was already drinking, smoking cigarettes and a few were smoking pot. This was the first time I ever smoked it. I honestly didn't care since I was supposedly "living the good life as a man". I had barely made it through my junior year, but I made it. I have a hot girlfriend who satisfied me, my own...er... my girlfriend's car, friends, getting buzzed off of beer and pot, I was finally free from the vicious circle of boredom!

## The Acid Trip

Michael and I had these parties so many times. Then that too, became boring. I just lived through it without thinking. Then Michael introduced me into acid or LSD. He passed me a small, square-shaped piece of paper. "This is better than pot. It's absolutely amazing!", Michael convinced me. By then, I was already buzzed from drinking beer and coming off of pot. "just put it on your tongue and let it dissolve...", he instructed me. not thinking about it much and just about sleepy and exhausted, I took it and closed my eyes...for exactly 44 minutes...

"Holy f**k!", I think my mouth or brain said it...my eyes were wide open! I was so amazed to see what I was seeing. I looked down at Michael's living room floor that had already been previously stained from vomit, blood, cigarette ash, beer, soda, whatever the f**k was on the dirty, stained floor was moving like an ocean...gently rolling. I was a bit nervous so I took out a cigarette and tried to light it…I could not for the life of me light my cigarette! "what the f**k………?" my cigarette that in the natural world should be straight…but it started to lean and curve. Each time I tried to move my lighter to the direction of the end of my cigarette, the end of the cigarette would slowly turn in the other direction.

…it was an amazing sight…

The party had ended at about 2am in the morning yet Michael and I were still on acid so we wanted to check other things out while on our acid trip and headed over to the local 24-hour Kroger's supermarket. There inside was a tank full of lobsters. We thought it would be kind of us to let them free so we both reached in the tank with our hands and only took out one each. Our minds changed at that point and compared them to each other. Michael's lobster's legs were moving quite frantically as it perhaps thought that we were going to place it in a pot of boiling water…so we decided to race them with each other.

Sure enough, Michael's lobster was really fast and mine appeared to just lay there and talk to me. "Michael….MI----CHAEL…" I used my ventriloquist-like voice to make it appear that my lobster was talking to Michael.

Though I thought Michael was playing along, he was very serious and began to sympathize with the lobster apologizing to it. "Mi… chael….give me a cigarette, Michael…", I replied using the lobster… Michael pulls out a cigarette and tries to give it to the lobster but the lobster turned away and then stopped. Michael finally realized that it wasn't the lobster and we both laughed so hard and loud that the meat section guy at Kroger saw what we were doing and we ran out of the supermarket, still laughing to the point where we almost threw up.

After catching our breaths from that hilarious event with the Kroger lobsters, we started to head back to Michael's house which was only a block away however, we ended up 10 miles away at a friend's house instead. Michael's mother was furious as he had broken his legal requirement with his P.O. (probation officer) as Michael was not supposed to be drinking alcohol, doing any illegal drugs or being outside after curfew. Michael had been in juvenile court several times for theft, burglary possession of drugs before the age of 17. Though Michael had been arrested for several offences, he was giving probation as long as he is to not do any drugs and honor his curfew. So that is how we ended up at our friend's house, Dougy.

## Dougy's Place

Dougy was an awesome, 20-something guy. It was my first time to meet him and he apparently had his life situated and on a fairly good path to somewhere – own car, nice apartment, decent job, middle-weight boxer who would laugh at anything funny or stupid. He always had a smile and was a very welcoming guy. Even when we knocked on his door at 3:30 in the morning, "knock- knock- knock- knock- knock...... knock- knock", Michael politely knocks on Dougy's door. 20 minutes passed and we could hear some commotion inside.

The door finally opens and this big dude with a big smile on his face in his boxer shorts and Dougy answers, "what happened?"

"I f**ked up and my mom is pissed...", Michael responds. Dougy says nothing and points to the pair of couches in his 1-bedroom apartment. Michael then says, "we can crash here".

And so we did, for the next several days without informing our parents of where we were. To face them now would certainly get us grounded for the whole summer and Michael would go back to jail.

"It'll get better once everything blows over" Michael says. From then, we were dead-out from exhaustion and coming off of our party.

The next day in the afternoon, I called my parents to tell them that I would continue to stay the night with my best friend, Michael. They strongly disagreed and told me to come home. Already being 16 and legally able to drive, I felt that I was already a man and I didn't want to be treated as a little boy – a fact which every parent dislikes to realize.

I love my parents from whenever I could remember to up until my death. Sure, we have had a lot of disagreements which I have always lost however, I finished my junior year and felt that since I was getting laid, could drive, felt respected by people... I have become a man, but a careless one.

"Come home", my mother said. I could tell that she was holding back a few tears and frustration that her little boy was heading in the wrong direction. Still pissed and anticipating that there would be repercussions for not returning home, I hung up. My parents didn't know where I was. They knew where Michael lived and they knew I wasn't there, so all that they could do is pray and just wait for me to come to my senses – which were blinded by all the fun that I was having. And this fun lasted past my senior year in high school, which I had not enrolled into.

Why go back to school and be faced with failure? Why give up a fun life of partying, staying out late, using my car...my girlfriend's car? Tripping on acid, smoking pot, drinking, no homework, no more being grounded and living with Dougy and Michael. It was fun!

Dougy's apartment was the center-most destination. Everyone came to that party and it sometimes became nuisance to a point where our sleep was disturbed. Regardless, if anyone knew anyone that liked to party, Dougy's apartment would be the place.

All sorts of creatures visit Dougy's place. He had a coworker who worked with him in Dallas who was a transvestite. Honestly, I had no idea what a transvestite was until he..she..he…showed up at one of the parties. I wasn't told that he…she…he WAS the transvestite, but I found her a little bit different in several ways. He dressed like an average girl (not like a drag queen), jeans, blouse, carefully-applied makeup and very kind. I was already tired from the night before, so a pleasant "hello" was provided. I don't remember his/her name but he/she went into Dougy's room with one of my friends (you can figure out who).

30 minutes later, he comes out with a satisfied look on his face. After he/she left, Doughy told us that he/she was a transvestite. My friend was surprised, yet it seemed like he was faking the surprised look aligned with his reply, "wha…t!? Na, bro…it was a girl…regardless, we didn't do anything…"

But after that day, we never spoke of it again.

Our stay was becoming an 'over stay' and Dougy hinted that we needed to contribute to either drugs, alcohol, acid, food, rent, etc. We had been there for about a month and didn't think that Michael and I would go anywhere else. We were living the life of freedom. No one knew where we were except for my sister who came to visit me from time-to-time.

## Car Skitzing

Michael suggested that we consider gathering some items and going to the pawn shop to sell these items however, we didn't know from where these items would come freely to our hands. Neither one of us were attending our senior year of our high school nor did we have any savings or money. We needed to make money fast! Dougy and our friends were not going to keep giving us free room, board, etc., forever.

One of the those opportunities came one night at Dougy's place. He had invited just a few friends to smoke pot with us. We were all in our social circles and Dougy lights up a joint, smokes and passes it...past Michael......and past me.

Apparently, we needed to start contributing. Michael and I went out to the balcony and shared a cigarette as we were running out of the cheapest brand of cigarettes known.

"We need to get money and I know how to get some money", Michael excitedly shared with me. "How?", my reply cut short with Michael saying "Let's go to some of the apartments".

At about 2am in the morning, we walked over to the 24-hour Kroger supermarket to get a donut and chocolate milk to fill up our stomachs before we went to work...doing something...somewhere... and then Michael explained the plan on how we can finance our new lifestyle.

"I need you to keep a lookout for me while I check my friend's car", Michael said as we entered an apartment complex across the street from Dougy's place.

I had no reply as it appeared innocent. It's just Michael's friend's car. What so strange about that?

The strangeness was that it appeared that Michael couldn't find his friend's car. He kept randomly going from one car to another car, and to another car, to another, checking to see which car door was opened.

I didn't think much of it, perhaps I was stupid, but whatever. Michael wouldn't be that much of an idiot to steal anything from cars…or would he?

From out of the 15 cars Michael checked, one finally was opened. Not many cars had a car alarm as this was in the 1980s. Michael got into the car and went through the car's glove compartment, under the seat, side of the doors, in the console and the back seat under a minute!

He didn't know what he had but it was something gadget-y, some pot and other small items that would barely make any money at the pawn shop.

"Hold this", Michael said without even waiting for my refusal. "Dude, what? We can't do this!", I said as he kept looking for other unlocked cars to go through.

There were so many close-calls where we would hear a neighbor talk or an apartment door close and open, but we never saw anyone.

We hit about 5 cars and we secretly went back to Dougy's place to inventory what Michael took.

We were happy to have found a quarter-bag of marijuana as during this time in the summer-fall, Texas had a dry-spell for marijuana access. Our profit would increase cause everyone was desperately looking for weed.

We celebrated our finds and smoked a bowl of pot before heading off to bed. We were going to be busy salesmen in the morning and needed our sleep.

The next morning, we placed all the items that Michael got from the cars into a backpack we borrowed from Dougy and walked over to the nearby pawn shop.

Upon entering the pawn shop, we saw boring-ass items such as saws, power drills, construction equipment, a few Game Boys and cassette tapes. Cassette tapes made pretty good money since they didn't have serial numbers and we had a lot of them. We place other items on the pawnshop's glass counter, including a collection of cassette tapes and a few CDs.

Our grand total was about $150. We were successful! Just 30-45 minutes of Michael grabbing items from other people's cars got us $150 and a quarter bag of marijuana! What an awesome return on investment that only cost us less than an hour of our time!

Michael took the money but didn't share with me the money since yea, he did all of the work, but he had another idea.

I was confused with the feeling of personal achievement. There was a tug between being good and being bad.

Being good meant going to high school and finishing my education, but realizing that I was a failure. I missed being with my parents, yet if I were to return home, I would be grounded for life. And during this time, I had called my parents who pretty much wouldn't let me back home until I changed my ways.

I would not change my ways as I was still doing okay on my own. Why go back to all of that failure I had been living through with myself when I had all the freedom and excitement?

## The Neighborhood Plaza

Michael and I bought ourselves each a pack of regular cigarettes (instead of those cheap-ass, nasty-tasting cigarettes), McDonalds meal and then started walking through the shopping plaza.

As we were walking by all of these stores; nail salons, car insurance place, cheap haircut stores, you know, the typical stores you see at the plazas? There was one store that shined – the military recruitment.

The pictures of the successful soldiers, patriots, protectors of our nation, man, they looked cool…but I lacked that "successful" part. I my life was of a criminal or a drug dealer. This was the only type of life I knew and seemed to be really good at it. But I was curious to "Be All I Could Be". What could I be? Could I be in the Air Force? A Marine? Army? Navy? Is there more to life than being a young thug roaming the streets of Dallas?

## Somewhere In Fredricktown, Missouri

A young, 19-year old man named Terry Helvey grew up quite similar to how I did. Helvey grew up running around with the wrong crowd and getting into trouble. Nothing which Helvey had experienced before signing up for the Navy was different from mine or any of my friends. We were basically "boys being boys" on a much extreme level than typical boys growing up before hitting their 18th birthday. Helvey might had known what a lot of us bad-boys got away with being under the legal age without being prosecuted for petty crimes. We had to venture and understand ourselves what we could and not could do and get away with before reaching 18. Though being considered a bad-boy, getting into trouble and fights, he was still well-liked by his friends and helped when he could. No one ever thought of him being a murderer.

The distinct difference between Helvey and my growing up with family however, was much different. It was a lot more dark, sad with ongoing abuse by the male-figures in his life. Though my father was working most of the time, Helvey's father-figures were practically non-existent and occasionally replaced by boyfriends and a step-father, Ron Lynch, who seemed to be a lot worse than his paternal and non-existing father figures.

From Helvey's age of four, his step-father, would take out his frustrations on him psychologically by calling him "Faggot" and "Fag". For a four-year old boy, the connections didn't make sense yet when Helvey was observing Ron's negative behavior, he would brand Helvey as being just that – "A faggot".

As the years moved on, Helvey continued to endure not only the psychological abuse, but also physical abuse. This wasn't a typical spanking on the butt for getting into trouble, they were actual punches from Ron's fists for minor faults of a typical boy who are bound to making mistakes. Some punishments would be executed using wooden paddles and boards. Once, Ron severed Helvey's index finger into a door so badly that it had to be amputated. At times when food was scarce for their family due to the inability to maintain work to support their hunger, Helvey wasn't allowed to ask for seconds. To save money on water usage, he wasn't allowed to use the bathroom and was told to use the bathroom at school or at friends' houses. One day, Helvey couldn't wait to go to school to relieve himself so he let this out in his step-sister (Ron Lynch's daughter), Becky's closet. Several days later, Ron discovered Helvey's feces in Becky's closet and forced Helvey to eat it – which he did, but decides to block out such trauma.

In the years that followed and moving from one family friend's house to another, Helvey found his calling. He wanted to do better for himself and hoped to work with other children who too, experienced abuse to protect them. After graduating from high school and reaching the age of 19, he then joins the Navy.

Besides all the hell and psychological sh*t that Helvey endured, his lifestyle was quite similar to mine, being thug-like and all. We both wanted to do something better with our lives.

# CHAPTER 2

# THE FAULTS

1990

Back in Texas, our friend Dougy was getting serious with his girlfriend and didn't want to totally kick us out since we were all friends, but yeah…Michael and I overstayed and the parties were dwindling anyways. The topic of Michael and I moving out continued, but we stayed a little longer. We honestly were not looking around, instead, we were looking for a place to hang out during the day.

I could continue but most of the next few weeks involved partying, drugs, rock and roll. Then Dougy connected us with another guy, Jerrold.

Jerrold was an awesome drummer in Arlington, Texas. We had hit it off as he and I liked Neil Peart from Rush, who is world's best drummer. Conveniently, Jerrold had a full drum set in his living room, almost the same size as Neil Peart had!

Jerrold played a Rush's "Tom Sawyer" and I was blown away! As picky as musicians are with not having anyone else play their instrument, Jerrold let me play his drums. Naturally, I played "Limelight" that seemed to impress Jerrold.

A friendship was formed.

Jerrold had a whole set of friends we never knew who came to his place to part. This wasn't your typical pot-smoking, alcohol-drinking party. These parties were the ultimate parties! Sometimes Jerrold's parties would cater up to 40 people and then rotate from those leaving the party to new people stopping by to party.

These people would not only bring pot, but they would bring cocaine, heroin, opium, ecstasy, pills, etc. – you name it, they were using it there. I was offered all of them – but I was too scared.

At one point that evening, there was a ruckus back in Jerrold's living room. From what one would hear loud music and drugged up or drunk youngsters yelling happily or talking about their funny stories went completely dead. All that we could hear is Rush music.

I turn into the living room and see my sister laying on her back on the couch crying as everyone stood around her in shock…

"I'm sorry, Jerrold…" The silence of shock went to a few asking, what happened

My sister's right foot was completely inside of Jerrold's living room wall.

"There was a cockroach and I tried to kill it with my boot", my sister said while trying to correct her tears.

"Well, that cockroach is definitely dead, now!", replied Jerrold as he helped my sister get her boot out of the wall.

Immediately, 2 people fell to the floor laughing as the rest laughed along. The rest of the night was uneventful except for people coming and going. Michael disappeared and I passed out on the couch at Jerrold's house.

The next day, I went back to Irving to Dougy's apartment to look for Michael to go back to work at our "business". We were successful for the next few months, then our profit started to disappear little-by-little. Michael had been making excuses to where the money had been going (from "I got jumped" to "I needed to help my mom with money"). But one day Michael just fell off the face of the planet. All the money that we had saved up together all disappeared with him. I was so pissed, yet was happy that I had kept some, a grand total of $80. It was a lot for a 16-year old but not for one who was living like an 18-year old adult.

## Hit Rock Bottom

I tried my best to hang onto that money but it was spent fast on food. Plus, I still had that addiction to cigarettes. I would go to the 24-hour Kroger supermarket parking lot and pick up used cigarettes off of the street and ashtrays. Marijuana rolling papers were more readily available than food so I'd return to Dougy's apartment alone, dismantle the used cigarettes, separating the used tobacco from the yet-to-be-burnt tobacco, place the unused tobacco into the marijuana rolling paper, roll it and smoke it. Ugh!

Eating was a huge issue. I could not face my parents to borrow money. My sister couldn't loan me any money as she had just graduated high school and was off to start her own life. My best friend Michael, disappeared. I could not ask Dougy for money nor eat any of his food. He mostly ate out and never brought food home since he would have 2 sets of starving dog-eyed punks asking for his leftovers...but I had to eat.

Dunkin Donuts was close by. I was hungry. I had enough money to buy just one donut and struck up a conversation with the lady who worked there. She was cool and she was concerned that only 1 donut was going inside my tummy. "Is that all you're going to order? You need more meat on your bones." I remember telling her that I only had enough for one donut.

It wasn't until a few weeks and several visits later that she knew that I was not eating well and kindly suggested that I try to get a job in one of the businesses in the shopping center. I had applied for those jobs but never was able to get hired. Once, Wendy's hired me do make drinks and quit the same day. It was a horrible experience watching the orientation video on VHS on how to make a freaking drink. Here, I had once had all of this freedom and power and now working at Wendy's pouring drinks for people on their lunch break.

I ended up at Dunkin Donuts only to afford 1 donut a day to eat. Nothing else. The clerk at Dunkin Donuts then says, "Every night, I dump donuts into the dumpster that are not bought during the day. You can take as many donuts as you want". I was a little hesitant going behind the Dunkin Donuts eating out from the dumpster but my stomach was very ecstatic!

"I'll take them!", said my stomach through my mouth. I continued to thank her and walked backwards out of the donut store as if she was a queen.

That night, I went dumpster diving and found a bag full of perhaps 40 donuts of a variety of flavors. I grabbed the bag and happily skipped back across the street to Dougy's apartment. Once inside Dougy's apartment, I went straight to the completely empty fridge and aligned the donuts from the bag onto the shelf of the fridge, segregating the different flavors. I was in total heaven!

This only lasted a month or 2 until the plaza began locking the dumpsters. I ran out of money, free donuts and everything else I thought made me happy while the rest of those my age were working on their senior year in high school.

Looking into a mirror, straight into my own eyes, I see complete failure with no food, no money, no friend, no family, no home, no school, no love and no hope for my future.

## Oklahoma City, Okay

Knowing that I could not return home not only because I was personally humiliated with myself but also my parents had given up on me. It was basically the end for me. My parents had been sharing my pitfalls to my father's sister Anne. But I knew little about Anne's lifestyle. I have only heard about her family's lifestyle from my parents – Anne was strict.

Anne was a 2$^{nd}$ grade teacher and her husband worked at the Oklahoma state capitol in Oklahoma City. They had 2 boys, my cousins but only had a 2 bedroom, 1 bathroom house. Unsure if living with them was a good choice, I really didn't have one.

There were a few conditions which I had to abide by:

1. No drugs or drug usage
2. No alcohol use
3. Attend Alcoholic Anonymous
4. Go to school and graduate
5. Help with the chores
6. Attend church

I wasn't much of an alcoholic, didn't have any pot to smoke anymore and living at Anne's house with her family seemed to be a better option than hanging out with my other friends. We would get into trouble anyways. The person that I'd end up leaving would have been my girlfriend, Yukiko. She was supposed to return back from Japan in a few months, but I had no other options for places to stay in Irving. Unable to tell Yukiko that I'm moving to Oklahoma City, I flew on a prepaid flight to Oklahoma City and stayed with my Aunt Anne, Uncle Bruce and her family for quite some time.

A month passed by. My aunt's family adapted to my mullet, piercings which I did myself with a sewing needle. There was no intentions of going out at night since the area which my aunt lived was quite sketchy. Almost every night a police helicopter would fly over with its searchlights shining through the window of the living room where my make-shift bedroom was, instead of my aunt's living room. Anne advised that I should attend an Episcopalian church to be part of her family and be a good example. I was too cool for that. Surely, this stint in Oklahoma City would cut short and I'd soon return to my girlfriend, Yukiko, back in Irving. Perhaps going to Japan would be an option?

Yukiko never made it back to Irving and in fact, she remained in Tokyo with no intentions of ever returning to the U.S any time soon. She went on to start her career as a secretary at Tokyo Prince Hotel, a well-known, five-star hotel. Our last call was quite sad. It was crushing considering that we both were our first love – or was it? …At that age, having sex equaled true love. Yukiko cried and I was trying to figure out ways to get us back together. I promised her that we will meet again. The phone call ended and my last thought of her in my mind, was exhaled

# CHAPTER 3
# SIGNING MY LIFE AWAY FOR THE BEST

## 1991

January 17, 1991: News coverage of bombings in Iraq by The United States was on every TV station. What a fascinating sight of power, patriotism and heroism as our soldiers bombed the sh*t out of Saddam Hussain. The constant media coverage was overpowered with my Queensryche's "Operation Mindcrime" album.

The combination of the "Operation Mindcrime" album and seeing the bombings inspired me.

"I want to go there! I want to be someone!", I thought to myself.

Since I was still finishing up my senior year in high school and my lifestyle at my aunt's house made me feel more comfortable, I'd continue to conclude my promise to her. I really wanted to finish my commitment not only to her and her family, but to my family and myself.

The next week during school, it was abruptly interrupted by an announcement on the school speaker. "Teachers; due to the recent events in Iraq, please allow your students to briefly step out of class whose fathers will meet them at the classroom doors". After the bombing in Iraq, the reservists based close by Oklahoma City were being deployed immediately for a ground war. These reservist had children in my high school. A reservist knocks on the door. The teacher opens it and he walks in and calls out to his child in my class. No words were spoken. The girl whose father walked in immediately stood up, ran to her father and hugged him. The both cried and walked out of the classroom.

This was followed by another reservist coming into the classroom and called out to his son. "Why are you going, dad?", he said in the most weak-sounding voice a teenaged boy could make. "Why?"… They both walked out. Our class was completely silent. The sounds of sniffing, holding back tears from everyone was the only noise heard.

The children of the reservists did not return back to class and spent what leftover time they had with their fathers before they went off to war. Hopefully they will come back – but some never did, so the little time that they had with each other was minimal and respected. It was an absolutely heart-wrenching experience for all of us.

Witnessing this good-bye to their children changed my perspective in life. We have very little time on this planet and regardless of how much control on life we think we have, it can be taken away from us instantly…and without our permission. The respect that I had for the reservist and sympathy for their children changed my outlook in life however, it took months to make the transition from being a drug-dealing thug into a young, successful man ready to make his mark in his life…you know, to be worth something!

Yup, I started to go to church. It was a cool church cause we could smoke inside the breakroom. I smoked with my uncle before and after church. Mostly, I was blind to religion as it made no sense to my life – that was so messed up. Living with my aunt's family however, was a blessing. Perhaps it was God's plan.

The people around me in church, at my aunt's house, at school was quite different than what I had in Irving. There was no power, control or the constant distrust in people to protect myself. Here at their house, there was no need for power nor control. And I could trust everyone. Even at the depressing, smoke-filled Alcoholic Anonymous meetings which I had to attend with real alcoholics, I could trust them.

I was doing better in school, worked on becoming a future architect, stayed out of trouble, I received my 1-year sobriety chip from Alcoholics Anonymous (even though I did not have a drinking problem), became more active at church – and I was finally baptized as an Episcopalian!

I was jamming out to Faith No More's "War Pigs" song getting pumped up in joining the military after I graduated from high school. With only 3 more months to graduate, there was a growing feeling that things were looking up! Nothing was going in the bad direction anymore and nothing could screw things up, now...Until my stupid allergies kicked in. Typically able to deal with allergies, this version kicked my ass and I needed medicine.

My uncle had Nyquil for colds since back then, allergy medication was quite rare to get and I personally didn't have enough allowance which my aunt provided. I took more than I should have but wanted to desperately get rid of this nose draining, coughing and sneezing badly before meeting up with my uncle at my cousin's athletic competition.

"God damn-it, Jon, You've been drinking!", my uncle looked at me sternly and with disappointment.

"No, I had allergies and took Nyquil", I pleaded with my uncle.

"Don't bullsh*t me, Jon. We will talk about this when we get home".

I was both angry but very, very sleepy from the effects of Nyquil.

We weren't able to discuss anything further that night as I had passed out from the over-abundance of Nyquil taken.

The next day, my uncle and I took a walk to a neighborhood park nearby and we discussed my so-called relapsing into drinking.

"You knew the rules and you broke them. You know that once you broke any of these rules, you have to leave".

"I did not drink any alcohol, I swear!", I immediately answered angrily. "Stop bullsh*tting me, Jon!"

My heart sank. I was mostly pissed but sad that he didn't believe me. Perhaps he was tired of having 5 people in a house that only had 2 bedrooms and 1 bathroom. Maybe my lifestyle wasn't syncing with his family. For whatever honest reason, I have failed again even though I believed I was in the right. The opportunity for me to be successful and graduate from high school has ended 3 months short.

"I'll give you one more chance", my uncle said after a 10-minute silence.

I continued to dig an abandoned stick into the grass as if it were some invisible person who had screwed up my whole life. I was tethering the decision of staying, but that would mean my uncle and aunt would continue to not trust me. Or I could just go out in flames and leave. I was unsure who was speaking for me on my behalf, but instantly the words out of my mouth were "I'm outta here!"

We walked back in silence to the house, packed my little things that I had including my new wardrobe which my aunt bought me to replace my punk, thug clothing. The goodbyes were quick yet calm and I was on my way back to Dougy's apartment in Irving, Texas.

"Man, my life is so f**ked up", were the words I had in my head.

## Going Back To Hell

I was amazed to see my mom and dad at the airport. They wanted to see me and figure out what had happened at my aunt's house in Oklahoma City. Hoping to gain sympathy from what happened, they still didn't want me to move back home.

They told me that my friend, Jerome Green was arrested for aggravated robbery and murder of 4 people at the Taco Bell restaurant not far from our house. I suspected he thought that he was one of the guys I used to hang out with.

Jerome Green was indeed my friend. He was a great guy, cool, fun to be with. One never imagined that he would have been capable of doing such a crime. He and another guy named Jessy Miguel forced 4 people into a freezer at Taco Bell and shot them in the head. All of them died in the head, short-ranged included an unborn baby inside one of the employees. They got away with close to $1400.00 but were captured soon-after the murders.

We all know that things get out of hand and things just happen, but what drives them to do such things? I was wondering if my father felt like I was heading in that direction. Maybe he thought that I could have been with Jerome Green…well, I could have been.

God was watching over me. He had something else in mind for me.

## Back At Dougy's

My parents dropped me off at Dougy's. It was embarrassing but Dougy was very welcoming. "Stay as long as you want!", Dougy smiled. I knew at the back of my head that I should do something quick to get out of this mess.

In hindsight, I remembered that the military recruiter mentioned that as long as I didn't smoke marijuana or had any drug in my system, that I would be accepted into the military. Thank God that my almost 1 year in Oklahoma City was a great place to detox all the party-fluids I had been doing in the previous year… and thank God that after the several times I had been checked by the police , I was never arrested. The only factor that was missing for me getting into the military was the lack of my high school degree. I was missing 3 months of school… damn it, just 3 months was needed to get a degree, but since I had been kicked out of the school system in Irving Independent School District. I had no idea how to get it but I truly hoped that the military recruiter could waive this.

## Recruiting Station At The Neighborhood Plaza

The military recruiting station was the 3rd office from the left-side of the shopping plaza. I had frequently walked by it but never walked in – I only called to find out information about 'the prerequisites in entering the military". I slowly opened the door to hopefully figure out if there was a way to get in the Navy. It was a bit dark inside, tan-colored walls with all the military paraphernalia "Be All You Can Be" and Uncle Sam's "We Want You!" plastered on the walls as if they were inspirational pictures. It was a huge contrast to anything in the area that I had seen.

There were a few enlisted personnel inside sitting at the desks. They sat up straight; looked powerful and so cool!

"Hello, recruit!", one of the officers said to me with a serious smile.

"Have a seat!", instructing me to sit down. He was a Navy Ensign with 5 ribbons and 1 medal from achieving something.

"Can..can I join?", as my words got confused on what to ask. "I only lack 3 months to finish my high school degree, I need a GED".

The Ensign leans over the desk where we were sitting, folded his hands together and says, "We have something better than that– a high school degree…"

"No shi…really!?", excitedly I replied.

"The military has a special program for people in your situation. They can send you to a school where they will assist in helping you finish your actual degree in Texas at a fast pace. You can finish your 3 months of education within 1 month!", the Ensign proudly explained.

I was super excited! I had no more drugs in my system, not dependent upon alcohol, no criminal record and most of all – no place else to go!

The Ensign explained more about how the military operates, the Navy specifically, the process that needed to happen before one is shipped off to boot camp.

First, I needed to take a test to determine my intelligence and occupational abilities called "ASVAB" (Armed Services Vocational Aptitude Battery and AFQT (Armed Forces Qualification Test). I scored miserably but I did qualify for a Master-at-Arms (like a cop), a cook and something to do with working on aircraft. The test results were sent back to the Ensign at the recruiting station. He explained that all of the ones that I qualified for started out as the E-1 ranking.

"E" means "Enlisted" and 1 means the very bottom of the ranks. The pay back then in the early 1990s was about $670 per month – not enough to party with. BUT, EVERYTHING is paid for such as medical, dental, haircuts, food, clothing... so $670 per month was for saving or, ahem, entertainment. That amount was very doable. By the way, the amount in 2018 for an E-1 was $1,560 per month – practically doubled! The Ensign added that there was a big demand for cooks and can offer the position as E3 which would provide you with a monthly salary of $843 per month instead of $670 as an E1. That was a no-brainer. I knew I could cook.

"I'll take it!", I answered too quickly. Honestly, I wanted to be a cop which was completely opposite from the life I had so far been in training for, a thug. Given the experience and history I had on the streets, it could be very beneficial to my career if I had become a police officer. But the $200 per month raise and 3 ranks up seemed a lot more enticing at the time. Who knows?

Now, the recruiting process needed to proceed to the next step: Finishing my high school degree – in one month!

My father was proud of my new direction in life, so proud that he drove me down to Elm Mott, Texas, which was just north of Waco. The only things that were there within walking distance was a truck stop, the school and a really bad, run-down motel where I would be staying during school. There were bugs inside the rooms; druggies and transients were living there. Others were there to attend truck driving school. Though it was a terrible place for anyone to stay, I was still determined. My parents took care of me by paying for the hotel, food and visited me almost every weekend. Things were finally beginning to look up for me.

Weeks later I received my actual high school diploma. Proudly holding onto the diploma, my parents picked me up from Elm Mott, Texas and drove me up to the military recruiting station, the MEPS (Military Entrance Processing Station), where a physical determination of potential soldiers would take place. The MEPS provided a pretty nice hotel room as there was going to be a lot of processing and testing to see if I could actually qualify to enter the military.

I was so glad that I had not smoked any pot upon my return from Oklahoma City to Dougy's house. I passed the drug test and prerequisite "butt check", etc. The next day, I was informed that I had passed all requirements and signed the contract to enter the military. I was then escorted into another room that was a lot more formal and ceremonial. The room was filled with plagues, awards, ribbons, all of the 4 branches of the military flags, the beautiful American flag, the Great State of Texas flag and pictures of the First President Bush and Vice President Dan Quayle. There were about 20 of us recruits, standing at attention, looking straight ahead.

Abruptly an officer enters the room.

"Good morning, recruits!", the officer said and introduced himself,

"You all have been the few selected to be part of our great military".

He instructed us to raise our right hand and repeat the oath. I was holding back tears because I knew I had made the best decision I have ever made in my life. I finally graduated from high school with a diploma, drug free, away from the bad environment and have become one of the few and the proud. I became a soldier. My feeling was not complete until I met my father outside and happily told him "I'm United States soldier".

I could tell he was so relieved and proud looking at his son who had changed his life. He had thought that I was going to ruin my life and now, I was someone worthy of his respect. I thought he was going to cry.

He told me that he and Mom had talked and decided that it would be best to move back home with them until it was time to go to boot camp. For the next 2 months, I was finally home reflecting on the journey I had made in the past year. It was a great 2 months getting to know my parents again but this time, as a real man with a real purpose in life.

# CHAPTER 4

# BOOT CAMP ORLANDO

Depending on the deployment date of new recruits, some would go directly to boot camp and others would wait. It wasn't until 2 months later until I had to report to the Orlando Training Center in Orlando, Florida for my boot camp. So I had to report to the military recruitment center at the shopping plaza each day. It was located right across the street from Dougy's apartment where it was evident the parties were still going on. I hid every time I had to report to the navy recruitment station. Strangely, I did not feel tempted to see what my friends were doing. My life had changed since I became a soldier.

After the first week of reporting daily to the military recruitment center/station, I was informed that I only needed to call the center at 8am each weekday. The best part of this was that I was getting paid by the military to wait! But I still needed something to do.

The only place that I could work was at the nearby Whataburger restaurant that was a 10-minute walk from my parent's house. I decided to work there at nights as the pay was $3 more an hour than working at daytime. When my shift ended at 07:00, I'd walk home, take a shower and then call the military recruitment center at 08:00. It worked out perfectly.

My sister had recommended that I work to make extra money for my own going away party, but only with a selected few. By the time I had saved up enough money, she took me to the beer store in Arlington, Texas (again, Irving, Texas was a dry county before 2008), bought a ton of hard alcohol and a keg. We then headed to Jerold's house and set up for my going away to the military party. We unsure of how many people would show up but it appeared that we had enough food and alcohol for 100 people.

Amber suggested that we buy red cups and charge people $3 each and they can drink whatever they wanted. So if 100 people showed up, it would flush-out what I had paid for the drinks - $300.

## Walking It Off

The night came and I had not seen so many people show up for the party. I would guess more than 100 people came!

"Who the f**k are these people!?", Jerold asked out of amazement.

Apparently, someone spread the word and it was a party to remember. Lots of people were there, a DJ and loud RUSH music playing.

Apparently, someone spread the word of a party that would be known as the 'party of the year'...not my going away party, but f**k it... I'll just pretend that it was my party.

"It's my brother's going away party! He's going boot camp!", my sister proudly shouts but only 10 people possibly heard that over the loud RUSH music playing...since RUSH was and still is my favorite band. They simply shout, "YEAAHHHHH!!" and forgot about what the party was actually about as soon as they finished yelling.

It was a great party. Although there was plenty and various types of drugs flying around, it was easier to resist as I had something better to look forward to in a few days.

The party slowly and gradually diminished. Our DJ who would be the one flipping the cassette tape over when the songs ended playing on the broken auto-reverse tape player was passed out and had his finger on the play button. It continued to click towards the end of the tape causing a 'clicking' noise. The leftover carnage of passed out the party members were spread out everywhere; the couch, floor, kitchen and toilet bowl. In the front yard, littered with the red Solo cups, were three bodies that had apparently never made it to their cars (which appeared to have been parked by five-year olds).

## Goodbye Free World

"We Love you", my parent's said as I was entering the gate at the Dallas/Fort Worth Airport at about 19:00 hours. My hands on the military orders mailed to me for me to report for duty at the Orlando Training Center in Orlando, Florida and my other hand around my parents. "I love you, too. Please write to me…" I asked them as we released our hugs.

Strangely, this was when we all cried unlike the other times I left home on a bad note. That made us cry more. Finally, their son was on his way into the military to do good for himself, his family and his country. I could tell that they were proud.

As I walked through the gate, we had a last sight and the sign language of 'we love you'. We were separated by a wall on the way to the airplane and that was the last time I saw them.

## Somewhere Outside Chicago, Illinois
December 1991

Allen Schindler was a six-foot, 180 pounds of confidence. His sandy-brownish hair was meticulously styled and dressed in polo shirts when he was out of uniform which matched his good looks and appearance. He was well-liked and would have given his shirt off of his back for anyone who needed it more than him. He fancied comic books, drawing and writing. Unsure of what he had hoped to be when he left the navy, he had intentions of using the military's Montgomery GI bill for him to attend college, possibly in the creative field.

Schindler's childhood was far from Terry Helvey's in regards to abuse yet he lacked the male-figure in his life. He clung onto his mother with so much love through divorces and difficult times with limited finances and struggles yet he maintained his positive and glowing character, loving animals, friends and family.

Allen Schindler enlisted as a Radioman in the US Navy who was stationed in San Diego soon after his graduation from boot camp in The Great Lakes Naval Training Center in Illinois. While stationed in San Diego, California, he was ecstatic.

Here, he was able to meet new friends, visit more clubs to his liking than he did back home even though he preferred being close to his mother, Dorothy Hajdys. Many of his friends said that he was well-liked, kind, creative and outgoing yet he kept some things to himself.

As a year and several months had passed while stationed in San Diego, he was given orders to report to the USS Midway where he would make his new home. He enjoyed his time there on the ship and met several shipmates who shared the same interests as he did. Learning that the USS Midway was going on its final voyage to San

Diego from Seattle where it was going to be decommissioned and made into a floating museum, he signed up for another 4 years with the Navy. Several months later, in December 1991, he was told to report to the USS Belleau Wood instead, cut from the hopes of sailing with the USS Midway on its final voyage.

He felt a bit cheated however, new opportunities could arise meeting new friends, going on adventures to new places gave him strength. But by then, things began to take a different turn for him which left him less hopeful of making the Navy his career. He and I will meet in the months to come on one of the darkest liberties ever.

## The Last Drag Of A Cigarette

During my 4-hour flight over the Gulf of Mexico, I looked down into the ocean thinking, "that will be my new home". Regretting my decision to join and not knowing what to expect somewhat drove me to go back home. But to what? Though I was frightened leaving my world, my safe zone, my history, my family, my sister and my friends, I had to commit and see it through. My heart continued to race about not know what new world to expect. Short and sudden turbulence only amplified my heartbeat.

Landfall breaks and we begin to descend to the runway. Landed. Exit airplane. I look around and see many sailors in their summer-whites freely and confidently walk around the terminal. I look nearby and see other familiar faces of 'not knowing what to expect'.

In our military orders, it told us to report to the airport USO which are located in almost all of the international airports. A few of us take our last drag of cigarettes and wait…and wait…and wait…

It took about 5 hours before we were picked up from the USO in the airport to get on a white school bus with a government license plate.

We all entered , found a seat and sat down. The bus was packed but no one said a word. Much like any child going to elementary school on their first day of school, not knowing what was going to happen.

It was a quiet and long ride watching palm trees go by. Billboards of Disney World attractions. Somehow, I felt I was going to prison. The Orlando Training Center was well-protected. Barbed-wired fences. Military guards with rifles. You could smell the fear in the bus as if someone had expelled gas. The sound of everyone's' heartbeats were beating faster and faster. The bus stops. A few jump up as if they felt the bus was going to drive off an invisible cliff.

A soldier dressed in a light-brown-colored uniform, with two red-braided ropes circling from his shoulder and arm indicating that he was a boot camp instructor walks on the bus at the front and yells, "Welcome recruits, to the Orlando Naval Training Center! When I say 'go', you will exit the bus and fall in line on the white line right outside the bus! Do not talk! Do not breathe! Do not kiss! And if I see any of you cry, I WILL give you something to cry about! Do you understand me!"

Silence was followed by a few weak, "yes sir…" and the soldier dressed in a light-brown-colored uniform yells, "$%*($##$&%, I'm not a 'sir', I'm a Chief Petty Officer and you will respond loudly to me as 'Aye-aye, Chief Petty Officer! Do you understand me?"

"Aye-aye, Chief Petty Officer!", we all proudly replied loudly.

The Chief existed the bus and we all rushed out of our seats bumping into each other to get off the bus as if a monster was at the back of the bus trying to eat us.

We all got onto the pavement and lined up onto a white line clearly marked "recruits stand here", similar to a red carpet for celebrities. The Drill instructor introduces himself along with a few others who were going to walk us through our first day at boot camp – what to do, what not to do which were all replied by us recruits as, "Aye-aye!". We then were escorted off of our white line and sent inside a narrow hallway lined with painted cinderblocks and a very, shiny polished tile floor.

"Place your manila envelope with your travel orders in your mouth", another chief petty officer instructed us to prevent us from gossiping, complaining, commenting or doing anything that would make a sound from our mouths. He continued, "Sit down, crisscross apple sauce", which we did; one row on the left and another row on the right.

We sat there for a good hour, while feeling the institutional smell whisk by us as other chief petty officers walked by us briskly. Our feet and legs began to fall asleep. Cramps starting to settle in to the lower parts of our legs.

"Get up, NOW!", a chief shouted. We all jumped up. A few of the recruits took too long to stand up which prompted not one, but two chiefs to rush over to these two recruits and start yelling at them. I had no idea what they said as the chiefs were yelling as it was the loudest that I have heard anyone yell in my life! The recruits appeared as if they were going to cry which allowed the chiefs to make fun of them and try to pierce their hearts, "are you going to cry you f**king pussy!? Do you need mommy to come and give you a hug!? Too late!". Another chief steps in and yells, "When we say do something, you do it! Understand, recruit!?"

The two recruits replied, "aye-aye, chief" followed by the chiefs, "what did you say!?" and was again replied louder by the two scolded recruits, "AYE-AYE, CHIEF!!!"

**Note:** Keep in mind that this was in the 1990s, when there were only a handful of females in the military. During boot camp, males and females were separated. We only see them during workweek or occasionally marching off to their PT (physical training). There were assumptions and reasoning to why they keep both males and females separate. Masturbation was obsolete as we were all together; shared the toilets that had no dividers, showers were we showered together and we obviously slept on bunks. So all that we could think about is 'when we are getting out of boot camp' and 'I'm tired'. If they added female integration into the training, well… I will leave that to your own thoughts.

You can forget about political correctness during this time as it didn't exist. And since we all signed a piece of paper that waived our own rights and to be owned by the government, we belonged to ourselves no more. We belonged to the United States Government – we were property of the military. We did what they told us to do. We couldn't be fired and we couldn't quit without any serious and criminal repercussions.

The silence was so thick in the hallway. All that we could hear were echoes from the sounds of drill instructors yelling in the other end and around the corner of the hallways. Certainly I was not the only one who had regretted coming here. This was very scary. No one could fight back. If any one of us got murdered by a drill instructor, no one would have ever known…and we all had 4 more years to go… At that time, I regretted it, whole-heartedly. But there was no escape.

Impossible to back out. Impossible to call a taxi to take me back to the airport with no plane ticket to go back home. There was no reverse. No control-alt-delete. No way to close my eyes and have all that I am in go away. I had to face it. I took a deep breath and simply followed-through to the next steps.

"Fall in a single line – left goes first, then the right line follows the last recruit in the left line and we are going to take a shower. Before you get to the wall next to the shower, pick up a PT bag (Physical Training bag) with your size of small, medium or large, remove the contents of the bag and place it in front of you", the chief instructed.

The PT bags included workout sweats, underwear, t-shirt, socks, flip-flops, tennis shoes, razor, shaving cream, a ruler (which was used for measuring when we made our bunks and perfectly aligning our clothing), wash cloth, towel, a bar of soap, athlete's foot powder and deodorant.

We didn't want what happened to the last 2 recruits who were scolded to happen to us so we executed the command perfectly.

## The 3-Minute Shower

The Chief continued after we emptied our PT bags, "when I say 'go', I want you ALL to take ALL of your clothes off and place them in your PT bag. THEN I want you ALL to take a shower, wash your hair, shave and get dressed in 3 minutes.

**Note:** yes, 3 minutes.

For the next 3 minutes, the only word we heard was "GO! GO! GO!" and everyone looked like ninjas on crack! Clothing was flying everywhere! The contents of our PT bags where dumped everywhere! It was all men for themselves as we rushed into the already-running water in the open, shared-shower, pushing each other to be the first inside. There was no time to conceal your penis or be careful of dropping the soap as we were all too busy trying to wash our bodies as fast as we could.

We rushed out of the shower, some of us slipping and falling onto the floor. At least half of us still had soap on our bodies as we went to the sinks to shave – shaving cream everywhere on our face. Shaved. Cuts. Blood. We rush out of the bathroom and back into the hallway where we started before this ninja fiasco in 3 minutes and got dressed and fell back in line where we were before.

The continued shouting of the chiefs, "GO! GO! GO!" could still be heard echoing from inside the bathroom from the last ones finishing up.

Done. Again, silence. Some of our eyes gaze at the others who have blood dripping from our faces, shaving cream in our hair. All of us mostly wet from not having enough time to dry off. "Let's go!", the chief tells us and we follow the chief into the next room for orientation.

In the next room, we sat in chairs with tables and were told to empty out our pockets and place the contents into plastic buckets. The chiefs inspect our articles and ensure that we have nothing from the civilian world hiding. We then place our civilian items in a postal box, wrote our home addresses on them and left for the next room. A berthing area, which is a room filled with bunkbeds.

It was now 01:00 in the morning and we are told to sleep. No talking – just sleep. And slept, we did.

**03:00 AM:**

"Wake up! Wake up! Wake up!", one of the chiefs yelled as he turned on the light. Though its cliché in war movies, the chief was hitting a yardstick of some sort against the top of an aluminum trashcan lid. He continued, "Wake up! Wake up! Wake up!"

They instructed us to stand in front of our bunks at attention.

"Due to unknown reasons, we have to move to a different berthing area. Let's go! Move! Move! Move!", the chiefs yelled at us.

We grabbed our PT bags and followed in line without speaking.

**03:30 AM:**

We arrived at another berthing area, confused, sleep-dirived and scared. The drill instructors could have just walked us around a little and made us return to the same berthing area just for fun, but we did what we were told. The drill instructors again commanded us, "Sleep!" and so we did.

**05:30 AM:**

"Wake up! Wake up! Wake up!, time for PT!", a new chief wakes us up by banging not one, but two aluminum trash can lids.

"Hit the head and sh*t, shower, shave and get at attention at the foot of your bunks by 05:40". In the Navy and Marines, 'head' means 'bathroom'. We were somewhat relieved that we had 7 more minutes to get ready than we did the night before!

The showers looked the same as the ones we used last night. Taking a sh*t was hard as there were no stalls or dividers –just a row of toilets against the wall. There were 6 toilets and only 1 roll toilet paper… but there really wasn't much time to do the math. This was an insanely odd, non-traditional yet good lesson about teamwork. We did our business and returned to the berthing area.

We were brought outside to a large pavement called the "Grinder" and stood in line. We had 5 lines of bodies, 10 bodies in each row equaling 50 recruits in our division. We were instructed to stretch our right arm out to our right and touch the other's shoulder. Then, we were instructed to extend the same right hand in front of us, touching the person's back. This provided us with enough room for... marching?

Our new drill instructors introduced themselves in the cool, Florida morning night.

"I'm Petty Officer (PO) 1st Class Demers and this is CPO (Chief Petty Officer) Forrest. We will be your mommies and daddies for the next 8 weeks. As a welcoming gift for coming to the Orlando Naval Training Center...Drop and give us infinitive push-ups!"

We started with push-ups, then jumping jacks, then squats, then sit-ups, then back to push-ups...rinse and repeat. We did this so much that we lost count. It was exhausting and honestly, it was the most I have ever worked out in my life.

We were done for our morning workout and instructed to return to our berthing division to shower and get dressed.

## 06:30 – CHOW TIME

"Chow Time!", PO Demers announced. "Fall in line and walk with us outside to the Grinder".

We were super-hungry after all that stress, lack of sleep and that intense workout session. Seriously, super-hungry!

PO Demers laughed in an evil tone and blurted, "When you eat, no talking. There's no time to talk. You will only have 10 minutes to eat breakfast. Don't eat too much cause you'll end up throwing it up after our next workout session!"

You could hear everyone's stomach cry. I think several of us had the thought of eating the person next to us...we were so hungry. We had to wait outside until the other divisions were done eating. That left us to stand at attention, in line for at least 15 minutes as our stomachs growled. All we could do is move our eyeballs without our boot camp instructors catching us to take a look around.

The Florida's sun rose and we were able to get a clear view of our new prison...er...home. The area had a 1960's architectural design. Mostly rocks plastered walls of buildings with gray concrete arches. The grass was so perfectly maintained that it looked like it was fake or candy. One would NEVER cut through the grass and if you did, you would be greeted by several senior officers and sent to "remedial training".

Remedial training was a place that one would go if you f**ked up some minimal tasks or continually didn't listen what you were instructed to do. You would either wax the hallways of the berthing area, clip grass with scissors, and worse of all: being assigned to the mess hall for kitchen duty...basically washing plastic cups and trays.

The most embarrassing and popular remedial training was being the "Bulkhead buffer" in the "Galley" (for you civilians, that's a 'cafeteria'). On all of our ships, we have bulkheads. To pass through any door or bulkhead you had to step a foot higher to cross the threshold. The "Bulkhead Buffer" was an awesome mind-f**k to train recruits to remember the bulkheads on the ship. It was made of a polished piece of brass, the same level as the floor but you had to imagine it was a foot higher and actually step over it. This strange, cult-like event was at the exit of the galley where recruits would drop off their empty trays to be washed.

We finally got inside to where we pick up the trays and simply presented them to the cooks behind the counter. Very simple yet warm breakfast; eggs. Sausage. Toast. Potatoes. Then we headed over to the drink area and selected orange, apple juice or milk. There was no coffee. Coffee was not allowed as the caffeine inside of it was considered a drug. I chose Florida orange juice for obvious reasons.

We ate all of our breakfast and headed to the place where you returned your tray and turned around to exit where we would muster with the others to head back to our berthing area where we were greeted by someone announcing from the ground on their hands and knees.

"Don't step on my bulkhead, shipmate. I work diligently to polish this brass…Don't step on my bulkhead…" a recruit on his hands and knees as he's buffering the brass threshold of the door on the floor. This is the punishment for anyone who steps on that threshold and the only way you could be relieved is when someone else accidently steps on it. Then it would be HIS job during chow time – breakfast, lunch and dinner. Everyone that eats at the galley will see and hear the "Bulkhead Buffer" as there is absolutely no talking or there is hell to pay, so everyone would always hear the "Bulkhead Buffer" yell out loud his instructions. A good recruit will walk-over the door's threshold, as if it were an actual bulkhead on a ship. You would not dare look into the "Bulkhead Buffer's " eyes.

"Thank you, shipmate! You have relieved me from my duties as a "Bulkhead Buffer", we heard one afternoon during lunch from the original "Bulkhead Buffer". You could hear the relief in his voice as if he the lottery.

Thank God it wasn't me...but I must remind myself to not step onto any threshold of a door...

Once we had mustered just outside of the mess hall, we proceeded to the administration building for processing, or as commonly known as "P-days".

## P-Days

"P-Days" are "Processing Days". The military would perform administrative work on recruits, further background checks, x-rays, dental work and address any medical conditions not found during MEPS intake when recruits enlisted.

Some recruits smoke pot or crack-cocaine to celebrate their swearing in the Navy then get kicked out during "P-Days" after taking yet another drug test. This will either result in a dishonorable discharge or medical discharge, depending on the laws that time.

For females, they could have unexpectedly gotten pregnant which could put their boot camp training on hold or discharged medically.

Others have been found to be psychologically unfit for duty such as sleep-walking, multiple personality disorders and back when I was in the Navy in the early 1990s – homosexuality. The military did not hate homosexuals. It was a taboo, a mental disorder and something which no one would want to discuss – especially in the military. The military was not equipped to educate nor provide separate berthing quarters for a 3rd gender. It was already difficult and expensive to provide a separate berthing section for females. Not many people would disclose their sexuality and therefore, not many publically existed as they were in hiding.

For the rest of us who had nothing medical to be questioned, we proceeded with the rest of the processing.

The next stop was to get our heads shaved. I loved my mullet hairstyle and the guy in front of me loved his asymmetric afro.

"Sit down", the barber said who appeared to have the experience of a sheep wool cutter shaved both my mullet and the guy with the afro clean-off under 10 seconds.

We all fell back in line. Everyone looked the same unless you were white, black, Hispanic, Asian, fat or skinny. It was difficult to distinguish who was from a wealthy family, a punk, thug, athlete, geek, loser...nothing! And as we didn't speak much to each other and dressed the same, we were practically the same!

Next, we went off to a very hot, small warehouse only air conditioned by utility fans. Here, we had to wait for quite some time to get our uniforms. The room was quiet and was overpowered by the sounds of the large, spinning fans adding to our sleep deprivation. It was incredibly hard to stay awake. The only thing that most of us were thinking was how pungent the smell of mothballs were. The mothballs were very apparent in aroma which helped maintain the uniforms which were kept in boxes for years from being destroyed by moths or bugs.

Summer whites, Winter blues and dungarees – which were the same clothing which prisoners wore, dark-blue bell-bottom jeans and a blue shirt. The only awesome ware which we received were the P-coats and black sweaters – hoping to God that they wouldn't make us wear them. This was by far, the most boring time in my life as we stood still in silence peering off to those trying to fit perfectly in their uniforms.

Then it's off to medical to get our shots. We would all stand in a row and walk between 2 nurses 5 times (that's about 10 shots). Bam! Bam Bam! And you are done. The worst of them was the "peanut butter" shot that went in your ass cheek. It feels like peanut butter when they squeeze it from the needle into your butt cheeks and for the rest of the day, it's hard to sit down.

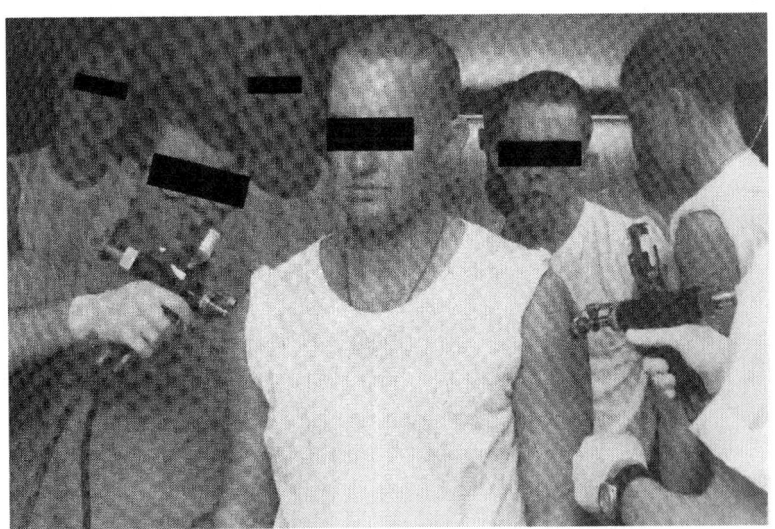

*This is an actual photograph of my C048 shipmates and I walk in line receiving immunization shots.*

It was fast and the most painful part is waiting for your turn. Afterwards, no pain…except for the peanut butter shot. I still wonder what that was.

P-days are very, VERY boring. This is where I learned the term "hurry up and wait" which I have been used to up to this date. In my opinion, hurrying up and waiting was the most painful part of boot camp. You would rush as fast as you could to various administrative and medical offices to end up just standing and waiting. Then you would have to wait for everyone to finish with their turn.

For any man who goes through this, in your future when you are with your significant other, holding her purse as she shops will become very, very easy. Perhaps this is some sort of girlfriend-shopping-training because boy, waiting while my wife shops is nothing as boring as P-days in the Navy!

Once this was completed, we were told to put on our winter-blues sailor uniform, as it was during the winter in Florida. Below, we wore shorts. Strange request but later, this was for our official Navy pictures – one smiling and the other a serious look.

Once P-days came to an end, it was time for more rigorous training to prepare us to be soldiers. I had never worked out this much in my life, but I felt very strong and healthy. Sit-ups, infinitive number of pushups, jumping jacks, running and these combined versions where you would squat, fall to the deck, push your feet back, pushup, retract your feet, squat up, stand, jumping jack and shout "ONE!" we did these 50 times, 4 times a day. We were all buffed!

Marching, marching and marching. Each division has their own cadence and we picked ours from the Adam's Family movie theme song. And we practiced this for the rest of our boot camp time.

"Recruit! RECRUIT!!!, Recruit Littell", PO Demers shouted and rushed towards one of the recruits that just stepped-out a little.

"You son of a bitch! I bet you like other men take turns F**ing your mom and I'm sure one of the losers got your mom pregnant which resulted in your sorry-ass!", PO Demers continued to yell.

"Get over here and prove to your shipmates that you're not a bastard child and count pushups for your shipmates!", PO Demers concludes his scolding.

We all glimpsed at the Recruit Littell appeared as if he just died. His face glowing with sorrow and regret...

PO Demers shouts the one word that has been stapled in our minds to this day...,"DROP!!!", PO Demers proudly shouts to the 49 recruits. And we drop submissively into the push-up position. PO Demers calmly instructs Recruit Littell to count-off as he stands while his shipmates are taking the beating..

"One...two...three...four...", Recruit Littell begins to count off as he stands in shame..

PO Demers shouts over Recruit Littell's counting at 60 as all of us are failing to push up with the counts, "you f**k-up together, you f**k together! You fight together! The man next to you is you! You will never, ever let down your shipmate...and your shipmate will never, ever let you down! He may save your life instead of letting you down by ignoring you!"

"67...67.5.....67.76..." we all continue to sound off our ever-breaking up push-ups. You can hear grunts and a few crying when we got to 110.

P-days are starting to seem like heaven, now.

"Everyone on your feet!", PO Demers instructs us resulting in the sounds of heavily breathing, sweaty men. Recruit shamelessly returns to our crew wanting badly to apologize for letting the rest of us down. Yeah, we were super-pissed, but it could have happened to any of us and upon returning to our berthing area, we never spoke of this again. But somehow, it brought us closer. We are brothers, now.

We supported and helped each other out with cleaning duty, polishing our boondocks (black military, still-toed boots), helping us memorize the chain of command, the UCMJ (Uniform Code of Military Justice) which was a list of military laws which we abide by in addition to local civilian laws. If stationed overseas, we had 2 sets of laws to abide by; UCMJ and the country's civilian laws where we were stationed. There was a lot to learn and prone to making many mistakes. We couldn't do this alone – we needed our shipmates.

## Hell Week

The 4th week begins at 5am before morning chow. Strangely, we didn't start our morning off with PT time on the Grinder...We have heard rumors of this "hell week" and how intense it is that we didn't want to start the day.

"Chow time", our Yeoman (a recruit selected to lead schedules for the crew).

"Eat light, cause if you eat too much, you're just going to throw it up later", PO Demers reminds us.

We walked like zombies outside and lined up on the grinder for morning chow. The costal weather calls for squalls. For some reason, we waited outside on the grinder at attention in line more than we used to... about an hour. It begins to rain. And then what seemed like a tidal wave, it rained on us. No rain coats. No umbrellas. We became part of the stationary scenery of the boot camp just standing in the rain. Our heads heavy from the rain collecting in our Dixie Cup (white sailor hats), we lean our heads forward to empty it. Completely soaked uniforms, we appeared sad but was overcome with our hunger for food and what was yet to come today.

"March!", the Yeoman yells. Large puddles of rain on the grinder is smashed like the remnants of explosion, systematically and in rhythm as we march cadence to the galley.

We enter the galley. Grabbed our trays. Received the food. We sit and wait for the Yeoman to instruct us, "Eat! But we don't, fearing what was ahead of us today. Continued Silence.

We stuff our face with a piece of bacon and a toast.

We head to the tray drop to waste the rest of the meal.

"Don't step on my Bulkhead, Shipmates. I buff the brass", the victim of the newly replaced 'Bulkhead Buffer' yells out at the end.

We line up outside the galley to wait for the others on the grinder.

"No sh*tting today, recruits!", PO Demers yells at us evilly. "This is the day that we determine if you're ready to be a sailor of the finest navy in the world, or still a baby that needs to go back home to mommy…"

We were scared but determined. Pumped.

"Forward…MARCH!", the Yeoman yells and we make our way to the grinder.

"DROP, motherf**kers, DROP!!!", PO Demers shouts and we just dropped.

We were doing all of the exercises that we had been doing since we arrived at boot camp except longer and more yelling. From our last bite at morning chow until lunch, we did all the exercises, non-stop for hours.

Then it was time for lunch. "What, wait!?…that's it!?", we all thought. CPO Forrest confidently says, "That's it! Let's go eat! Enjoy your nice lunch!"

We entered back inside the galley and happily ate our lunch out of relief, stuffed and tummies satisfied. Hell Week was out-faced lie, a rumor. That last PT we had on the grinder before lunch wasn't that bad! We felt confident and sure that we met the Navy's expectations.

The weeks to follow were going to be more educational and attend some classes. We would need to learn how to save those who were gruesomely injured or attacked, First Aid, CPR, learn about types of fires, shoot off guns, learn about sexually transmitted diseases, how to not hook up with prostitutes, identify enemies and potential harms, and other classes.

We were all ready to return to our berthing quarters to tidy up, write to home, chat with our shipmates and any other small details we had forgotten to do before the rumored Hell Week event.

As we march back to our division, we looked in front of our building. It appears that they're moving things out or into our building…but whoever moved these pieces of furniture must have had an accident.

"LEFT, LEFT, LEFT RIGHT, LEFT, left, left. Left righ…..t… lef….t", our Yeoman's voice slowly turns down his guiding march as the closer we got to see this mess in front of our building…

Two bunks were thrown out of our building, sheets, clothing, lockers, all thrown – not placed – were thrown out of our building and onto the beautifully manicured grass. It was a terrible art sculpture awkwardly and hurriedly created on a systematic canvas. It didn't match at all.

"Go upstairs and get on the toe line", Chief Forrest calmly instructed us as if he had reached beyond his limit repeatedly teaching us how to maintain our gear, racks (bunkbeds), folding our clothes and everything which the Navy provided us for boot camp.

Since the first day of our boot camp, we were taught how to fold our clothes. Everything was folded using a ruler (again, that's what that ruler was as part of our gear that they gave us during our P-days) and stacked perpendicularly perfect. Nothing was off 1/16th of an inch. We would get yelled at for not maintaining consistencies and we were punished for this. Our sheets on our mattresses were tucked tightly. If you view one rack and align a long string from the first bunk and took the other end of the string to the last rack of 22 racks, NOTHING was off by 1/16th of an inch! No exaggeration which can be confirmed by other sailors who went to boot camp before 9/11.

After Chief Forrest instructed us to go back to our barracks and stand at attention on the toe line (imaginary line where we line up our toes against), we knew that someone made a slight error, which was a common fear in boot camp besides the Hell Week rumor. If one shipmate made a slight error, everyone was punished.

All 50 of us recruits returned to our barracks and stood on the toe line in front of our racks. A lot of us were relieved that our racks were still there. 4 others, not so lucky. You could see them stand at attention, sweating and shaking at the unknown of what wrath will be cursed upon them once Chief Forrest and PO Demers returned.

"Witte! You're at main watch!", the Yeoman calls me out to take watch at the main entrance to our barracks. Man, I was super-lucky to be assigned to a watch while our drill instructors execute their worst punishment. We have 3 watches that rotate every 2-4 hours; Starboard (right side of the barracks), Port Watch (left side of the barracks) and main watch (the entrance where other officers or visitors would enter and that was my watch for now). Yeah!

PO Demers storms up the stairs and slams open the door at the other end of my watch where only recruits enter and exit for PT, chow and classes, "What the f**k, you piece of sh*ts!?"

It felt as if the lights went out and the sun ran away into the clouds, not wanting to see the humiliation.

"I have f**king told you, a goddamn million times...", PO Demers continues to scold as I continue to check the guest names while standing my watch at the entrance.

"Man, I am so lucky not to be with them. This scolding will last at the most 2 hours and I am super-safe!" I relieved my mind as I stand at an "at-ease" position staring out into the entrance.

PO Demers continues yelling in a disappointed tone, "I don't know what to do... You are f**king embarrassing me! I f**king give up. Just f**king go back home to your slutty mommies".

I continue to look at towards the entrance and I hear several footsteps coming down the hall towards our entrance to our barracks. If someone enters our barracks, they must say their rank, name, social security number and reason for entering followed by "permission to enter". If the reason was not acceptable or they did not follow the universal request which we learned in boot camp, it was our job to yell "Enemy On Deck!". This would prompt all others in the barracks to rush toward and surround the enemy with our hands towards them to prevent the enemy to move anymore forward.

"BAM, DA BAM!" the doors at the entrance flies open and lord and behold, real officers! Not the enlisted like PO Demers or Chief Forrest – these were Ensigns, lieutenants and one lieutenant commander! "HOLY SH*T", my mind bursts the fear inside my brain! The officers rush toward me and only a table with a lamp, a pen, a log book of previous visitors stood between us.

I freaked out with the 5 officers rushing towards me with several lines of ribbons and medals on their chests. I didn't say the typical command to ask the visitors their purpose as they were rushing too fast for me to ask it, so I yelled at the top of my lungs; "ENEMY ON DECK! ENEMY ON DE....", unable to finish as a lieutenant bent over and threw the desk on me hitting my pelvis, wrists and leg.

"GET TO THE TOE LINE!", the other lieutenant shouts at me as the others make their way to my shipmates.

I tried to prevent them from entering and tried to hold one of them by their chest, but he escaped. Nothing more for me to do but go to my toe line.

When the officers joined our boot camp instructors, all we heard was constant yelling by our seniors to each and all of my shipmates to perform the most ridiculous tasks and exercises. There was one shipmate who was going to each of us embarrassing saying with his undershirt collar in his mouth, "This is my shirt. I love my shirt. I will always wear it correctly". Apparently, this shipmate wore his undershirt inside-out. From time-to-time, you would see these recruits with their undershirt collar in their mouths marching about in other divisions as a form of punishment for not wearing their shirt correctly.

Another of our shipmates was the Master-at-Arms (like a cop for our division) wearing a paper Burger King crowned hat on his head yelling at each of us for not listening to him. He appeared to be crying as he got the bulk of the punishment but he was simply exhausted. His body and uniform completely soaked in his own sweat. There was another recruit piggy-backing on another shipmate walking around the room making horse noises. It was a strange experience.

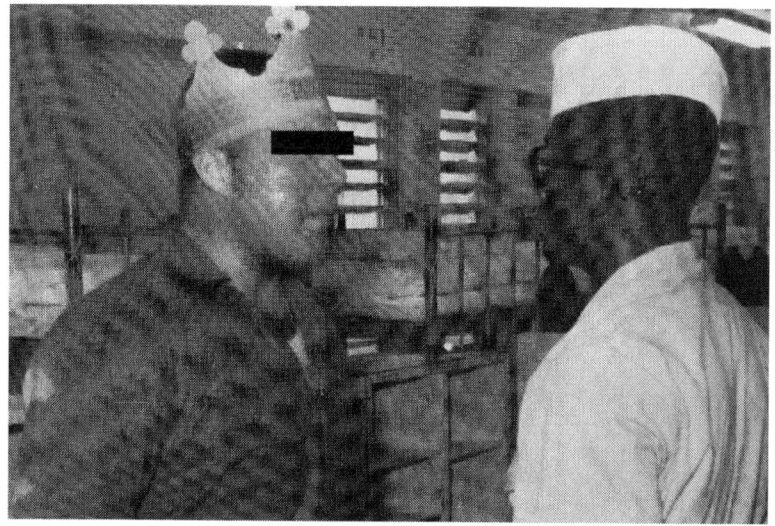

*Our C048 Master-at-Arms wearing a paper Burger King hat, drenched in sweat*

The rest of us were doing PT hard core! Squats, jumping jacks, pushups (and we did over 100!), folding and unfolding our clothes and other strange tasks that I forgot as there were so many of them.

"Keep your head up, recruit!", one of the officers yelled at me while slugging the front of my shoulders. Another one of my shipmates got pushed down to the deck (the navy word for floor) to pick his clothes up that were thrown scattered on the floor by another officer.

"KABOOM!!!", another rack falls victim to an officer who pushes them over to the floor. Clothes, lockers, racks and shipmates are all animated in our barracks. The rumored 'Hell Week' officially begins, except compressed into 10 hours of intense PT (physical training), yelling, pushing, humiliation, cursing…much like a riot where recruits couldn't fight back – only endure. The stench of sweat, heat and regret left in the air as there was no air conditioning and the windows were closed. I honestly thought that we had the worst treatment than those who had been to prison…and this had no end. No one could complain to anyone else superior as we knew that we were government property – easily to be disposed of.

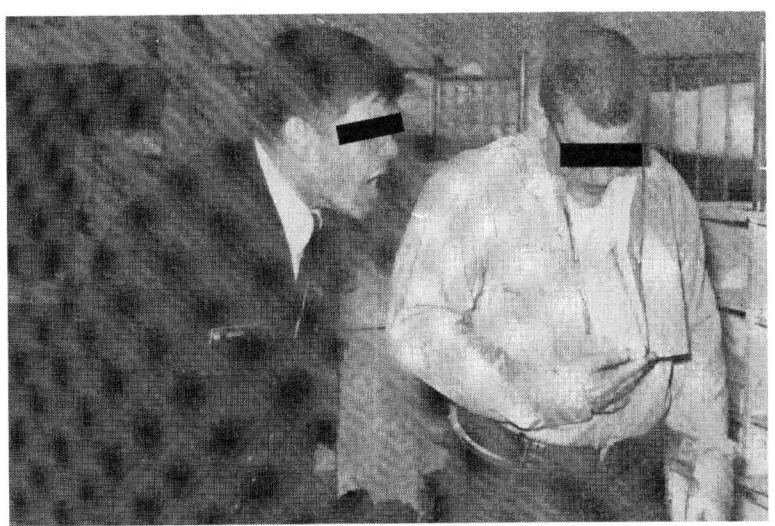

*Another petty officer during our 'Hell-week' yelling at one of our shipmates for not properly folding his shirt. This resulted in not only a scolding but by continually holding his crooked shirt between his chin and chest as a reminder.*

At about 12am midnight, the officers left one-by-one until they were satisfied. The carnage of lockers and racks lay on the deck. Most of us laid on the floor. A few were left squatting on the balls of their feet, hand extended straight with a pencil between their index finger, crying from the pain. We all had done that punishment before and trust me, it's hard and it hurts.

Hell Week (Hell Day), was completed. All of the officers had left. Chief Forrest and PO Demers had left. All those who were left were us recruits. Again, silence. Each of us looked at each other as if we just had a taste of death.

For the next 2 hours, we cleaned up our racks, folded our clothes, try to repair lockers and a few racks, mopped up the sweat and vomit and then took showers. We completely skipped dinner, but that was fine as we had just eaten a lot of sh*t from our seniors and didn't feel worthy to eat. We only wanted to sleep.

During our sleep, I was sure that I wasn't the only one thinking of ......(we all then fell asleep...)

## Work Week (Week 5)

"Good Morning, girls!", PO Demers greeted us in the morning in a cheeky greeting. "This week, you all will need to go to work."

By this time, we were pretty much in routine; Sh*t, shower and shave, fall into the toe line for inspection by our Master-at-Arms recruit (the one who wore the paper, Burger-king crown hat), go to the grinder for PT led by our Yeoman, go to breakfast chow at the galley and report back to our barracks on the toe line for further instruction.

We all got assigned to different locations to assist with the boot camp administration – much like apprenticeship. Some were assigned to the galley, help with new recruits, file paperwork, buffing tile floors and other miscellaneous tasks to help run the boot camp. Such work was also a way to gauge a recruits performance working under instruction and competencies.

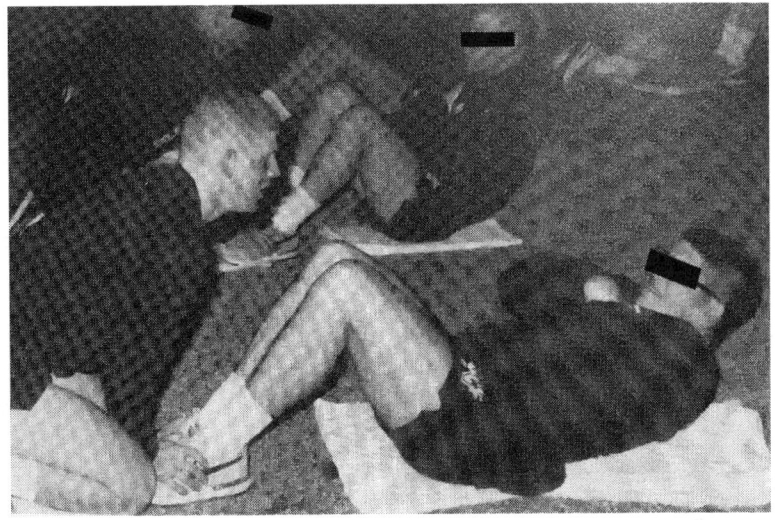

*Me holding my shipmates feet to perform countless sit-ups.*

My job for the week was to stand watch on recruits under discharge processing for those who gave up on boot camp and 'pretended' to be mentally or emotionally disabled. Others perhaps were mentally or emotionally disabled, but that was not for me to determine. My job was to watch and prevent them if they were to find something to kill themselves. Other times, I would have to escort them to the psychiatrist.

The reason I mentioned that they 'pretend' to be mentally or emotionally disabled was that the 3 recruits I was watching told me that they had enough of boot camp. By claiming that they were insane, they would be discharged as "Medically Discharged" which would not negatively impact their work history. If they were not mentally or emotionally disabled, they would be discharged as "other than honorable" or "administrative discharged" which resulted in a negative work history. But, like I said, it was not my job to report this as it was the doctors' determinations.

Some of us had more than one job as well as I did. Master-at-Arms (military police) was the rate that I initially chose but it was a rate as E1 but I chose to be a cook at E3 rank (MSSN) upon graduation. The plan was that once I was stationed on the ship, I would study for the E4 rank (MA3) for the Master-at-Arms position instead of working from the lowest rank. Smart, right? My other job during Work Week was as a Master-at-Arms. I loved it!

Female and male recruits were trained separately, but during Work Week, we worked together…it had been 5 weeks since any of us saw any women and it had been 5 weeks for the girls, as well. If either sex hadn't seen one of the other sex for 5 weeks, cooped up in a prison-like setting and both sexes see each other in a secluded location during Work Week, you can expect what would happen.

Being an MA during boot camp, I was able to go almost every-where, doing my rounds. My supervisor didn't make the effort to check the time that I left or returned from my watch, so I was able to do other 'extracurricular activities' with a female recruit between my posts due to the psychological isolation and simply how human nature runs its course.

After work-week, the next 3 weeks we continued to attend inten-sive classes learning about sexual diseases, how to remove sharp objects from eye-balls, identifying potential enemies, procedures in "General Quarters" (battle readiness) and everything else needed to be soaked into our very exhausted brains.

As for as sleep deprivation goes, it is basically through the whole time we were at boot camp. Some almost dose off while standing at attention. Our boot camp instructors frequently tell us that if we sneeze, cough, must scratch ourselves anywhere on our body to just

– fall down as if we passed out. With the limited sleep that we had, the heat from outside, after lunch and into class in an air conditioned and dark room, watching an old 1968 movie about UCMJ (Uniformed Code of Military Justice), with the lights off, you can easily pass out.

"WITTE!!", PO Demers shouted at me. Let me add that I was not the only one, but for this situation.

"Yes, Petty Officer Demers!", I half-opened my left eye back up.

"Stand up in the back of the room", he instructed me and so I went to the back of the classroom and stood up.

"Damn…I can't stand up anymore…I'm going to pass out from lack of sleep…", I think I dreamt in my head.

PO Demers saw me struggling trying to stay awake as I begin to sway into sleep standing up.

PO Demers grabs a push pin from the bulletin board which probably had been there since the movie we were watching was made in 1968 and walks over to me and whispers in my ear, "push the needle of the push pin between your pinky-finger nail and finger."

The UCMJ has two articles that we are bound by legally:" Article 113 and Article 92 which describes a soldier's obeying instruction, commands, and character on-watch. Without going into much details, it simply means that a soldier can be put in jail 6-12 months, reduction in pay and rank reduction. This depends upon the gravity of the situation and is determined by "Court Martial".

I did not want to be discharged, placed in jail 6-12 months…I wanted to finish boot camp. I was willing to prevent all that I had worked hard on. With only 1.2 months left in boot camp, I had to do everything and anything possible to finish.

"Sh*t, Damn, F**k, Hell!" I yelled loudly inside my head as the others heard me suck air through my teeth loudly. I had pushed only ¼ of the push-pin between my left pink-finger nail and finger but it hurt like a son-of-a-bitch. Admittedly, it worked….however, I had to do this twice. There may have been other techniques to stay awake, but this one worked for me.

## Boot Camp Graduation Ceremony Day

The next day, we woke up, sh*t, showered and shaved then we ate morning chow and got our uniforms tidy and in ship-shape like we have been doing for 8 weeks.

This was it! Besides a couple of recruits that dropped out of our division in boot camp, 48 of us made it to graduation. It was finally here! I was unsure if my parents would make it as they would have to fly all the way from Dallas, Texas to watch an hour ceremony.

We all proudly walked down out of our berthing division and to the grinder. Our flag-bearers held the United States flag, our Division-CO48 flag and all of the 1st place flags which we all won in competing with the other divisions and stood in formation. Ready for our boot camp graduation ceremony.

"LEFT, LEFT, LEFT-RIGHT, LEFT!", the Yeoman calls.

As we entered the position on the field marching with the other divisions, you could feel the power of accomplishments of every recruit. Actually, we were no longer recruits – we were soldiers. The audience was filled with families, friends, spectators, several officers and the boot camp commanding officer.

*CO48, my boot camp division graduation at the Naval Training Center in Orlando, Florida in December 1991*

This wasn't television or an ROTC ceremony – it was an actual ceremony which was very serious. The speech which our commanding officer (the captain of the boot camp) was loud, confident and proud. Though our heads remained in formation (straight), our eyes wandered to our families. A lot of them cried with joy and happiness. And when you see your families cry, it makes you want to cry as well. You could hear sniffles amongst the others marching. We were indeed proud!

The Commanding Officer ended with a final note, "Congratulations completing your training and may God watch over you as you protect our great country…"

As we left the ceremony and the field, our tears of joy, happiness and accomplishments began to dry. We were now ready to go celebrate with our families in our uniforms, but we needed to march over to the visitor's building for our first day of Liberty (or leave, meaning 'time off in civilian life') to meet our families.

After the ceremony, we march up to the gate and as our heads maintained order looking straight yet our eyes wander around the visitor's building looking for our families.

"LEFT, LEFT, LEFT-RIGHT, LEFT...HALT!", our Yeoman yells and we proudly stood at attention. "COMPANY CO48 IS HEREBY AT LIBERTY!", the Yeoman yells and the rest of us yell, "YEAAAAHH!!".

As if we had been gone for years; no cigarette, no alcohol, no drugs, no current music, news, nothing! We were in boot camp, under a rock for the past 8 weeks. We were all so eager to see the new world and our families. But where were my parents?

"Jon...JON, JON!", I hear someone say inside the sea of happy recruits and families hugging each other. "MOM, DAD!" I yelled back when I saw both my parents smiling and heading towards me with open arms.

I could see the tears they were holding back as they looked at their new son who went from a complete, druggie, uneducated, thief, thug and loser to a man who was now proudly serving in the United States Navy.

"Let's go to Universal Studios Florida, Seaman Witte", my father said proudly. And we had a wonderful time catching up and getting to know each other after all of these years. All in a Summer-White sailor uniforms, my parents and I left the Orlando Navy Recruitment Training Center for the night. There was so much to catch up on in my brand-new body and character as if the last Jon had died and another was reborn.

## Last Day At Boot Camp

The last day at boot camp was extremely relaxing. No PT at the grinder, no mustering on the toe line. It was time to pack, clean our berthing area and get our orders to our A-school (Apprentice school) for training.

"Men, gather around", both Chief Forrest and PO Demers calmly asked.

As there were no chairs in existence in boot camp besides inside the galley, all of us sat down crisscross-apple-sauce and looked up at our drill instructors.

"How many of you got laid by the girls during boot camp?", half of us laughed cause some of us did. I was a bit frightened thinking that someone found out about the other female that I met on my rounds during the Work Week, but apparently, it's common. As long as we didn't get caught, it was okay.

"Well, you all are not the first," PO Demers jokingly said and reached for the pile of legal-sized envelopes stacked on a table next to him.

PO Demers continued to call out each of us recruits when he read the names on the envelopes one-by-one. Inside were our orders to report to different A-schools (apprentice school) cross the country. The majority of us were sent to the A-schools in San Diego, California while the others went to Virginia or the Great Lakes in Illinois.

My orders were for sunny San Diego, California.

All of us newly graduated Navy recruits grabbed our gear, said 'good-bye' to our shipmates that we transitioned with from boy to soldier, hit the bus for the Orlando airport and flew home for a week before we reported to our next duty.

...And we didn't look back.

# CHAPTER 5

# APPRENTICE SCHOOL SAN DIEGO

After a week of leave/Liberty in Irving, Texas with my parents, I was to report to NTC (the Naval Training Center), San Diego (now known as a civilian hot spot called "Liberty Station") was now my new home. It was here where a lot of sailors gained their knowledge in their skills before they were stationed on ships all over the world. It was also to become where I would get a much larger taste of reality in the world.

There were a lot of accommodations at NTC; a movie theatre at a discounted rate, bowling alley, pool hall, bars, restaurants, cafeteria, cleaners, barber, you name it – NTC had it inside a recruited military gate restricted to military personnel only.

We felt bad-ass going in and out of the gates. We could get into a fight and hide away on base. Cause any trouble in the civilian world, then run onto base blending in with all the other sailors. We felt we could get away with anything. Just flash our badges and we get in.

It was our A-school which kept us civilized. Our classes were Monday to Friday but we still had a swing-shift to do watch (guard the base, important buildings and our berthing area). One of my shipmates in school and I were positioned at the main gate.

We had rifles that were just simple, one shot at a time. We wore these on our shoulders and was mostly to scare those without authorization to attempt getting on base. Those that were allowed and showed proper credentials with their military ID cards, we would move our hands horizontally across our chess to give them access.

One smart-aleck tried to drive through the gates flashing a folded-up dollar bill in their wallet, but thankfully I caught this before he drove through the gate.

"Halt!", I yelled as he smiled flashing that folded up dollar bill. He continued to drive through. "Enemy on deck!", I yelled and my other shipmate drew his rifle after me pointing at the a**hole and remembering what boot camp had taught me.

"SCREECH!" his tires made as we pointed our rifles at his body.

I was so pissed that he didn't give me a chance to give him the horizontal hand gesture to allow him to drive through.

"Surrender your credentials", as we still had our rifles pointing at him.

We didn't scold him as we were mostly concentrating on getting ready to shoot him. It was a huge rush and I was so ready to shoot. Not on my watch, was I going to let this threat enter my home base.

"Here….here… calm down, Seaman", said the threat and presented a real military ID. His name read 'Lieutenant (name withheld) . But I didn't give a f**k what rank he was. He was a threat and we were prepared to shoot him. He then drove onto base.

Seaman Hughes, who was also ready to shoot the lieutenant said with relief, "Man, I need a f**king drink. It would have been my second time shooting someone…"

"What!?", I surprisingly replied. "Have you shot someone before!?"

Seaman Hughes snapped back, "Yeah, and that's what got me into trouble and landed me here in the Navy."

Seaman Hughes further explained," I was at home when my sister came back crying about breaking up with her boyfriend for cheating on her. I take those issues quite personal since family is family. Then her boyfriend arrives a few hours later trying to take her, so I grabbed my pistol and shot at him – not hitting him directly. Later the cops show up and I get arrested."

"So how were you able to get into the Navy with that criminal offense?", I confusingly asked. Seaman Hughes further explained, "I ended up in court. I did have my sh*t straight and was only trying to protect my family, but the gun was my uncle's, not mine. So it was an illegal discharge of a weapon. The judge saw the personal reason to shoot at someone trying to take my sister away and understood that the law was not on my side so he gave me a choice; go to jail or join the Navy... and of course you can see which decision I made".

I too had a similar issue which I explained to Seaman Hughes, "I was with one of my friends, Jeremy and we were shot at walking across a big field in Grand Prairie, Texas, later to realize that it was private property. Some old geezer yelled at us and Jeremy gave the old man the middle finger. The old geezer gave a few shot and we started to run. One of those shots grazed Jeremy on one of his nipples. I was relieved to live through that with both of my nipples intact".

We were trying to achieve bragging rights to see who had the most wildest lives before joining the Navy which led us to go drinking.

"Let's go get a bottle of Southern Comfort and go walk around drinking", Seaman Hughes suggested.

"Um, I'm only 18. We would get into trouble", I shot down Seaman Hughes' invitation.

"Dude, look at your DOD card (Department of Defense card, also known as the 'military card). Do you see an age on it?", Seaman Hughes said as if I was some dumbass and continued to explain, "If you are old enough to fight in a war, you better damn expect to be allowed to drink alcohol".

1986 was the year which the United States raised the drinking age from 18 years of age to 21 however, if you were between 17-20, you were allowed to drink alcohol on base legally. Though we were not allowed to drink alcohol outside of base, we still did. Regardless of the bars or restaurants, we would flash our military ID and that would mostly allow us to drink alcohol in the 1990s. This of course, depends on the establishment serving alcohol.

It was an awesome benefit which no one told me about and took up the offer to go walk around the neighborhood with my fellow shipmate and drink!

Our watch at the main gate had ended and we ran back to our dormitory to change into civilian clothing. Since there is a Commissary (grocery store on base), we were allowed to buy a litter of coke and a bottle of Southern Comfort.

At 21:00, Hughes brought another shipmate, Seaman Rogers and we placed the drinks into our backpacks and headed off base into some neighborhood across the street from the NTC base.

We lit up our cigarettes, opened and shared the bottle of Southern Comfort by pouring a shot into our mouths and then mixing the coke into our mouths. We shared stories of our home life and how we ended up in the Navy. We raised hell laughing, yelling and talking loud excited to hear about each other's stories. We were quite sure that we woke up or disturbed a lot of the neighbors but none of them would come outside to confront 3 drunken sailors raising hell.

## Run For The Border

We had finished up the bottle of Southern Comfort and our conversation got worn. "Hey, let's go to Tijuana!", Seaman Rogers excitedly suggested. Seaman Hughes added, "There are a lot of 18-year old college students that go there to drink since it's illegal here in the states to drink under 21!"

"Nah…I'm good", I said as I was already getting a little sleepy. The expression on their faces looked quite disappointed.

"What are you, gay!?", Seaman Hughes sharply asked as he had not heard of anyone rejecting an offer to go party.

To me, going far away for drinking was too much work for just a few drinks talking to pretty college student girls. So I explained, "What's the difference going there or going here?"

"To get laid and drink cheaply", both Seaman Hughes and Rogers said as if I was dumb.

"f**k it, let's go!" agreeing with Seaman Hughes and Rogers and dumped the empty bottle of Southern Comfort and the half-empty plastic litter of coke onto some lawn where we had decided to commit in going to Tijuana and headed back towards the base.

A few blocks from us and on the way to the NTC base was a light-rail train station that took people from San Diego to San Ysidro which is a border town just before you get to Tijuana. We hopped on the light-rail train and headed to the border.

Once we got to the last stop in San Ysidro, my shipmates advised eating something at the only establishment back then - Burger King. We picked up a few burgers and fries and headed to the California-Mexico border. On our way there, we saw many, many busses full of South Americans getting off the busses and walking to cars, the light-rail, taxis and by foot. Looking at the ratio, it was every 3 Americans going to Mexico and 100 non-North Americans crossing the border.

"Sh*t, I don't have a passport…", I disappointedly said.

"no need. Your DOD card is an international passport", Hughes insured me. I didn't believe him that much but apparently both Seaman Hughes and Rogers had previously made several trips to Tijuana.

We walked up to the Mexican custom personnel and were just automatically waved-in with no questions asked. They already knew our reasons going into Mexico – to party!

Now in Mexico, we hired a taxi out of what it seemed a million taxis to take us across "Sh*t River" (literally, the river had sh*t in it) and we go out on Revolutionary Boulevard. The Boulevard was lined with clubs, bars, strip-joints advertising their names in neon. This being my first time to Tijuana, I followed the guys into a bar called "Pink Cloud" in the red-light district known as "Zona Norte" (North Zone). Yeah, I should have known what bar I was walking into with that name "Pink Cloud" in Zona Norte, but my mind was busy seeing all of the under-21 people partying. And there were many, good-looking women eyeing us as if we were the only attractive men on the strip. Of course, their intentions were not to start a relationship, but to use one for a price.

As we entered the "Pink Cloud", we saw a stage with mirrors on the ceiling, floors and walls. The music playing back then was "I'm Too Sexy" by Right Said Fred as the loosely-dressed, sexy-looking, cheaply-candy-perfumed Mexican girls danced on the stage centered in the club.

We then sat at a square-shaped table that still left the stickiness of other patrons that had spilled beer or a sweet-mixed alcoholic drink on top. We ordered a pitcher of Tecate beer and returned our eyes at the girls dancing. My memories of my ex-girlfriend popped in my head as I gazed at the dancing girls breasts bouncing.

My gazing at the girls dancing was disrupted by another Mexican dancer who came to sit next to me and asked in a heavy Spanish accent in English, "Drink for me?"

"Hu...?", I confusingly replied.

"Dude, by the girl a drink and she will stay with you", Seaman Roger interrupted and instructing me that this was the first step in getting laid.

"Is she a prostitute?", I asked Seaman Roger who then replied as he rolled his eyes, "uh...yeah..."

"My name is Maria", she said.

"I'm Jonathan...", I replied and honestly didn't want to give her my name as I wasn't all that interested in this sort of business.

Maria's drink arrived at the same time two other dancing friends joined our party. All three of these ladies were indeed hot. The only thing that turned me off from Maria being close and touching me in the 'no-no' area of my body was the scent of her cotton-candy perfume which overwhelmed the stench of the bar.

We continued to drink and boast about us being in the Navy which the girls most certainly were accustomed to. I look up across from me where Seaman Hughes signaling someone from behind me. As I was too busy looking at Maria, I didn't have a chance to confirm to whom he was looking.

"UUGGH!!!", I lightly yelled as two bar guys pulled my chair back at a 45-degree angle, grabbed my head and started pouring tequila and some other hard drink into my mouth.

"Go, Go, Go, Go, GOOOO!" both Seaman Rogers and Hughes chanted loudly as the alcohol continued to pour into my mouth. Yea, I kept swallowing until the stopped pouring the alcohol down my mouth. Then a third bar guy took a kitchen towel around my face and began shaking my head all around, left and right, up and down for a good ten seconds before removing the towel and replace my chair to the correct 90-degree position and then left. It was a strange feeling of excitement and energy!

Laughing, Seaman Hughes asked, "How did you like the 'Tequila Popper?"

"Oh, wow…, WOW…damn I feel good!", I happily replied.

By the time I came-to, I noticed that Seaman Rogers had left. Sailors typically stayed together, so he must have been close-by.

"Where's Seaman Rogers?", I asked Seaman Hughes.

"Upstairs getting his thing taken care of.", Seaman Hughes replied as I was oblivious of what goes on in these type of establishments.

"You're next!", Seaman Hughes replied and continued, "it has all been taken care of."

It was if I couldn't back out of this situation. Hughes was also my senior and had to take orders and tasks at work and outside of work.

This however, was out of the Navy's scope as it was personal. But I didn't want to hamper the environment that we were in and wanted to be like the rest of the guys in the Navy. Seaman Hughes had already paid, so it would have been more awkward to say 'no'. Quite honestly, it had been some time since I had a woman's touch. Why not!?

Maria took Seaman Hughes hint as he nodded upwards to the balcony upstairs. Maria then guided me out of my chair and upstairs. I knew exactly what was going to happen even though I had never had this type of experience. I was horny and ready anyways, especially after that 'Tequila Popper'. The only issue was getting up the stairs as I was getting quite drunk. Maria helped me up the stairs and onto the second floor.

The upstairs was like an inside balcony lined with U-shaped booths. You could see downstairs and the stage where other women continued to dance.

As Maria guided me to an empty booth, I saw other sailors and their dancing beauties having sex in the dark. Pretty soon after beginning the "dance" with Maria, a waiter stops by and I have to give him $5 for a shot. That constant interruption was a mandatory transaction that would continue until I had paid him over $40. Quite intelligent, actually to suck (pun intended) money out of us sailors. All shots were consumed by Maria, who was apparently either very sober or he was pouring shots of iced tea.

It was challenging, but I finally completed my mission and returned to our table downstairs where Seaman Roger and Hughes waited with glowing smiles.

"Let's go back home to the base", Seaman Hughes suggested and we left with satisfied smiles on our faces. As we were heading to the taxi stand on Revolutionary Boulevard to go back to the border, we were approached by a nicely, dressed, 20-something Mexican guy.

"Donkey woman f**k-f**k", he said excitedly.

"What..?", Seaman Hughes asked confusingly.

"Donkey. Woman. F**k-f**k", the nicely, dressed man said.

"I think it's a show where a donkey f**ks a woman", Seaman Rogers said dissecting the broken English.

"No f**king way, man! We gotta see this!", Seaman Hughes excitedly said.

"I don't believe it. Let's go!", Seaman Rogers said as he was leading us with the nicely dressed Mexican man.

I could not compute what had happened nor what we were going to see. Already drunk about to pass out, I should have gone back to the base but I had no idea how to get back by myself. Besides that, I could barely talk, much less argue. I just followed along the excursion deep in the alley of the red light district.

## The Donkey Liberty And The Dame

We make our way into a dingy, 1960s style movie theatre. The smell of sweat and wildlife was so thick that we strained to hold our breath. The room was filled with local Mexican men and a few groups of Marines. All looked serious. We looked very curious. We sat down at our table and ordered a few more beers. 10-minutes pass in silence as we look around the dingy theatre.

Before long, the curtain was drawn back and a donkey stood there with a woman.

SO, let's just say, all the stories you have ever heard about a donkey and a woman in Tijuana is absolutely, positively true. Horrified, we all watched as if it were some traffic accident.

The remainder of the night was like a movie. Our laughing and loudly commenting on what was going on with the donkey and an actress on the stage irritated others who were interested in such an activity. No one complained about our loud laughter except a few Marines who too were calmly watching the event happening on stage. Their complaint was louder than the actresses moans that caught the attention of practically everyone in the room.

"Shut the f**k up, squids!", one of the Marines yelled to us. Of course we yelled back. Three Marines waltzed over to our table. One of them said to me, "Stand up, Squid." I felt that this was intimidating as he stood over me. When I stood up, the Marine pushed me down. I stood back up and shoved the Marine. The Marine falls back onto the wall and right before we started to fight, Seaman Rogers slugged one of the guys which got all of us ready to fight. The Marine I shoved came back to me and swung, grazing my left cheek on my face and I replied with a punch to his throat. Soon after that, all of our fists started flying.

Soon after several exchanges of punches, the Marine who I was fighting with and I backed off from each other. We looked at our shipmates who were already on the ground wrestling. I was ready to take a direct hit back to the face when the theatre bouncers came and got into the middle. "Phew", I thought to myself.

"Policia, we call", one of the bouncers said which prompted all six of us to run out of the theatre together and disappear into the alleys.

"WITTE!", both Seaman Hughes and Rogers yelled at me as they were running in one direction for me to catch up with them. The Marines headed in the opposite direction never to see them again.

Seaman Hughes, Rogers and I ran a few blocks until we got back to the main strip on Revolutionary Avenue to catch our breaths.

"Damn, that was close. We need to get out of Mexico", Seaman Rogers said. "if we get in trouble, we will be heading to a Mexican prison and you don't want that..."

As we made our way down Revolutionary Avenue, we encountered a Mexican street cop from across the street. He looks at us as we had guilt painted all over our faces.

Seaman Rogers mumbles what guilty characters in television and movies say after committing a crime, "..Act..natural...don't run..."

A taxi separates the space between the cop and us and the driver asks us in broken English, "need ride?"

"Hell yeah", Seaman Hughes says as we all dive into the backseat of the taxi.

"To the border!", Seaman Hughes exclaims as we all laughed and sighed with relief.

We finally arrived at the Mexican-American border. A little boy stands tall playing a child's guitar, strumming with all his heart to no notes or chords known to man. His mother sits crisscross-applesauce on a blanket, asleep. He and his mother have been at the Tijuana-side of the border all day trying their best to make ends meet selling trinkets and souvenirs from Mexico.

We all had $5 leftover and the little boy melted our hearts playing his guitar and placed each of our $5 in his collection cup.

We walked away looking back at the little boy in satisfaction from his expression gleaming excitement. We accomplished something better than the crazy night we had.

We all had $5 leftover and the little boy melted our hearts playing his guitar and placed each of our $5 in his collection cup.

We walked away looking back at the little boy in satisfaction from his expression gleaming excitement. We felt that we had accomplished something better than the crazy night we had.

We got back onto the light-rail and took a quick nap back to the base. Everything went dark.


"Wake up, sailor, you can't sleep here", said a voice standing over us as we woke up next to the commissary. I didn't respond as I had to get an understanding of where I was and where my other shipmates were. I could not remember how I had gotten back to the base. All that I remembered was passing out on the light-rail.

"We just rested a little", I heard another voice to the right of me. I looked for that voice and saw Seaman Hughes was wiping his vomit off the side of his face. Seaman Rogers was nowhere to be seen.

"Ha ha ha ha! You guys had fun last night, didn't you?" the voice said standing over us. He was an MA (Master-at-Arms) making his rounds waking up sailors like us who had painted the town and crashed on base. We all knew how to get back to base, but we sometimes can't find where our barracks are. As long as we made it back to base before our mustering (reporting to rollcall).

"Sh*t, where's Rogers?", I said worried either that we had wandered off or we left him stranded somewhere.

"Rogers went back to his barracks but you and I were hungry and decided to wait for the commissary to open, get a bite to eat and head back to the barracks before mustering.", replied Seaman Hughes.

"Well, the store is open and you shipmates can't be sleeping here", the MA instructed as he helped us up.

Sailors work hard and party hard. This was true up until after the tragic events on 9/11. Finding sailors passed out drunk in strange places was not uncommon. Nowadays, not so much. If sailors were to be punished for drinking too much and passing out, the majority of sailors would be in jail. As long as there were no altercations, issues, damages, or serious crimes and as long as we reported for duty and muster, we were okay. I was one of these sailors and this trip to Tijuana was one out of many I took while at A-school.

The MA informed us that it was 07:00 and that we needed to eat and muster at 09:00 so we picked ourselves up, got a bite to eat and headed back to our barracks to take a shower, dress and prepare for mustering.

Our crazy sailor days in A-school were soon to be completed. We had to finish our MO (Military Occupation) education as we were prepared to finish school in 2 weeks. I was enjoying these days and nights in San Diego, but soon was all going to end and we were going to be assigned to our ships. As long as we stayed out of trouble and completed our A-school, we would be fine.

## Choose Your Rate, Choose Your Fate

On our last day at school and after our final exam, we headed to our senior officer's office to learn about our final grades.

On our way down the hallway towards our senior officer's office, we heard a man cry and agonize from the bathroom.

"Ahhhh, huh u hu…", we hear echoing from the head.

A few of us go inside and we see one of our shipmates sitting on the left side of his butt while holding onto a toilet bowl. We then hear him cry again and vomit. When he did this, we saw that he soiled himself. He looked as if he was exploding from every whole from his body.

"Don't eat street food in Tijuana…wwwooooooaaa", the poor shipmate advised us and finished his sentence vomiting even more in the toilet bowl.

"Wahahahaha!" the three of us laughed out loud while witnessing this shipmate suffer was hilarious. We did feel sorry for the shipmate and took him to sickbay (clinic) in the adjacent building that caused us to be late to learn about our exams. But he is our shipmate and we need to help each other in time of need.

This was rewarded with our senior officer delaying the exam final report learning of our efforts. Our sick shipmate scored the top rank out of our class, believe it or not and was able to choose his destination where to be stationed.

"Whaaaat!?", I shouted out with surprise. "We can choose our destination!?", I followed up with my exclamation.

"Yup!", the senior officer replied. "the higher your exam score, the first pick you have of the available destinations.

"Sh*t…", I said silently to myself. I took more effort drinking in Tijuana than I did studying. Honestly, I really didn't care where I would end up. But on the list of available destinations that stood out from other places like Hawaii, Alaska, Virginia and California were both Sasebo, Japan and Yokosuka, Japan.

The majority of the other shipmates that scored higher than I were fighting for stateside destinations. Only 1 spot was available in each Sasebo and Yokosuka, Japan.

As the shipmates who scored higher than I ticked-off the destinations, I remembered Yukiko and her being back in Japan and wanting to be with me again. But in our youth ages, it was not easy to make the trip to each other's' country alone. This could be the opportunity to be together again! This was fate! But I didn't remember where she lived. Yukiko had shared some of her personal pictures of her hometown which struck my curiosity in visiting Japan. It was very different from the states. I revisited those afternoons after high school where we would go up to her room, listen to Japanese pop music, eat snacks, have sex and look at the pictures of her back in her Japanese hometown. Who knows? Maybe I could meet her again? If not, Japan seemed like an awesome place to visit. Europe didn't seem to be that interesting to me. Asia wasn't really part of the American culture and was overrated. I wanted adventure. Asia was calling me.

I looked on a map next to the destinations which the other shipmates were checking-off as their names were being called in order from the highest score to the lowest and looked at the country of Japan.

Sasebo is a small town nestled inside of Nagasaki, the second-most southern part of Japan. Yokosuka was situated south of Yokohama, which is south of Tokyo. I just couldn't remember where she said she lived. My name was coming up next to tell our senior officer where I'd wanted to be stationed. My heart raced as I tried to decide, "Sasebo? Yokosuka? Sasebo? Yokosuka?..."

"Seaman Witte, you're next! There are only a few places left. Choose your destination!", the senior officer asked.

"Sir, can you give me a moment? I cannot decide yet", I pleaded with him.

"Seaman Witte, if you cannot decide in the next 5 seconds, I'm going to make that decision for you!", the senior officer commanded and began counting down, "5….4…3…2.."

"Sasebo, Sasebo, sir", I interrupted him.

"Clip, clip, shuffle, clip", went the sounds of several stacks of paper and placed in a large manila envelope.

My fate was sealed. The next day, I was ordered to report for duty at the Naval Surface Forces just down the street from the NTC. My feelings shared both regret for choosing the wrong Japanese city and excitement about the new adventure that I was going to partake in.

As my other shipmates were walking out of the senior officer's office and building, I heard them asking each other about where the other shipmates were going to be stationed. We all wanted to be stationed on a bad-ass aircraft carrier like the USS Ranger where the Top gun movie was based on or a deadly, bad-ass ship like a destroyer.

Though being stationed in Japan interested me, I too, wanted to be stationed on a large ship. The bigger, the better.

## PART 2

# THE NEW AND UNTAMED WORLDS

*"Ah, but a man's reach should exceed his grasp, Or what's heaven for?"*
—Robert Browning (1885)

# CHAPTER 6

# THE USS BELLEAU WOOD LHA3

After my 5-week A-school in San Diego, California, I was to report to my permanent ship: the USS Belleau Wood. The USS Belleau Wood was ported along with 13 other ships just right down the street off of Harbor Drive at the Naval Surface forces.

"Next stop, Naval Surface Forces…San Diego", said the military shuttle driver as we arrived at the front gate. Five of us grabbed our gear and stepped off the shuttle confidently and prepared to report to our new ship. We had no idea what kind of ship the Belleau Wood was…Small, large, boring-looking, awesome-looking like a battleship, we had no idea except we knew that it wasn't one of the most bad-ass aircraft carriers that we all wanted to call our home.

We were told by the military shuttle driver which pier out of several that we needed to head for and we began walking.

Three of the shipmates headed for another direction as they were to report to a smaller ship and another guy named Seaman Marion or "Rat-boy" (a lot of our other shipmates called him "Rat-Boy" ,but his closest friends called him Marion) and I headed for the other pier.

"Are you going to the Belleau Wood?", Marion asked.

"Yep", I replied as we walked together. Towards the pier where our new ship was ported.

We walked a ways, perhaps a 10-minute fast walk. We didn't want to run to the ship as if we were new recruits, but we were excited so we walked briskly towards the ship.

We paused. We awed.

The mass of the ship peaks 14 floors through the maze of 2-story repair buildings. As we walked closer, the length of the ship spanned more than 2 football fields. It was one of the most powerful things that I had ever seen that it slowed my approach as if it were a monster waiting to eat me. It was called the USS Belleau Wood, LHA3, a Tarawa-class amphibious assault ship. And it was bad-ass!

*USS Belleau Wood returning from Deployment to the San Diego Naval Warfare Base*

The USS Belleau Wood housed 930 officers and sailors, shipped 2,000 marines and their equipment to any place in the world. The Belleau Wood also carried 30 helicopters and AV-8B Harrier jets that would land vertically. The length of the ship was 820 feet, width was 106 feet and displaced 40,000 tons of bad-ass!

The USS Belleau Wood was nicknamed the "Devil Dog" from Germans during the first World War who referred to the Marines as "Teurfelshunde" or "Devil Dogs" for their intense fighting in one of the epic battles of that war. Since the naming of the ship in 1973 (coincidently one month after I was born). Since then, the USS Belleau Wood has been on many missions and exercises during its deployments. It also had a reputation for being one of the roughest ships in the Pacific Fleet.

*The USS Belleau Wood's official mascot which is displayed on the forward of the island of the USS Belleau Wood*

The history or the reputation didn't seem to frighten me. It wasn't really a choice for me or anyone else who was stationed on the ship. I personally was happy to be part of a large ship. I could also handle any issues with my shipmates, troubles with my seniors or situations that I may experience.

Small vehicles driving about, welders welding, sparks falling onto other parts of the ship and its deck, sailors cleaning the outside of the ship or touching up with paint, trucks unloading equipment, trucks loading and sailors restocking, a whistle sounding off of officers going aboard the ship or basic and scheduled announcements…It looked very similar to science-fiction space movies when their space ship is docked, being restocked and ready for its next deployment.

My part in the USS Belleau Wood now seemed very important and depended on me to do my best. It was an amazing sight and an amazing feeling. I had never felt so excited in my life!

Quickly reflecting on my previous bad years doing drugs, getting into fights, trouble with my friends back in Dallas was NOTHING compared to the sight that was in front of me – the USS Belleau Wood was indeed a bad-ass thing to see.

As we walk towards the cat walk which takes us inside the ship, we hear Nirvana's "Come As You Are" playing from a utility truck driving by us. Coincidently, I was coming as I am.

"Make a hole!", the driver of the utility truck said as he zipped by us, making us lose our step and our awe as we walked towards the second gate to the pier.

The ship appears to get bigger, larger, more powerful as begin our ascend up the 4 flights of stairs on a 'gangplank' (a small bridge that connects the shore to a ship). We see the American flag gently waving from the harbor wind that hanged off the side of hanger deck. The humming of the ships engines were quite apparent. The closer I got to the ship, the louder and more powerful it appears.

Marion and I stop and salute to the flag then proceed to the ship's OOD (Officer Of the Deck) who we saluted to again.

## Welcome Aboard

The OOD stands on the Quarterdeck and checks those coming aboard or going ashore. He makes sure that those who are restricted to the ship (Liberty Card taken away), stay on the ship. And those who come aboard must have the Ship's ID card to pass through the OOD and the Quarterdeck. All personnel stationed on the ship were provided both a "Liberty" and "Ship" card.

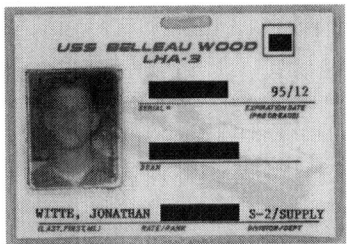

*USS Belleau Wood Ship Card (left) and Liberty Card (right)*

"Seaman Witte, reporting for duty", I saluted followed by Seaman Marion, "Seaman Marion, reporting for duty".

The OOD then took our military orders from our hands that we received from our A-School and said, "Ah, you are both are to report to the galley....Timmy! Timmy!", the OOD said to another sailor who had just passed us by. His name was not 'Timmy', but due to his long, hard-to-remember name and that he was one of the shortest sailors on the ship, he was called "Timmy".

The OOD continues, "Take these new sailors to the S-2 Division's berthing area and get them situated"

"Yuu gais com wid me", Timmy said with a strong yet kind Filipino accent.

Marion and I followed Timmy into the hanger deck.

The smell of aged oil, gas, steel, iron, grease, sweat and the sea wind gently made its way into body and soul. Straight ahead locked 3 AV-8B harrier jets to the deck with large chains to keep them stationary at sea.

Barely lit, the hanger deck also housed missiles, fuel and engineers maintaining all the complex parts of the ship and jets. I was amazed with all of the activity and deadly equipment and machinery were so animated in a limited space.

Timmy, Marion and I make our way by one of the AV-8B Harrier jets and I touch the low-hanging wings. "This thing that I am touching flies and bombs targets", I said to myself in awe.

We continue down to the galley. The smell of institutional food lingered along with the jet fuel, oil and steel.

We turn right past the galley down through a "Portal hatch" (an entry point that connects lower and above decks) with steep stairs leading down to our berthing area.

## Muster

The smell of steel, oil, pine oil cleaner and a boys high school gym locker room. Sets of bunks, 3 levels for each sailor stood closely next to each other row-after-row. We were amazed to see so many bunks squeezed-into a small room.

"Yu take any abailable bunku but not boddum bunku – dat por senior bunku", Timmy tells us. The seniors with a higher rank had first pick of the bunks and preferred the lower bunks to get into quickly without climbing into the 2<sup>nd</sup> or 3<sup>rd</sup> level bunks.

I quickly grabbed the middle bunk as it had easy access to stow away my gear. I didn't mind climbing into the middle bunk. The top bunk was too high for me to stow anything and required a high climb into the top bunk.

I stowed all my gear and clothing underneath the mattress door that opened-up, closed it and locked it with a Master Key lock claiming it 'mine'.

Timmy waited until we were done and instructed us to change clothing,

"Changie to yur dungarees. We muster at 14:00."

Confused to where anything was in the berthing area, I asked, "Where do we change our clothing?"

Timmy laughed and suddenly got serious, "Yu changie here en de space".

Just like boot camp, we still get naked in front of everyone. The whole ship was practically a freaking high school gym locker.

Marion and I quickly changed our clothing in the open and went to look for the 'head' (bathroom for navy and marines) to pee.

Across the narrow hallway was a recreational room with a small 20" tube TV hanging off the corner of the ceiling and wall. There were 2 small tables with chairs to play cards and 2 fake-leather and plastic chairs that were attached to each other allowing 6 sailors to sit on to rest.

The room adjacent to the rec room was the head. Inside the head were 4 sinks with mirrors, 4 toilet stalls separated for privacy and 4 shower stalls. If you needed to sh*t-shower and shave in 10 minutes, this was very complimentary. All sailors who were sh*tting, showering and shaving would most definitely touch one another when the ship was at sea and moving. Definitely too close for comfort, but we are all men and no women to tease our penises when we are at sea for months at a time.

After changing into our dungarees (Navy work clothes) and freshening up, we went back up to the hanger deck where we mustered. When in port, we muster once a day, but at sea, we muster three times a day to ensure no one is sleeping or fell off the ship. It was also to see how many of us returned for duty or to see who went A.W.O.L. (Absent With Out Leave) or were stuck in the Tijuana jail for causing trouble – something that squids (Navy sailors) and jarheads (Marines) habitually did.

"Count-off!", our division Master Chief Petty Officer Cusaga commanded us. One-by-one, each sailor in our division would count off as we stood in 2 rows at attention. I was the 3rd one to count-off and Marion was the 5th.

"Fresh meat", I heard one of the sailors behind me in my division say quietly as a few others snickered. This was my first day and wanted to present a good impression to my shipmates.

"Shut the f**k up, faggot. You're going to get us in trouble", I heard another say.

"Wat the god-damn madda pucka did ju say!?", Master Chief Cusaga scolded the ones that were talking. Yup, another Filipino with a heavy Filipino accent. Master Chief Cusaga continued to scold our division shipmates in the back row, "Ju god-damn madda puckas jus shut da fak up".

A few giggles returned at Master Chief Cusaga's cursing in a heavy Filipino accent. Master Chief Cusaga also smiled and giggled a bit.

Just like thousands of other Filipinos who joined the Navy, they worked hard to become American citizens. Yup, they had green cards and promises from the American government to provide them American citizenship in exchange for 7 years of active duty in the military. We loved working with Filipinos in the military. They had good hearts, worked hard, usually religious and the majority were Catholics. We really didn't care if they had green cards or not. They had the same goal and purpose in the Navy which was to protect America and our allies.

"Git to worku!", commanded MC Cusaga and we all reported to our stations except for Marion and I.

New to ships and at a lower rank, we had a task to perform. It was both like an initiation and a way to learn about the ship. Marion and I were scared, nervous and overwhelmed being assigned to the ship. Unfamiliar with the culture of the team and the ship, our brains and hearts were pure, if not previously tainted.

## Steam Shells

"Hey shipmates, I need you guys to do something first...", a senior one rank above me instructs us. "go collect 3 steam shells; 1 from the ship engine, 1 from the anchor room and the last one from the state room…GO!"

Marion and I freaked out when our senior said 'go' and we tried to collect the 3 steam shells.

We first went back through the hanger deck, to the stern of the ship (the end part of a ship), then down 4 levels to the engine room.

It was a very loud area. There were large hopper-like cylinders that held steam which ran the ship; heat, power, for the ship's propellers. Everyone was wearing headphones to protect their ears.

"Do you have any 'steam shells'?", Marion asked.

"G$*FJLDJLJFLDWPD, here!", yelled back one of the engineers as it was extremely noisy from the engines.

"What!?", I asked back loudly.

The engineer got closed to my ear so I could hear better, "There aren't any 'steam shells, here".

Unsuccessful, we decided to return to the engine room later and head off to the anchor room.

It took us about 20 minutes to walk to the forward of the ship to the anchor room. Without anyone giving us directions to the anchor room, we would have gotten lost as the ship was very, very large and room limited (2 football fields long, 14 stories tall) It was a labyrinth!

Right before we entered the anchor room, we entered the weight room.

"Looking for 'steam shells', shipmates?", a shipmate asked us as he was working out.

"Yup", Marion replied.

"You guys just went on a wild goose chase", the shipmate laughed and informed us that we were naïve and fell for the typical-new-sailor initiation.

"Those f**kers…", I quietly told Marion and we tied to make our way back to the galley area where we were supposed to work.

Once we made it back, all of our shipmates in our division laughed and snickered.

"Sh*t, we got a few dumbasses on our crew", said one of the ship-mates in our crew.

Marion and I couldn't reply back as we just fell for the ship's oldest tricks in the book.

"Jou dum-ass mader phukers…leabe dem alone, phucker…Marion, Witte, go get the stock for the galley", MC Cusaga instructed us.

Just a few blocks away on the same deck, we retrieved stock for the galley. This was our job for the next 3 weeks before we set sail for Pearl Harbor.

During the minimal, one-potato-two, tasks that we were assigned as new sailors, we made friends. And these friends new how to party in Tijuana, too! Much like we did when we were in A-school.

It was a cycle; work hard, finish your watch (walking around the ship and ensuring it was safe and secure), withdraw money from the Navy Federal Credit Union, take the light-rail down to San Ysidro, take a taxi to Revolutionary Avenue, get drunk for cheap, get laid, try to behave crossing back into the United States, get back on base, act sober as much as possible when you got on the ship and log in with the OOD on the Quarterdeck, try your best to find your bunk, sleep off your hangover, wake up with a hangover, take a shower hungover, muster hungover, work hard, finish your watch…and so on.

As the days got close to shipping out to sea for our new port in Sasebo, Japan, we did this almost every day! What else could sailors buy at sea? There was no alcohol and no women to entertain our needs. A lot of us thought that we would ship out to some war and never get to spend our money that we save while at sea, we became experts to spend every last penny of our $600/month pay.

The day before our departure for Japan, we were restricted to base. No one wanted to be left behind and having to pay an expensive one-way commercial flight from San Diego to Sasebo, Japan…but we needed to drink as much as possible before we shipped out to sea where there was no alcohol, so 99.9% of the ship's crew headed down the pier to the Waterfront Recreation Center conveniently located on base.

*The USS Belleau Wood (left) in port at the San Diego Warfare Naval Base in 1991*

The smell of warm beer, sweat and ashtrays filled the room. Half of our division walked together inside and needed to stick together in case any one of us get out of hand or wander off. We hit the bar to pick up 2 beers each and watched the other sailors dancing on the wooden dance floor. I have never seen such sausage fest in my life. There had to been sixty sailors inside and maybe two girls who served our last mainland American beer and food. It was a ridiculous sight to see!

"Man, we won't be seeing this any longer," PO3 Martinez sighed.

"What, men dancing!? Are you f**king gay?" another PO3 in our division laughed. We all laughed. We knew what PO3 Martinez meant, but we took what he said out of context. We were all having a good time.

PO3 Martinez was a Mess Management Specialist and my direct supervisor. He was of Spanish decent and carried on the cool, calm and matureness of a man who grew up at a young age to help his family financially. He would never speak ill of anyone. If there was ever an argument or disagreement, he would completely stay out of the situation unless he was dragged into it. He would easily diffuse conflict and execute it professionally. He was quite young yet held a higher rank than I did which could have been reflection of his hard work and maturity.

His smile was light otherwise would render a subtle expression. His persona was calm. If anyone would have felt troubled, they would simply stand by PO3 Martinez and one would feel calm. All around, Martinez is a great guy and a good supervisor.

"Well, you would be surprised to know that there are some faggots on our ship", Another PO2 continued. We had thought it was just a joke, but our fun became a little concerning.

"Dude, why are you talking about this!?," the other PO3 asked disappointedly and looked at both Martinez and I and continued, "you know, if you know of anyone that is gay, you don't want to be associated with them and you must report it or you will get in trouble… possibly kicked out of the navy with a other-than-honorable discharge".

PO3 Martinez ended the conversation with a, "just shut up and drink your beer…"

We all slammed our 3rd beer and ordered another round.

"Head Like a Hole" by Nine-Inch Nails started playing and everyone went to the dancefloor to let out our 'goodbye to the mainland'.

# CHAPTER 7

# BECOMING SALTY; OUT TO SEA

The Boatswain of the USS Belleau Wood blows the whistle informing us that Captain Douglas Bradt, the commander and leader of our USS Belleau Wood has come aboard our ship. Everyone shuffling, pushing and commanding others in preparations for launching our Amphibious Assault Ship.

Captain Bradt was an experienced Navy officer who joined the Navy shortly after his graduation in 1966 and had served in the Vietnam Campaign from 1969-1970 with 110 combat missions flying various aircraft including F-14s and FA-18s. He looked like anybody's grandpa – not fat, not thin, a smile behind his aged and gray mustache. When you were in his presence, you could sense his importance in the navy. Under his command and the sailors who served beneath him saw him as a celebrity and sometimes as a god. It appeared cult-like however Captain Bradt earned his medals and respect from his military career. One would think twice before calling him out on a mistake. One would rather make his mistake their own.

Second in command of the USS Belleau Wood was Captain Robert Franklin, also known as the "XO", shortened for "Executive Officer". Captain Franklin was a photocopy of Captain Bradt however a bit shorter, no gray hairs and less experienced. For unknown reasons, we seemed to fear Captain Franklin more than Captain Bradt he spoke more than the Captain Bradt did when executing orders or communicating with his subordinates. When either Captain Bradt or Captain Franklin got onto the 1MC to communicate with the crew of the USS Belleau Wood, they sounded calm, confident and professional. Captain Bradt's reputation was 'a cool man' and was nicknamed by the majority of the young sailors as "Dad".

*Captain Douglas Bradt presenting me (right) with the Battle Readiness Award in 1992*

"Witte. Marion, go ahead and get into your Summer Whites and man the rails…", instructed PO3 Martinez (petty officer 3rd class Martinez). It was time to depart.

Manning the rails is a tradition where sailors (regardless of country) line up, side-by-side in the at-ease position around the sides of the ship. It is a ceremonial expression of ships passing which that started , well, since sailors first sailed the seas. Manning the rails is typically expressed for ceremonies, but for current Navies, we do this when entering and leaving ports.

Marion and I changed from our working dungarees into our Summer Whites and raced up to the flight deck. We met other sailors from the other divisions on the ship and lined up, side-by-side. We then extended our left arm to touch the other sailor to our left to ensure that all sailors were dispersed evenly around the deck of the ship. If our ship were carrying Marines, we would have one marine to our left and to our right. Since our ship was already filled with officer's cars, personal house items like furniture, only us sailors were manning the rails.

As the ropes connecting the USS Belleau Wood to the pier were thrown into the ocean and the tug boats pulled our ship away from the pier, we looked down at the family members of those stationed on the ship. They were holding banners and signs they made the night before reading "We love you!", "God Bless America", "Daniel, I'm Pregnant" among others. There could have been over 100 families on the pier.

You could hear sniffles and others manning the rails strongly hold back their tears. Even though I knew no one yet, I too, shed a tear. It was a powerful moment. The family members would meet us in about a month in Sasebo, Japan after our trek across the large Pacific ocean. Others waved their final goodbyes with very minimal chance of seeing each other again.

The USS Belleau Wood silently, slowly and powerfully sails underneath Coronado Bridge. Just before we got to the entry to the San

Diego Bay, we were relieved from our manning the rails and returned to our stations.

My shift had yet to start so I went to smoke a cigarette off the starboard side of the ship (starboard side – right, portside – left) where there was a small open-aired window about the side of a Volkswagen bus.

"Hey sailor!", an Ensign Wilson greets me with him lighting up his cigarette as well. We exchange what our MO was (Military Occupation) and the places that we were going. Ensign Wilson was a cool cat and unlike other officers or even our chiefs. The only difference that he had from my smoking and having a much higher rank was a 4-year college degree. I felt comfortable talking to him and heck, we became smoking buddies.

Ensign Wilson and I also exchanged some Japanese conversation. I thought I was the only one who spoke Japanese the most on the ship, but apparently, Ensign Wilson was almost fluent in Japanese. Jealous, however, I had plenty of time to learn and improve my Japanese speaking skills.

There is no saluting inside ships. The only time one with a lower rank of captain would greet our captain is by slamming your back against the wall in the passageways (hallways on boats) and standing at attention to let the captain pass. But as for officers below the rank of captain, it was basically like a co-worker.

"Japan is awesome! You'll enjoy it there!", it's safe, clean, fun and a lot of exotic women", Ensign Wilson continues as another seaman in my rank come out to smoke with us and joined our conversation. We began a 4-way conversation about the fun ports (places where ships land) that they had been. I was so excited at this point from hearing about their adventures that I completely forgot about my boot camp experience.

I continued to look out into the ocean poking my head out looking towards the stern of the ship (towards the back of the ship) to see a thin line of the Californian coast. Then I looked towards the bow of the ship (towards the forward of the ship).

Suddenly, 3 dolphins start jumping out of the ocean similar to how neighborhood dogs chasing trucks. It was an amazingly, peaceful experience to see the dolphins jumping in and out of the water alongside our ship as they have done since boats sailed.

"That's the sign of 'good luck' for the ship and its sailors", Ensign Wilson educates me on sailor superstition.

"Wow, that is f**king cool!", I excitedly said.

We smoked last of our 3rd cigarette, flicked it into the ocean and everyone but I left. My shift had yet to start so I looked out into the ocean seeing the last of the coast when the ship began to gently rock side to side. It didn't rock too much like a fishing boat would on a lake but it was still noticeable. Thinking that large ships would not move so much, this one still rocked somewhat noticeably in still water.

I returned to my post and began my shift. It was a tight shift. 16-on, 8-off. Meaning for every 16 hours I worked, I had 8 hours to sh*t, shower, shave, eat and sleep. For others in other divisions, they ran a much tighter and f**ked up schedule which were 6-on and 6-off. Others, 3-on and 5-off. Keep in mind that this is EVERY DAY! If sailors were out to see for 3 months or even 6 months, sailors worked every day like this. And due to the crazy shifts that sailors endured, they would have to...well, wanted to "hot-rack" or "hot-bed" where they would share the same bunk. While one of the 3-on and 5-off was working the 3-hours shift, his "hot-rack" mate would sleep on that shared bunk for 5 hours. Then when the 3-hour shift was completed, he would wake the sailor who was sleeping for 5 hours and have him be relieved from duty. Then the sailor who was relieved, will sleep in that same bunk for 5 hours. Yea, they could walk 20 minutes back to their division berthing area and sleep on their beds, but 20 minutes was very, very critical – not a second wasted.

Luckily for some of us in the supply division, we worked 16-on and 8-off. Yea!

"Witte, ju need a hayercut. Go now", MC Cusuga instructed me. My hair was not that long, but I'd rather be sitting down getting my haircut rather than moving heavy-ass boxes or doing watch.

It took me 30 minutes to find the barber shop located on the ship. The outside looked just like a barber shop! It had the traditional blue and red swirls and you could hear "Mother" by Danzig. These barbers were not your typical, old man barbers... they were heavy metal dudes...

"Duuude!", Seaman Knight said. "We just smoked with you upstairs on the side of the ship!"

Seaman Knight was a cool guy who liked the same music, had the same opinion about things and we seemed to have a lot in common. When it was my turn to get my haircut, I sat down and we kept talking about common things like work, our seniors, back home, and just about anything. He loved the way that he looked and had a bit of rebellion in him, just as I had.

SHSN Knight was a seaman with the same rank as I was. He looked either Italian or Moroccan. I never asked him. He loved his mustache and hair, he loved them more than anything else. Knight always wore cologne, radiating a macho, musk or Old Spice scent. He was tall, confident and rebellious. Though his main duty was to cut hair, his hair was against Navy regulations. Every time I took his picture, he always wanted to appear cool and masculine however his heart and manner was kind. He was always up for adventure just like any 18-year old.

Knight knew everyone. He constantly networked with everyone he met by either cutting their hair, drinking at ports or walking around coincidently meeting people. His memory was so perfect that he knew everyone's names and where they were from. He was also great at keeping tabs with rumors before they were announced which is why he was well-known on the ship.

"Hey, Knight", another voice entered the barber shop.

"What's up, Szerlag!", Knight replied.

SHSA Szerlag was a seaman apprentice, only one rank lower than I was, but it didn't matter to anyone unless there was a strict command or instruction. If I got into trouble, only my senior would be responsible for my mistakes. If Szerlag got into trouble, I would be solely responsible for him, but Szerlag was an angle on an 18-year old's testosterone who enjoyed life at every moment. He was always positive and concerned for others before himself.

Both were assigned in the field as a Ship Handler stock and restock every item that is used in the navy stores on shore and on ships, clean the laundry, managing tailor and barber shops. As for both Szerlag and Knight, they were both barbers in the Navy. But to me, they become the brothers I have never had which is quite typical for those who are in the military.

Both Knight and Szerlag worked together but Szerlag had different tasks such as schlepping heavy boxes above and below decks. Such a task was not easy. Szerlag never complained about all the heavy boxes and refilling coke machines. He always had a positive attitude. He too liked to have fun and had the same things in common which Knight and I had. Since then, we remained friends till this day.

## In The Middle Of F&ſɑ#Ing Nowhere
### AUGUST 06, 1992

*The USS Belleau Wood leaving the San Diego Naval Warfare base for Hawaii, and then off to its new homeport of Sasebo, Japan.*

On the USS Belleau Wood's course, we plotted our location in between San Diego, California and Pearl Harbor, Hawaii…in the middle of f**king nowhere…Everyone began to appear differently. Once excited when we left port, now everyone overworked, tired, sleepy, stressed, everyone is yelling at everyone.

There were several occasions when fights broke out. Once was between an officer and an enlisted sailor in the passageway near our S-2 Division. No one seemed to care and basically stepped over the scuffle between them on the floor.

Up until the sometime in the mid-1990s, seeing a female on a ship was very rare. In fact, we had about 8 women on our ship – the majority of them were pilots and officers. A few we had seen when we launched from San Diego were butt-ass ugly. 5 days later in the middle of the Pacific, they were the absolute, most beautiful women we had seen in our lives. 99% of the men that saw here were crafting up some pick-up line to get her and have sex with her however the repercussions would send both to captain's mass and receive a deduction in pay and be restricted to the ship. That punishment really didn't matter in days without seeing a female. She was a beautiful model!

You can also forget about masturbation. There's very limited privacy and besides, everyone is working all day, every day, being yelled at and the irritating feeling of the ship's rocking in the sea… So the pressure without alcohol, women or television took a physical and psychological toll on everyone's well-being.

## USS Arizona Shipmates

(Boatswain whistle blows for an announcement)
This was what we had been waiting for! Though it only took 8 days to reach Hawaii, it felt like weeks.

"Good morning, shipmates!", Captain Bradt announces on the 1MC (a Public Announcement system on the ship) across the ship. "We will be making port in Pearl Harbor. For the majority of you, this will be your first time in Hawaii. We will be 'manning the rails' for a significant ceremony to our shipmates who died in the Pearl Harbor bombings by the Japanese Imperial Navy. Those who wish to man the rails, request a dismissal from your seniors of your division... dress appropriately".

Not thinking much of this event, I requested to 'man the rails'. I changed from my working dungarees to my 'summer whites' and ran up the stairwells to the flight deck. It was better to be topside (top of the deck) than moving heavy supplies inside the ship.

Those manning the rails, again stood side-by-side, extended our left arm to touch the side of the sailor's shoulder, then stood at the 'at-ease' position facing out from the ship and to the ocean. Our ship slowed its passage just as we began to enter the narrow straight of the Pearl Harbor entrance. Land was what it seemed, within our reach from the ship as the straight was very narrow.

*Both Sailors and Marines manning-the-rails on the USS Belleau Wood*

We could see a civilian neighborhood on the starboard side of the ship. They came to greet us in their backyards. Some were holding large poster boards which they made reading, "God Bless the USA", "Welcome Navy" and "We Love You". There was one woman who ran out of her house to her back yard and got close to us as much as she could and lifted her blouse exposing her beautiful, American breasts. It made us smile and we secretly saluted her with our penises in our pants, but we still stood strong as soldiers and 'devil dogs' of the sea.

Our ship continued through Pearl Harbor much slower than usual as several tugboats guide us. Abruptly, the boatswain's whistle blows:

"SALUTE!", commanded one of our chiefs as we entered the shipyard of where the Japanese Imperial Navy bombed our shipmates only 50 years ago. My shipmates and I rendered honors by turning around to face the USS Arizona Memorial to the portside (left side of the ship), stood at attention and rendered the best salute to our shipmates who had died during the Pearl Harbor attack.

It was a very strong, somber and surreal moment that I had ever experienced in my life as our ship slowly and quietly made the passage by the USS Arizona. Water was in our eyes trying to maintain our composure. It could have been us, but it wasn't. It was our brothers.

The boatswain's whistle blows for the second time and we move to the 'at-ease' position for a few more moments passing the USS Arizona. Then we hear the boatswain's whistle again to be relieved and prepare for our leave in Hawaii.

"Time to get f**ked up!", a shipmate exclaims followed by other shipmates, "Yeahhhh!" We all ran down to our berthing area to change into civilian clothing and patiently waited for the gangway to connect to the shore.

Knight, Szerlag, a new friend and shipmate named Seaman J.R. and I reserved a rental car so that we could drive around the island of Oahu that seemed to only take us a few hours but due to traffic, it took us until the evening until we got back to return the rental car. It was a beautiful island to see and such a relief from seeing other men in a steel ship, working every day. Having not prepared to visit the beach, I wore my acid-washed jeans and just laid down on the warm sand. The other guys wore shorts. It looked strange and I clashed against my shipmates, but at least I could say I had experienced lying on the Hawaiian beach!

It was getting to that time when we needed to quench our thirst for alcohol. It would take quite a bit of time to get back to the ship and decided to leave the beach. We met up with a few other of our shipmates and decided to hit the bars together.

"Sh*t! I'm out of cash..", I declared as I looked through my wallet. I had carelessly spent money on a cassette tape by the music group Electronic.

"Dude...", Knight replied in disappointment.

"Here, I'll spot you and pay me back when you get cash...", Knight comforted me realizing that it would take about 2 hours to get a drink if they had waited for me.

"Naw, Knight.", Szerlag added. "I need to get money, too. I only have enough for 2 drinks."

Knight was a little disappointed but he could not be separated from us. Knight threw his hands up and said, "Alright...let's go back to the ship to withdraw money from the ship's ATM. You f**kers owe me a drink."

Little did we know that this would have been a mistake…

## Hurricane Iniki
### SEPTEMBER 10-11, 1992

As we enter the base gates, we see a sign, "USS Belleau Wood sailors, report to the ship, immediately". We had already passed through the gates when we began to wonder what that sign meant.

A marine guarding the base's main gate overheard me saying, "this should only take 10 minutes", referring to the time it took for me to go to the ship's ATM and exit the base to go drinking.

"NOPE!", the marine said.

"What do you mean, 'Nope'", Knight replies sternly thinking that the marine was messing with us.

The marine explains, "There is a strong hurricane heading this way and your ship is shipping out to ride the waves in 2 hours. You are to report to your ship immediately to assist."

Knight and Szerlag shake their heads with disappointment. Then I ask the Marine, "What about our shipmates who are still on leave?"

The Marine seemed to not care in giving us any more details and concludes his duty informing us. Jarhead!

Knight, Szerlag, J.R. and I walked quite casually back to our ship. We noticed a lot of hustling.

"Szerlag says calmly but concerned, "I got a bad feeling about this…"

Captian Bradt gets on the 1MC announces that we are shipping-out to the seas and wants all of us to assist in other duties where needed.

"All hands on deck. Due to the drastic and sudden change in weather, we need to ship-out. The OOD has informed me that we only have 400 sailors on board stranding 500 of our other sailors who are currently on Liberty.... I'm not going to sugarcoat this news. We are in for a ride. Secure all equipment immediately and then report to your stations."

Szerlag and Knight go to their division, J.R. goes to his and I go to mine. In hindsight, everything was secured as it has been. MC Cusuga instructs me to secure equipment in the marine's berthing area, though we had not any on board during this deployment. I was also to secure X-ray hatches (doors that are located in the lower part of the ship), Yankee hatches (doors that secured the mess deck) and a few Zulu hatches (doors that are frequently left open for busy foot traffic). Afterwards, I was to standby with the other shipmates in my division.

The gangway was lifted and we were escorted by the tugboats out of Pearl Harbor. There was no time to render honors to the USS Arizona as we needed all hands on deck to prepare for what seemed like a typical sail through a small storm.

Hurricane Iniki, a category 4 hurricane sustaining winds of up to 227 miles per hour, was about to make landfall to the island of Kaua'i. This hurricane killed six civilians and caused more than $3.1 billion USD. But before that, the USS Belleau Wood and half its crew were going head-straight through it.

After we were towed to open sea, it was calm but within 30 minutes, the ship began to feel the effects of the waves coming from the storm. The ship began to rock back and forth, then up and down. Gradually, it worsened and made some of us a little sick, but all we needed were Saltine Crackers which sailors can eat to endure and beat seasickness. These crackers were readily available unlike any motion sickness medication one would buy over-the-counter. If we were to take the medicine, we would be considered not sea-worthy so everyone just ate crackers and tried to keep from throwing up.

As there was nothing to do inside, I wanted to go outside and smoke. The smoking section had been secured in preparations to prevent water coming inside the port (a hole in a ship intentionally created), though it was 4 floors above the ocean, I couldn't imagine why it needed to be closed. I needed a smoke so to kill two birds with one stone, I made my way up on the top-most part of the ship above the bridge on the island. Being a restricted area on the ship, especially during the sail through hurricane, it would be a wonderful place to enjoy a view of Hurricane Iniki while smoking.

The wind strong, gusting over 140 miles per hour which was hindering my ability to light my cigarette with my Zippo.

"Dammit", I muttered to myself while rotating my body to block the strong winds. I looked down to the flight deck's bow as I finally lit my cigarette. Then the cigarette tilted downwards from my mouth as I realized that our ship headed straight into large 35-foot swells, 3 stories high just a mile ahead. It was a frightening sight. Just only taking a few hurried drags from my cigarette, I threw it into the ocean and headed downstairs to prepare for what I thought was going to be the sinking of our ship.

The USS Belleau Wood began to move upward sharply, then drop downward to the starboard side. There was a slight feeling of stomach butterflies while dropping downwards. It became difficult to walk as the other sailors quickly ran to their divisions.

"Make a hole, shipmate. Make a hole!", you could hear through every passageway as sailors jumped through hatches and doors. By the time I returned to my division near the galley, the ship moved even more; slowly moving upwards, then downwards with the feeling of riding a rollercoaster as it dipped to the starboard side. Then things got worse.

"Bam! Crash! Boom! Crash!", went whatever wasn't secured onto the deck. It was a bit scary but not as scary as what our crew heard right after the lights went out. Immediately the boilers began to shut down, generators went out and then it was deadly quiet. Our ship had succumbed to the wind and waves. Knowing that more than half our crew were left on the Island, we had no idea what to expect next. We were a bunch of young men and weren't nearly prepared for this and then we heard, "Brace for heavy rolls, brace for heavy rolls!!!", Captain Bradt alerts us on the ship's 1MC system.

Then there was complete silence…

The ship continued side-wards, upwards, then downwards way beyond the feeling of riding a rollercoaster as it dipped to the star-board side. The temporary relief that the Saltine crackers gave me began to wear off and I felt my lunch making its way out of my stom-ach and quickly in the wrong direction. As I made my way through the passageway to the head, the ship suddenly started to tilt to the starboard side to the point where the walls took place of the deck – I could practically walk on the wall!

There was more equipment noise as things were falling from everywhere. Then the ship returned to its stationary position and tilted towards to the port side just as it did on the starboard side. Trying to continue my way to the head, I extend my left and right hand against the bulkheads (walls of a ship), stumbling a few times. But by the time I reached the head, the power comes back on and we continue our course hitting the swells of the ocean caused by Hurricane Iniki. My lunch still considering exiting my stomach, I sit on the chairs in the lounge next to the head.

"Why the f**k did we go through this hurricane!?", a shipmate said as he too was sitting on the chairs gazing at his lunch on the floor. Not able to reply, I sat close to him. As the ship continued move upward sharply, then drop downward to the starboard side, the chairs that we were sitting on moved back and forth on the floor of the lounge; to the left and then to the right. My shipmates vomit spread its evidence as a live artwork being created. Neither of us could get up so we continued to sit.

"Witte!", MC Cusaga requested. "come wid me to da portside". I felt so incapacitated by the seasickness but I was needed by my senior and it sounded important.

Trying our best to make our way to the location where I was needed, I looked down one deck through the portal and saw that some of the sea water had made its way into one of the storage areas. There was only 2 feet of water but it needed to be dumped back out to sea.

Szerlag was already there filling pails and walking them up the stairwell through the hatch to dump them out of the portside port into the ocean. We continued to fill and empty the pails into the ocean for the next 3 hours without conversation. The hours after and as the hurricane continued on its path through the Kaua'I island, we conducted damage control and reported extensive damage to our seniors.

## Kaua'i Island Humanitarian Relief

The next day before we returned to Pearl Harbor to pick up the other half of our crew, there were disgruntled shipmates pissed about having their liberty cut short. We were supposed to continue our 7-day liberty however, we were requested by the Kaua'I Island to assist in humanitarian aid.

Our seniors concurred and allowed us to shop at the Pearl Harbor base PX (Post Exchange which is similar to a Target store but smaller and for military offering tax-free products) for only 1 hour, which took a lot of negotiating.

As we were leaving, we saw the other half of our crew make their way through the gangway and reporting to the OOD on the Quarterdeck. They were soaked, muddy and seemed awfully exhausted. All of our crew except for one made it back to the base as required in emergencies. That one shipmate who did not report to the base was Allen Schindler. Apparently, Radio Man 3rd Class Schindler was at a hotel waiting for the storm to pass. That pissed off a lot of our shipmates. RM3 Schindler came back to the boat dry as a whistle and a bit hungover from his partying at a nice hotel while the other 500 reported to the base and spent the biggest part securing the Pearl Harbor base filling sandbags and cleaning debris.

*The USS Belleau Wood in the distance standing by while helicopters drop relief necessities for the civilians on the Kauai Island. A sign warped depicting the strength of the hurricane.*

Typically, sailors who did not report for duty in emergencies were considered A.W.O.L. (Absent With Out Leave) even if they were on liberty, something he hadn't known when he was previously stationed on his previous ship the USS Midway.

RM3 Schindler received some mild backlash from his division because of him not helping out on the base, but nothing physical.

After Knight, Szerlag, J.R. and I returned from our 1-hour speed-shopping at the PX, we returned to our ship. There were a few cranes loading supplies (toiletries, canned food, blankets, etc) which we were going to provide the Kaua'I Island with. With only a few hours, we were on our way to the Kaua'I Island.

For the next three days, we anchored on the sunny weather and calm seas flying helicopters carrying pallets of supplies and medical equipment to the ravished island that suffered incredible damage that cost $3.4 billion dollars, killed six civilians and destroyed 5,152 homes. It also destroyed the Coco Palms Resort which Elvis Presely stared in the "Blue Hawaii" movie. Steven Spielberg's "Jurassic Park" movie set had also suffered great damage and parts of the Hurricane Iniki storm can be seen in the movie battering the coastal walls.

One-by-one, each helicopter launches from the deck with a full cargo of supplies as another helicopter lands replenishing its empty cargo pallet. Though all of us sailors missed out on several days of liberty and relaxation in Hawaii, we all helped out on the ship to ensure our citizens had the essentials they needed to heal and repair their island which has become the worst disaster it ever experienced in history.

All sailors aboard were awarded the Humanitarian Service Medal for this action.

*One of the many 12 CH-46 Sea Knight helicopters stationed on our ships makes several trips from the USS Belleau Wood to the island of Kauai dropping toiletries, food and blankets for the civilians affected by the damaging hurricane. The ship in the distance were one of the ships assisting the relief.*

## 2-Q-T-2-B-S-T-R-8

After assisting in the humanitarian relief for the island of Kaua'I, we set sail for Japan. We would spend another 15 days at sea. All was fine for the first 3 days but for some reason and for somehow, 'sh*t ran downhill' (something that our captain was pissed about, he got pissed at his juniors. Then the captain's juniors got pissed about that and got pissed at our seniors. Then our seniors got pissed about what their seniors got pissed about and got pissed at us). Thinking that all of us should have been rewarded for our humanitarian aid, we got scolded for no reason.

Well, this became clear only by rumors of what one sailor did.

We heard that Allen Schindler's security clearance was revoked, effective immediately. That was the rumor that was floating around the ship. One of the MS's (Mess Management Specialists – those that cook) overheard this discussion. And the rumor that spread was that RM3 Allen Schindler had transmitted a personal code to the majority of the 7th fleet (the Pacific Fleet). That message was "2-Q-T-2-B-S-T-R-8" ("too cute to be straight").

There was immediate backlash from the other ships questioning the safety and security of the ship and the 7th fleet.

The message itself ("2-Q-T-2-B-S-T-R-8") wasn't the issue. The issue was the unauthorized transmission of information on a secured frequency. At the time, no one really knew what it meant but it did not take that long to decipher it by the crew. When someone told me about it, I didn't understand what "too cute to be straight" really meant. To me, it meant that RM3 Schindler was funny and that he didn't want to follow the orders like all sailors. Not thinking much into its meaning, I carried on with my duties, sh*t, showered and shaved, ate evening chow and went out for a smoke with one of my buddies, Knight in the starboard side port smoking section.

Knight asked, "Did you hear about the shipmate who blasted over the secured line that he was gay?"

I replied, "Er…no…" Now, I did not know about that and it sounded as if there were 2 guys pranking on the secured frequency. I couldn't connect the two as I was so naïve about the homosexual lifestyle (it was considered a lifestyle according to culture and a mental disability in the early 1990s according to the DSM III – a book which all American psychologists used to diagnose those with disorders).

I continued, "Is this the same guy that transmitted 'too cute to be straight'?"

Knight lights up a cigarette, inhales and places his Zippo lighter back into his pocket as he exhales the smoke trailing with, "You know he's a fag, right?"

I replied, "a 'fag' as in a cigarette or a 'fag' as a homosexual in British?"

Knight smirks as he thinks he's talking to some child and says, "Dude… he's gay…come on, dude…"

Acting as if I was pretending to be naïve, "oh wow, he's f**ked".

Knight agreed, "yup! It's automatic 'Captain's Mass'. He could get kicked out of the Navy".

One of Knight's 'kinda friend' who was a marine on our ship joined in the conversation and explained that it wasn't the transmitting personal information over the secured frequency that would result in being other-than-honorable-discharged from the military - it was publically admitting that he was gay.

Confused as to why would anyone work hard in the military just to suddenly give up everything by telling everyone that he was gay? "RM3 Schindler was supposed to present this in MEPS during our medical and psych analysis before signing up with the Navy".

Knight replied, "Well, there are a lot of us that lied when we were checked. Did you tell them at MEPS that you smoked pot?"

"I can't remember but I'm pretty sure I didn't confess", I replied and then was cut-off by Knight pointing his finger at me with his last drag of cigarette between his fingers, "Exactly!"

Knight further explained that he had nothing against homosexuals, but everyone knew that if you were branded as a homosexual, you would get harassed.

A few other shipmates (whose names I have forgotten over the years) had told me that a few gay sailors had been thrown off of the ship before arriving in Hawaii. If no one liked you, they would gang up on you, beat you and in extreme cases, throw you off the ship. At that time, there was no way to confirm this rumor. You simply wouldn't piss anyone off or be gay and you would be fine.

A very loud emergency alarm goes off across the ship followed by an announcement over the 1MC, "General Quarters, General Quarters. Report to your stations immediately!"

All of us smokers flicked our cigarettes through the port and into the sea and ran to our stations in preparations for battle. The vent system which provided us with air had been shut off. No air conditioning. Hatches and doors closed and we stood by for orders from our seniors. This final 'general quarters' was going to determine if the USS Belleau Wood and its sailors would win yet another award for "Battle Efficiency" or the "Navy 'E' Ribbon". A ship that wins this award will become a flagship meaning we will host an admiral. The Captain wanted to win this award for his career as much as we wanted it. We all felt confident that it was going to be OURS!

# CHAPTER 8
# GO AWAY, YOU GAIJIN YANKEE

Three days before we arrived in Japan, we were to report to the hanger deck. On an amphibious assault ship, there are several hanger decks. The topmost hanger deck was for storing AV-B8 Harriers and helicopters. The other lower decks were for Marine troops to muster and prepare themselves for battle and tanks, Humvees, artillery, etc.

On one of the lower decks, each division's personnel were to muster and take a crash-course on Japanese customs. Nine-hundred sailors who never left their country were going to make an impression on a small town of 280,000 in Sasebo, Japan. It would be an impression which would affect a small town regardless of the instructions that we were given.

A lot of Japanese in Sasebo have never seen any other race besides their own. There were some 'unspoken rules' which we needed to abide by without offending the locals. Some of these rules were; not eating or drinking while walking, no spitting, no loud noises or ruckus and most importantly – not committing a crime.

We learned the basics such as removing our shoes when entering a Japanese home and bowing to the locals when we struck up a conversation. The course took a mere hour. After that hour of the crash-course, we felt that we were ready to pick up women without upsetting their families.

Two days before we reached land, everyone was very excited. Thinking that it was unlike visiting Tijuana, Mexico, we would embark on a new experience that was so unreal. We heard only wonderful things about Japan, how safe it was, how cold the beer was and how hot the women were.

In the berthing lounge, "Star Trek – The Next Generation" TV series was playing on the 16", tubed television that was snugged between the ceiling and bulkhead. Patrick Steward was playing Captain Jean-Luc Picard in the "First Contact" episode which began to make me think that what our ship was in a similar scenario. We were going to meet different species on a different planet except we were on Earth. We would learn their language, their customs, their habitat and colonize their town. We had 900 sailors that were soon to make Sasebo, with a population of 250,000, our colony.

It was something interesting to think about as I fell asleep.

(the sound of dominos forcefully slapping a laminated table from the lounge), "sh*t... F**k you, mother f**ker!", "BWahahahaha!". "Dude...." "BAM, BAM, BAM!!", we sleeping sailors in our berthing area overhears from the lounge across the passageway.

One of our seniors mutters from somewhere from the bottom bunk, "F**king noisy, pricks..."

The noise continues, "BAM, BAM, thud, patter, patter, patter" as we hear some noise which sounded like a wrestling match.

I had to pee anyways so I got up and joined the curious others who were awaken by the ruckus.

On the floor were two sailors hitting and wrestling each other. One of them were 4 ranks above the other.

"Stand down!", an off-duty Master-at-Arms yelled in his cute jammies. This order did not stop the fight and then two others joined in the fun. One of the guys hit me in the back of the head as I was making my way to take a piss. I wasn't involved with the fight but after one of the guys hit me in the back of the head, I was wrestling for my revenge.

Able to get a few punches back to the guy who had hit me, more seniors jumped in to break up the fight. Unable to understand why I hadn't walked away, it felt good to get in the scuffle. It was quite a stress relief and apparently the same to the others.

"Break it up, break it up, stand down!", several seniors said as they were separating us individually.

"That's it, lights out!", commanded one of the seniors said and we all left and I got to take my last piss for the night.

"How can people like us make a positive impression on the Japanese people if we cannot control ourselves...", I thought to myself once I returned to my bunk. But with the everyday, all day working with no breaks, no alcohol and being demanded to work by our seniors was taking its toll on not only me, but everyone.

Satisfied and relieved of stress from that small fight, I was able to sleep soundly.

Strangely the next day, everyone treated the fight as it never happened. No one was reported (any snitch would surely pay the price of being thrown off the ship) and when asked by our Chiefs on to where we received our battle marks, we simply said we "fell out of our bunks". Our chiefs knew exactly why we did it and always expect such incidents that they just ignored any answers that we would have. Fighting, pushing, verbal abuse, whatever, our senior chiefs would simply ask and then not listen to the answers or reasons. That would mean more paperwork for them and they too would get in trouble for not controlling their juniors. We simply took care of our own business.

I've witnessed other fights or "hits" when sailor pissed of a few people. As they would sleep, the perpetrator would go to the victim's bunk and punch them, then run away.

Such ruckuses, hazing, bullying and harassment was quite typical on our ship. All a sailor needed to do was to muster a few friends and you'll have a gang. Sailors would never report such issues to their seniors – we are supposed to deal with these issues ourselves and reporting such would be frowned upon by our seniors.

The next day, we will arrive in Japan! Everyone seems to be in high spirits. Not only would we be on a flat surface that would not rock continuously, but we will be able to drink beer! Oh, and get laid… but beer was the #1 priority on every sailor's minds!

I was a little too late getting up that I missed my morning constitutional. Knowing that a lot of our berthing areas would be secured for cleaning not allowing anyone to use them, the only berthing area head I found was in the Division 7. The portside of the head was opened while the starboard side passageway was closed, secured for swabbing (mopping and buffing).

Finally, a stall is open for me to go inside with my Walkman and begin playing my favorite music group, RUSH. I start air-drumming to Neil Peart's many songs, especially "The Trees", which is a song I hold true to my heart. I see graffiti written on the inside of the door reading "Schindler is a faggot". The name I vaguely remembered but to whom, I had forgotten. We men have seen these before many times in public restrooms at gas stations or other high-trafficked areas where all walks of life used. Not thinking too much into the name which was hard to pronounce, I continued air-drumming.

Finally, with my morning's constitutional out of the way, I wiped myself clean and opened the toilet stall door. To my surprise, I was greeted by a line of five-people long, waiting to use the stall which I used for my personal concert.

A short Filipino sailor says, "The toilet is for this (imitating poop coming out of his butt), and not for this (imitating male masturbation)..."

How...embarrassing...I wasn't but who else air-drums in a bathroom stall?

Knowing that the five guys patiently waiting for my air guitar grand finale solo would jeer to my explanations that I was not masturbating, I just left and stepped onto the deck of the port side passageway.

"What the f**k are you doing, motherf**ker!?", I was aggressively and loudly scolded by one of my shipmates who had just gotten through swabbing the deck of the port side passageway. He was still swabbing the passageway deck on the far end. It was Terry Helvey.

He was an Airman on the USS Belleau Wood and a large guy reaching a shy over six feet, 200 pounds. His eyebrows seemed angry and his expression never to change. I had never seen him smile, but if he did, it would have presented a different and positive persona. If no words came from Helvey's mouth, he would appear like the rest of us except he seemed a bit disgruntled.

"Oh, sh*t…sorry, shipmate…I thought that it wasn't secured", I replied subordinately as I felt bad that I had walked on a beautiful, newly-shined deck.

Apparently, my sincere apology and explanation did nothing to make up for my mistake into which he added, "I'm going to tear-off your arms and slap you with it, motherf**ker…I'll f**king kill you!!"

I said nothing and walked into the Division-7 berthing racks while looking back at him. There wasn't anything for me to reply to as I was confused to why someone would have gotten so angry and threaten me with such violence…and death.

A voice that greeted me in the berthing racks who had heard what the violent shipmate said, "Helvey is always like that. Don't worry about him."

"But did you hear what he said!?", as my heat still raced.

The shipmate continued to explain about Helvey's demeanor and how he always got upset doing work on the ship. He continued to explain that Helvey had a rough up-bringing, but wasn't a valid excuse as a lot of us had similar growing ups.

Still confused about Helvey's threat, I explained this to Knight in the starboard side port smoking section.

"Ha ha ha ha ha!, yeah, that's Hevley, alright", Knight explained as if he knew him in–person. Knight continued, "just don't worry about Helvey. He's like the rest of us and wants to get laid and drunk.

With Knight's reassurance of Helvey's empty threat, we all prepared for tomorrow's Liberty in Japan. My shift was taken by my senior as he was compensating for my taking his on a previous night when he was ill. I had my civilian clothes washed, my Electronic band cassette tape in my Walkman, placed enough cash to get f**ked up on Liberty and hit the mattress to charge-up for the big day tomorrow!

## Welcome To Japan! We Mean, Go Back To America
### SEPTEMBER 30, 1992

*Sasebo River separates the town of Sasebo and the base (I took this picture in 1993 from the east side of the base). Sasebo remains a fishing town as it slowly becomes a thriving city, yet too small for a large ship such as the USS Belleau Wood.*

"Dude! Come outside and check this out!", a shipmate says as he runs up to the port side port. "We have a welcoming parade!" he says excitedly.

Szerlag, Knight and I rush to the port side port and look out into the bay of Sasebo. We were amazed to see such a huge fiasco happening around our ship.

"A welcoming parade!", I said in amazement.

A shipmate corrected, "Um…That's no welcoming party. That's a protest…"

Looking out again, we saw the expression of the hundred protestors in small fishing boats, on the land surrounding the bay and on the piers who were holding huge banners in Japanese and shouting.

Another shipmate joins the view, "don't these F**king morons known that none of us can speak or read Japanese?"

We all just smirked confused with the shipmate's comment and the fiasco around our ship.

The group instigating the protests were the "Uyoku Dantai" or the "Japanese Ultranationalist Far-Right" group who are slightly connected to the Japanese Yakuza (mafia). But this group isn't necessarily against the American military, they are keeping us in-check and warning us to behave ourselves in their town. Though appearing as a protest, they were supporting the US military against the Chinese.

"Look! Some of them are waving", informing my shipmates.

We waved back and smiled. We mean no harm nor will we intentionally create any burden to the Japanese community.

Several news helicopters fly above, right outside of the Sasebo Naval base recording a half-parade, half-protest.

The tug boats gently ported our ship across from the USS Dubuque, an LPD-8, an amphibious transport docking ship, which was preparing for its excursion out to sea and would be our competitors in fights and brawls to come.

The USS Dubuque already had a bad reputation from its 1988 incident where it had neglected 110 Vietnamese refugees that had drifted into the open waters of the Pacific. Their captain, Alexander Balian did not provide adequate supplies for the refugees on its way to the Persian Gulf which resulted in 30 deaths, some of them cannibalized by their own.

We were about to go on Liberty after we ported to the pier, but we would not go out alone as we weren't certain about what was waiting for us outside of the base.

"Ding-ding. Ding-ding, Ding-ding! Captain Bradt has left the ship!", calls the Boatswain on the 1MC. Once our captain left the ship, it meant it was time for Liberty! But no one wanted to go out of the base alone as we didn't know what to expect from the "Uyoku Danti". Perhaps they would gang up on us and beat the sh*t out of us? Spit on us? Kill us? Regardless, we really wanted to get out of the military base and venture out into the new country.

Szerlag, J.R. and Knight had watch and duty so I mustered a few other shipmates who I hadn't really mingled with on the ship. And since I did speak some common Japanese phrases which I learned from my first girlfriend Yukiko, I was the only one in the group who could remotely translate anything.

We left the ship off the gangway onto the small Sasebo Naval Base and headed to the base gates. Our hearts were pumping. We were preparing for anything outside of the base.

Japanese taxis and small, compact cars were flowing by us on the wrong side of the road. Birds tweeted differently, the smell of Ramen (Japanese noodles) filled the air…and nothing more. No "Uyoku Danti". No civilians. No one met us outside the base that were not US military.

"Whaaaat…? Where are the protestors?", said one of the shipmates.

Others followed, "I don't know…"

The "Uyoku Danti" seemed for certain that they wanted to fight us, but there was no one in sight!

Our young, adventurous hearts placed the fear aside and headed to the downtown section of Sasebo for drinks. We wanted to eat something besides the institutional, military food that we had been eating for the past month. We saw a restaurant nestled in the small, 5-storied buildings that seemed to have edible food. Mostly rice, but it had meat and looked delicious.

I stepped in the restaurant first as the other five followed. We were greeted by a young host who hurriedly walked to us.

"Damme, damme...dette kudasai, (do not, do not, please leave)", the waiter said in Japanese as he made an "X" with his forearms. He continued to deny us by speaking simple yet hard-to-understand English, "Japanese only".

*A picture that I took in 2009 of a bar from Sasebo town section we sailors called "Sucky Town" as they prohibited non-Japanese from entering their establishments. They had similar signs scattered throughout Sasebo bars and restaurants. These still exist today! Can't blame them, really.*

We were furious to be denied as we have never in our lives been denied access for being, just patrons. That was a huge culture shock.

We began to yell American profanities as we were holding back one of our shipmates who was ready to kick the host's ass. We then left with a bitter taste in our mouths and headed over to the only Mc Donald's in town – a little American taste satisfied our tummies.

As the evening began to set its sights on the small city, the neon lights in the drinking district attracted our movement just as moths to a porch light. We made our way to the nightlife area called "Saki Town", A.K.A. "Sucky Town".

Uncertain as to what would be waiting for us, we made our way looking for a place to get a cheap drink and mingle with the women.

"Japanese Only" a few bar signs read. Others read "No Americans" and "No Military". We were quite confused. It wasn't the warm welcome that we had expected. From our last disappointing experience at the restaurant, we were more sad than angry and didn't think twice to attempt to enter any of these bars. Surely some place would accept our American dollars.

"Ah… this is why this place is nicknamed 'Sucky Town', one of the shipmates concluded. "Yo, Witte, ask directions to a place where we can wet our whistle!", he added. Since I was the only one who spoke at least one phrase in Japanese, they volunteered me to ask a Japanese street cop. The street cop was stationed in a small building the size of an American Kitchen that was built in the middle of a median as Japanese taxis whizzed by in both directions.

In my sh*tty Japanese, I asked the cop, "Osake doko ni desuka (drink where)?"

My shipmates were amazed in my ability to actually say something in Japanese. The cop replied while I listened attentively but had no clue what he said. Thankfully, we figured it out when he used his hands and arms to give us directions to "Sailor Town", where sailors were always welcomed.

With a strong thirst of beer, we again walked quite a distance across Sasebo town through the Ginza shopping mall (not the actual Ginza located in Tokyo) lined with every store you could imagine – from small and highly advanced personal electronics and coffee shops to game centers and small fast-food joints that were willing to take our American dollars.

On the other side of the Ginza shopping center, you could hear drunk American sailors yelling in celebration with loud American music. We had finally entered "Sailor Town"!

The scene of Sailor Town was lively. There were many sailors walking with young, beautiful Japanese girls leaving one bar and going right into the next bar. A few sailors hanging out just like us scoping the area for unchaperoned girls who we could take with us into bars, tell us about Japan and hopefully take us back to their place for a nightcap.

The Shore Patrol were actively strutting their authority with their batons, whistle, radio and "SP" lettering on a black armband. They wanted to ensure that we drunk sailors didn't get out of hand. There was no hesitation for Shore Patrol to use those batons on those of us who got into fights.

*Shore patrol from our ship patrolling the streets. Typically patrolling in various groups and shifts of 3-4 and led by a chief (second from the left). Note the baton on the third SP from the left used for beating sailors to break up brawls.*

*"Snack Shipmates" bar (door to the right), one booth to the left behind the wall, which sadly closed in 1998. Picture taken in 2009.*

One of the bars that we selected was "Snack Shipmates" as the music wasn't blaring that loud allowing us to complain about being at sea and the adventures we had in Sasebo. Snack Shipmates was very small and seated about 10 drunks sitting at the bar, 5 at a booth in the front of the bar and other standing sailors behind. The bar had a 20" television that played car racing crashes muted to allow the karaoke to be sung horribly by its patrons. So many of us sang "Stairway To Heaven" by Led Zepplin that we complained when we heard the intro to the song., "F**k, again?"

"Mama-san" was a lady about 60-years old and her welcoming smile was always present. She sometimes offered us free snacks and beer. This was the place where I first learned how to use chopsticks by the competition that she held. Mama-san would challenge us, "if you can move 10 uncooked beans from one plate to the next, you get a free beer. If you move 5 ice cubes from one beer glass to the other, you get a free shot!"

If we ever got too wasted, she would let us rest our heads on the bar table and wash our faces with a warm hand towel. She was considered our mother away from home.

My shipmates and I took her up on the 'chopstick challenge' but failed miserably. This meant we had to buy our drinks, again and again and again until we were just about sh*t-faced. We drank and sang karaoke for a good 2 hours. It was a wonderful beginning to our new lives in Japan!

"American sailors!!!", we hear as five Japanese Navy sailors in their uniforms walking happily into the bar. "Brothers!", another of the Japanese sailors say as they come by and hug us from behind. It was a strange sight and expression for them to do this greeting considering that only 50 years before this, our grandfathers were killing each other in the Pacific and now, we are 'brothers of the seas'.

The Snack Shipmates bar has now become the center-most location in our hearts where US and Japanese sailors come to drink and sing together while sharing sea stories for the weeks, months and years to come!

We all continued to sing "Piano Man" by Billy Joel until the morning light arose.

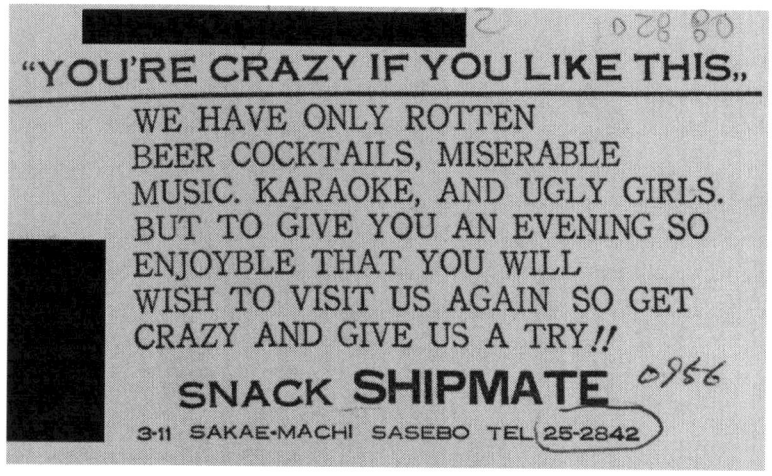

*The "Snack Shipmates" business card (I can't believe I held onto this card since 1992) .*

## Damn Women

### OCTOBER 09, 1992

The USS Dubuque had just left port for a little "at sea" time simply because the small city of Sasebo couldn't host nor cater to two large ships at port at the same time. Not only could the citizens of Sasebo cater to two large ships, but the USS Dubuque and the USS Belleau Wood were competitors.

Sailors aboard the USS Dubuque had all of the curious Japanese women that envied sailors and no waiting in line for alcohol. If either sailor from either ship saw another from the other ship, there would be equal, smirking at each other. Other times at bars, there would be a few scuffles and arguments.

So to remedy these incidents and to adhere a verbal agreement with the Mayor of Sasebo, both ships wouldn't be ported at the same time. If they were, it would only be for a few weeks. On one October night, this theory of having issues with both of the ships was proven true!

Alcohol consumption on base was a very cost-efficient way to get wasted. While beer cost $5 in the bars in Sailor Town, the on-base bar named the "Harbor View Club" provided beer for $2. About 99.9% of sailors going out to drink at the bars in Sailor Town would first tank-up (drink as much as possible) on-base and then clumsily make their way to Sailor Town to drink with the Japanese girls.

On this occasion and to reduce costs of paying for one particular sailor's girlfriend and himself all night, a sailor from the Belleau Wood would bring her to the Harbor View Club. He was trying to impress her by chauffeuring her around the base and paying for their drinks. Little did he know that she also had another boyfriend on the USS Dubuque. Not much for him to worry at the time nor did he really care that he was with another guy's girl while her original boyfriend was out at sea.

Once, the USS Dubuque was less than 100 nautical miles out at sea when they encountered a mechanical failure on their ship which required them to make an emergency port call back at the home base in Sasebo. As the ship needed to stay ported for several days to retrieve parts to repair the mechanicals, the USS Dubuque sailors poured off the ship and since it was at night, they all went for a drink. Instead of calling his girlfriend, he just went to the Harbor View Club with his shipmates from the USS Dubuque. When the boyfriend of the Japanese girl was nestled closely to her other boyfriend from the USS Belleau Wood, he walks in and sees her smiling up at her new boyfriend.

The Dubuque shipmates rush in. We sailors from the Belleau Wood didn't understand what was happening and thought that we were under attack by the sailors from the Dubuque so we all stood up and prepared for...something.

The boyfriend from the Dubuque and his shipmate grab our ship-mate who was touching the Dubuque sailor's girl and all hell breaks loose. Everyone was hitting everyone. If you didn't know who that sailor was, most possibly, that was the guy you were supposed to hit. Chairs begin to fly across the bar, beer bottles, ashtrays, cigarette ashes and sparks, French fries, ice cubes all went airborne.

Only four people knew the reason why we were fighting however, there were about fifteen to twenty sailors from the Dubuque and twenty to twenty-five sailors from the Belleau Wood fighting for unknown reasons. It looked like it was a saloon fight right out of a spaghetti Western. I had never been in such a large fight before, but it felt good fighting with my brothers against my other brothers from another ship.

Shore Patrol started rushing into the Harbor View Club with their night-sticks playing "whack-a-mole", randomly hitting sailors yelling, "Stand down! Stand down!".

"Dude, let's go!", some sailor from the Dubuque yelled at us and we all started to run out of the Harbor View Club and onto the base in the direction of Sailor Town (which was a fifteen-minutes run).

We get to the main entrance to get off base and they had secured it as Shore Patrol reported the bar brawl.

We then ran back along barbed-wire fence looking for another escape and then we hear, "This way!", from another sailor. We all ran over 3 lined, barbed wire fences, one by one. When we spread out into Sailor Town, we looked like cockroaches when you turn on the kitchen light in the middle of the night.

For the rest of the night and into the morning sunrise, we all drank and sang karaoke. When we returned to the base, it was still secured. Single file, we all went through the gate and answered the Shore Patrolmen's question, "Were you at the Harbor View Club last night", which we all answered separately with bruises and cuts, "Nope!".

Two days later, we found out that the reason why the fight that broke out at the club was because of the two boyfriends on separate ships sharing the same girlfriend.. Since then, the sailors from each ship continued to have angst against each other.

## Dancing In The Street
### OCTOBER 24, 1992

Huis Ten Bosch was a theme park thirty minutes away from the small city of Sasebo. Typically, retired married Japanese couples would visit this place as a cheap alternative to vacationing in Europe. It looked like the country of Denmark in every detail.

At times, plays, concerts and events were held here. One of these was a play called "La Cage Aux Folles" which brought an interesting bunch of folks from the United States that clashed between the monolithic Japanese and crazy, loud, drunk sailors. No one was expecting the interesting folks that openly expressed their art in the streets. But they too, loved to party just as much as we did. During their stay, they mingled in Sailor Town which both entertained and pissed off other sailors.

"Look at those queer dancers", as some of the sailors said when they saw them dancing in the streets. Some sailors on our ship felt intimidated by them. "Get out of the street, f\*\*king faggots", I hear other shipmates yell from outside of the other bars.

The dancers were with a few other of our shipmates who we recognized from our ship. They avoided the insults but they didn't look back and continued to some other bar far from Sailor Town.

"Hey, isn't that the fag that got restricted leave?", one of the shipmates hanging with me said referring to RM3 Schindler announcing "2-Q-T-2-B-S-T-R-8 (Too Cute To Be Straight)".

"Yeah, I think so…I thought he wouldn't have been off of restricted leave so soon..", the other shipmate replied.

The dancers continued on to another bar called "The Captain's Bar" hidden around the corner. And as they disappeared, we had landed into another bar where our conversation changed to our next voyage which was a month away, to the Philippines.

## PART 3

# HOW SOON IS NOW?

*"If you can't be yourself, then who are you?"*
—Allen R Schindler (1992)

# CHAPTER 9

# MY CONVERSATION WITH ALLEN SCHINDLER

October 25, 1992

It was a lonely evening. I did however, wanted to check out a bar that I had not gone to before which was the Bar Sakura. By then, I had been to Bar Shipmates too many times and wanted a change of atmosphere.

Upon entering Bar Sakura, the overwhelming smell of cheap, candy perfume filled the air with Yakisoba (an easy noodle and meat meal typically eaten by sailors). A Filipino woman sings an ABBA song loudly, off-key unnoticing how horrible her singing is as a few other patrons clap to the beat.

I see a few shipmates talking to each other whom I had seen around but never drank with before. No one seemed drunk at the time.

Before ordering a beer, I had determined that I would stay here and drink slowly and then pass by Bar Shipmates to see if Szerlag, Knight or J.R. had gotten off work.

One of the shipmates grabs the beer-smelling karaoke microphone and chats with his friend as the intro to "Stairway To Heaven" by Led Zepplin began thinking, "I am not going to listen to that song again". I finished my beer and slammed the 500-Yen coin.

I thanked the Mama-san and headed out the door in search of another bar that I had yet to venture.

As I am walking away from Bar Sakura in the small alley filled with other bars, I heard a door slam open from the Red Dragon Bar.

I turned around to see who had opened the and thought I recognized a fellow sailor. I continued to walk down the alley to the main street trying to think of who this guy was – I just couldn't remember.

"HEY, SHIPMATE!", the guy said behind me as he caught up to me and threw his arm around my shoulder like buddies and shipmates typically do.

*This is the alley in Sailor Town where Allen Schindler and I met. The Red Dragon bar (right) is where Schindler exited. I was already half-way down to the end of the alley when he called out to me. I took this picture in 2009 and not much has changed since.*

The smell of beer was presently apparent. Shipmates do touch each other like friends and brothers do when we are having fun as this guy did however, this guy continued to keep his arm around me as we walked through the alleyway and around the corner to the main street.

Feeling a bit uncomfortable with his arm around me, I instantly changed my mind of finding another bar and headed to Snack Shipmates where I hoped Szerlag and Knight would be by now. By getting inside any bar and sitting down, I expected my new friend to remove his arm from around my shoulder. I did not want to be rude but honestly felt uncomfortable with the situation.

"Where ya going, shipmate?", the guy said. He definitely wanted some company to drink with him.

"Snack Shipmates", I replied with a smile hoping not to break the atmosphere.

"Let's go!", he said. I couldn't instantly come up with an excuse to escape him and perhaps either Knight, Szerlag or J.R. would be there to save me from this guy who seemed desperate in finding friends.

"Please, oh god, please be there guys…" I thought to myself as we arrived to the front of Snack Shipmates.

We enter Snack Shipmates and were greeted by mama-san. No one else was there and I was a little wary of my new friend (who was obviously a few drinks ahead of me). I was disappointed that my friends weren't there but decided to wait for them.

The walls were littered with beer posters and Mamma-san is preparing small snacks like peanuts, salty seaweed and other Japanese snacks that are spicy as hell. The bar is small and perhaps built in the 1950's yet renovated for the 1980's. The small-tubed, 20-inch television was playing motorcycle racing with the volume set at 0. The bar is empty except for mamma-san. Though no business is coming in, she is humming happily. The bar is a bit chilly yet cozy and quiet enough to have a conversation.

We sit close to the end of the bar next to an old, pink Japanese phone that only dials locally within the neighborhood. I sit next to the bathroom and my new friend and shipmate from the USS Belleau Wood sits next to me on a tan, greenish-colored bar stools. They both squeak as we sit down. We lay our cigarettes, lighter and wallets down onto the bar.

## The Dialogue

Following the murder and trying to figure out what could have been the motive, my mind kept going back to this conversation. I had spent several hours talking with him and I kept thinking that maybe he could have said something that would give me a clue as to what and why the murder had occurred. Nobody was telling me anything for weeks and I was so worried about it, I kept thinking about the things he told me over and over. The following is how the conversation went to the best of my memory:

> Schindler: "I'm Schindler. What's your name?"
> Witte: "MSSN Witte"
> Schindler: (takes out a soft pack of regular Camel cigarettes and smiles) "Want a fag?"
> Witte: "What!?"
> Schindler: "A fag – a cigarette, in British"
> Witte: "Ha, ha, ha!, I thought the other meaning, ha, ha, ha!"

Schindler: "You would love me and I would fall asleep"

Witte: (unknowing what Schindler meant).

As Schindler lights his cigarette I noticed his Navy tattoos – a dagger with the number "41" on his inner, right arm which was the USS Midway's insignia and as he put his lighter on the bar I could see the other tattoo on the other side of his right forearm – a tiger, for his love for animals.

Witte: "So what do you do on the ship?"

Schindler: "I'm a radioman"

Witte: "Cool"

Schindler: "And you?"

Witte: "I manage the operation of the kitchen"

Schindler: "Yeah, I have seen you several times"

Unsatisfied with my MO (Military Occupation), I continue,

Witte: "I'll be taking a test to become a Master-at-Arms. I entered the military as a cook as they would give me a salary ranking of E3 and then transfer over to a Master-at-Arms as an E4. My job sucks, at the moment".

Schindler: "I know what you mean. I'm getting out of the Navy"

Witte: "Is your 4-years up?"

Schindler: "Well, I guess you could say that."

Witte: "What do you mean?"

Schindler: "I'm getting out on an administrative discharge"

Witte: "What's wrong?"

Schindler: "You would love me and I would fall asleep"

Again, I still couldn't understand what he meant by that phrase. It seemed as if Schindler did not want to tell me about it so we changed the topic by "swapping wallets".

In the Navy, we didn't have much entertainment in the Navy – especially when deployed at sea. Instead of asking other shipmates about themselves allowing them to sugar-coat their perfected lives, we simply swapped wallets. By looking through the other shipmates wallets, we could go through everything and then ask questions about who and why things were in their wallets.

I opened Schindler's Velcro and polyester wallet and started to go through his cards. He had three slots which accompanied six pictures. He had a picture of a middle-aged woman and another who appeared to be the same age as him. This prompted me to ask:

Witte: "Is this your girlfriend?"
Schindler: (sounding upset and defensive) "NO, man..."
Witte: "Oh, well, who is she?"
Schindler: "That's my sister, dude! What are you talking about?"
Witte: (pointing at the middle-aged woman) "And her?"
Schindler: "My mom."

Schindler seemed sad yet happy in the same facial expression. One could tell that he missed them dearly. Everyone loves their mother and family but to have pictures of them seemed a bit odd.

Schindler: "I miss them!"

I too, began to think about my sister and questioned myself for not having a picture of my sister and parents. Though I should also have a picture of my ex-girlfriend Yukiko, I did not.

Schindler: "Don't you have a girlfriend? Where is her picture!?
Witte: (trying to come up with excuses and lied) "I just met my girlfriend and I see her a lot so I don't have a picture of her yet."
Schindler: "I bet you like guys instead…"
Witte: "What!? No! No! Hell, no man…"
Schindler: "Well, I bet you would like it…"

Feeling uneasy on how the conversation was going, I ignored what he said and continued to look further in his wallet. I see a ring impression on the outside of his wallet which indicated that he did not use that rubber for quite some time.

Witte: "Ha, ha, ha! You hadn't gotten lucky for quite some time!"
Schindler: "Yeah, well, you would love me and I would fall asleep"

Again, I ignored his strange comment and we exchanged back our wallets. Just at that moment, mamma-san asks, "What drink?"

Schindler: "Screwdriver"
Witte: "Bacardi Rum and Coke"

"You got it!", Mamma-san says as she turns around to make our drinks from the make-shift bar/kitchen.

Schindler: "I bet I could drink you under the table"

Witte: (with doubt) "Yeah, right…". During this time in my age, I drank four beers and three rum cokes. I was quite confident that I could drink more than Schindler but needed to keep my head clear in preparations of ditching Schindler once my friends came.

"Bacardi Rum and Coke. Screwdriver", mamma-san says as she places our drinks on top of the coasters which are neatly organized on the bar.

Schindler pounds his drink to the very last ice cube as I watch him in amazement sipping my drink from a tiny red straw.

Schindler: "Told ya"
Witte: "Damn, Schindler! You're gonna get f\*\*ked up!"
Schindler: "I don't care. It has been some time since I had a drink"
Witte: "Been working hard?"
Schindler: "Nope."

Some Japanese rock music was playing in the background piercing Schindler's answer. My mind wonders a bit on why he hadn't drank in some time but begin to think about our next deployment to the Philippines on the 28th of October, 3 days from now.

The Snack Shipmates Bar door abruptly opens and another ship-mate looks in searching for his drinking buddies. He looks around and calmly yet in a drunken slur and asks us, "Have you seen Vins?"

I said to myself, "F\*\*k! That's Helvey!" He was the shipmate that had threatened to practically kill me for walking on the nicely shined deck! Quite a large, quiet yet short-tempered, six-foot, 200-pound walking time-bomb. I wasn't for sure if it was Helvey as there were a lot of guys similar to his type of build, but I knew that I had seen him before.

He didn't ask politely for his friend Vins, so my reply was monotone as if I really didn't care was, "Nope".

Hevley just looked at us and then shut the door.

Schindler: "I don't like that guy…"

Witte: "What? Who?"

Schindler: "Hevley. The guy that just came in the door looking for Vins".

Witte: "Ah, yeah. He threatened to kick my ass for walking on his deck that he was swabbing."

Schindler: "There's a lot more to that guy than you know."

Witte: "What do you mean?"

Schindler: "He hates faggots."

Witte: "Oh…?"

Schindler: "He's told several people that he hates faggots and that they shouldn't exist"

To my knowledge at that time, I had never met a gay person and to practically everyone on the ship, if you were gay, you would get thrown off the ship and into the water. And when you're overboard, no one can hear you since the ship's engine is so loud, no one could hear anything. Even being associated with someone who was homosexual would pretty much brand you as a homosexual. If any heard one being or associating with a homosexual, you would be sent to Captain's Mast. Without any credible evidence saying otherwise would get you kicked off the ship and sent for military discharge out from the Navy. The rumors on the ship were if you were considered gay, you would get harassed or physically thrown off the ship and into the ocean. This type of mentality was not taught in boot camp, A-school or from anyone I knew before going into the Navy. It was simply rumored on the USS Belleau Wood. Knowing that I knew of no one being gay, the topic wasn't something I was interested in discussing.

> Schindler: "Mamma-san, Sex On The Beach"
> Mamma-san: "Haaaaai" ("yes" in Japanese)
> Witte: "Damn, already for another drink?"
> Schindler: "Yup! It has been some time since I drank."
> Witte: "Yeah, I know what you mean. I drink a lot too."
> Schindler: "No, you don't know what I mean."
> Witte: "O...kay"
> Schindler: "Do you want to know why?"

"Sex On The Beach, desu", Mamma-san retrieves Schindler's empty glass of the Screwdriver he just slammed down his throat and replaced it with the Sex On The Beach.

> Schindler: "Have you heard of the guy that announced '2-q-t-2-b-s-t-r-8' over secured lines?"
> Witte: "Oh yeah! Damn. I feel sorry for that guy..."
> Schindler: "Well yeah... that was me. Initially, it was just a joke. Of course my drinking didn't help and probably was one of the two evils that made me do it, ha ha ha ha!"
> Witte: "No, sh*t!"
> Schindler: "Seriously, that was me!"

I was really starting to get nervous. This was one of my shipmates rumored to be gay and he was talking to me. Helvey saw us talking when he walked into the door a while ago. Perhaps he too, knew that Schindler was gay and now he thinks I'm gay for simply talking to Schindler. Since Schindler (and a few others) had been branded as what they called, a "Faggot", the average guy did NOT want to be associated with them. It is unfortunate to think about this in today's world, but back in the 1990s, it was serious.

Silence was thick.

Witte: "So…what was your punishment?
Schindler: "Ship Restriction for 30 days. It wasn't completely for the transmitting a personal announcement over secured lines, it was doing it while drunk!"

The Japanese rock music stopped. I was getting antsy to get away from him because I didn't want to be associated with someone that had been restricted to the ship and especially someone rumored to be gay. I was trying to think of a way to get out of the situation and away from Schindler without being obvious.

He tells me again that he will be leaving the Navy.

Then he says, "I'm gay."

My heart stopped and I began to feel I needed to run away. I knew then that this conversation was something that needed to be kept extremely quiet.

Witte: "Oh, sh*t, dude. You need to keep that to yourself"
Schindler: "Yeah, I know. But it's too late. Practically everyone aboard knows, thanks to the officers during my Captain's Mast."

Witte: "Huh?"

Schindler: "You wouldn't understand"

I leaned back in my chair looking towards the door hoping that my crew would come in at any moment to rescue me from this very awkward situation.

Schindler: "Are you expecting someone?"

Witte: "Yeah, a few of my guys are going to show up"

Schindler: "Aren't I one of your guys?"

Not replying nor saying anything further, I tried to divert the conversation towards mamma-san but she was back in the make-shift kitchen.

Witte: "Mamma-san, have any of my shipmates come by earlier?"

Mamma-san: "No, desu" ("desu" is a Japanese word to describe the end of a sentence)

Witte: "What are you cooking up?"

Schindler realizes that I'm trying to get out of the conversation and asks me if I'm trying to ignore him. I tell him no and ask him when he's getting out of the Navy.

Schindler: "I was supposed to get our earlier, but my discharge papers are taking too long"

Witte: "Are the officers holding something back?"

Schindler: "I'm not sure"

Witte: "Don't worry. Your discharge papers will go through"

Schindler: "I'm not sure, man. I'm not sure"

I sip on the melted ice of my Bacardi Rum and Coke. Mamma-san sees that my drink is empty and offers me another drink. The bottle of Bacardi Rum is from the base. Tax-free and a hell of a lot cheaper than buying from the liquor store in Japan which saves about $10. By bringing in your own bottle of liquor, you would not have to pay the $20 cover charge. Each bottle you bring into the bar is called a "Bottle Keep" where the mamma-san would write your name on the bottle and keep it behind the bar on a shelf. Mamma-san would make money by "pinching" or "taking" a few shots and provide that to other customers which she would make more profit. She also knows that I typically drink 2 glasses of Bacardi Rum and Coke so she places another drink for me on the bar.

Schindler: "Do you know what they do with gays on the ship"

Witte: "Yeah. Are you scared?"

Schindler: "Nah, I think they're rumors"

Witte: "Yeah, me too"

Schindler: "Sometimes I get a little scared because there are several shipmates that hate me. I think that if they hate me that much, they would throw me off of the ship"

Witte: "But if you're worried, you should at least tell your senior"

Schindler: "If I tell me senior then he would know that I am gay. And if that gets out more directly in my division, then everyone would know."

Witte: "Ah, yeah. But I think these are just rumors. I don't think anybody really would hurt you."

Schindler: "I'm not worried about getting hurt. I worry about getting killed"

Witte: "No one's going to kill you, man…relax"

Schindler: "I've heard a few conversations about people wanting to kill homosexuals"

Witte: "It's all talk."

He said that he was pretty sure that there are a few. He elaborated a little about a "gang" that were hell-bent on eliminating gays on the ship.

Sometimes there are others on our ship that do a bit of bullying. I had my share of it while we were at sea. A few shoves and an alteration that was ignited from nothing at all. When there are no women, no alcohol and no days off while at sea, months at a time, the ship becomes a floating metal gym locker filled with testosterone. If you haven't lived on a ship for over a month with all men, you have absolutely no idea how being at sea can alter a man's thinking and feelings.

Admittedly, I was curious to know why they wanted to throw Schindler off of the ship however, I did not want to know the precise details. Schindler already had a reputation for becoming a target by a group of shipmates on this ship. Recorded from the NIS [Naval Investigative Service, now known as the NCIS (Naval Criminal Investigative Service), Helvey had shown aggression towards Schindler as being 'bossy' and 'acting as a boss instructing others to do their job'. Schindler was a Petty Officer 3rd class and was indeed doing his job leading and instructing his subordinates. The manner in which Schindler executed tasks to his subordinates was not favored by Helvey.

Witte: "Well, we will be underway to the Philippines the day after tomorrow and you will be on shore duty.

Schindler: "That's the other problem. As I'm being separated, I'm supposed to be on shore duty.

Witte: "I don't understand…"

Schindler: "Way before the Captain's Mast (a legal procedure whereas the Captain of the command or ship gathers information and evidence of the accused and execute a punishment. This typically results in base or ship restriction for the accused), I told Captain Bradt that I was homosexual and that I wanted to be discharged from the Navy.

Witte: "Yeah, and…?"

Schindler: "He told me to tell no one. But things got worse. I really wanted to stay in San Diego and get discharged from there before moving to Japan. I'm not sure who knew that I was gay at that time.

Witte: "Do you think Captain Bradt told others about you being gay?"

Schindler: "I hardly think that he told anyone directly. I was hanging around a few civilian guys around San Diego who were gay. Maybe someone from our ship found out. I'm not sure. Soon after, some of the guys on the ship started talking behind my back. Few others would shove or push me in the passageways.

Witte: "And ever since, they kept pushing you around?"

Schindler: "After we left San Diego, it stopped a bit. But once we got to Pearl Harbor, it got a lot worse."

Witte: "Dude, that's messed up".

Schindler: "Right?"

Witte: "So, why did you blast that personal stuff ('2-q-t-2-b-s-t-r-8') over secured lines to the whole Pacific Fleet!?"

Schindler then finishes up his Sex-On-The-Beach drink and orders another drink. He then scoots his barstool closer to mine which pushed me to the wall of the bar's bathroom. It felt uncomfortable as it seemed if there was no way to escape. I could easily move out of my barstool directly left of me but if I had, it would have shown Schindler that I was no longer interested in his story and would have appeared rude. I lifted my left leg to rest my left calf onto my left knee preventing Schindler to move in closer, but there was enough room to maintain my distance from him advancing any closer. Schindler leans in over my leg and said softly without anyone hearing although no one was even remotely close to hear a word we were saying.

I felt very uncomfortable. I needed to get away somehow and fast! Schindler continued to explain while I was searching for ideas on how to conclude the conversation without being rude or pissing him off. Speculating that Schindler would say bad things about me on the ship if I were not to hear his whole story, I allowed him to continue.

Schindler: "I broadcasted '2-q-t-2-b-s-t-r-8' over secured lines because if I was going down, I wanted everyone to know who I was. I was already going to Captain's Mast after I was accused of A.W.O.L. (Absent With Out Leave) during Hurricane Iniki. So why not tell everyone who I am?

Witte: "Yeah, I guess."

Mamma-san places the 20-ounced, Kirin Beer bottle on the bar in front of Schindler. Schindler rubs the lip of the bottle in a circular motion and continues:

"During Captain's Mast, I was afraid that someone who attended my Captains Mast overheard and told everyone that I was gay. I told Captain Bradt 'you know what I am' yet he simply ignored what we had previously discussed. I suppose someone overheard that I was gay and that damage was pretty much done.

Witte: "So instead of being processed for discharge, you were restricted to the ship?"
Schindler: "Correct!"
Witte: "...and before you can begin the discharge process, you have to carry out your punishment?"
Schindler: "Correct, again, Shipmate!"

He gets out his wallet again and looks at the photos of his mom and sister, for a long time. It was obvious that he just wanted everything over as quickly as possible so he could go home. Just like any human would naturally do in a situation like this, I reached over and briefly patted his shoulder and said, "Don't worry, shipmate. You will see them soon. Everything will be fine."

"I hope so...", Schindler replies in a quiet voice and sniffs.

"Let me order you a drink".

"Mamma-san! Ni-hon Kirin, kudasai", Schindler requests two 20-ounce Kirin beer. Schindler slams the leftover beer he had on his previous bottle and says again, "I bet I can drink you under the table".

We changed the subject and started talking about our homes and growing up. We really had a lot in common and Schindler seemed like a great guy. Thankfully, the only person who saw us drinking and talking together was Helvey and Mamma-san. Thirty minutes had passed and we both were caught up on our growing up back in the states, the songs we liked and disliked, the televisions shows such as The Simpsons but the more he drank, the more the conversation was peppered with comments or questions that let me to believe he was trying to hit on me. Each time I would change the subject and it was becoming more uncomfortable.

He wanted to go bar-hopping and I told him no, that I was getting tired. I wanted to just get out of the situation and go back to the ship but I didn't want to be seen hanging out with him. I absolutely did NOT want to walk back to the ship with him not because he was gay, but because of the work culture of the ship (the known threat of being harmed for being gay or associating with homosexuals).

I began getting pissed at my friends not showing up. Perhaps they went elsewhere without me, feeling a bit left out and forced into this serious situation that I was presently in. Hopeful in every sip I took of my drink that my friends would show up, they never did. I was on my own and had absolutely no idea how to escape.

## Head Break

He finally had to go to the head (bathroom) and I found my opportunity. As soon as Schindler closed the door of the head to piss, I stood up and leaned over to Mamma-san four seats down from where Schindler and I were sitting and told her that this guy is gay and that I needed her help getting out of this situation.

Mamma-san's eyes got big and said, "Come here to the other side of the bar. I'll tell him that we are going to go eat Ramen." I then went around the bar and stood next to Mamma-san preparing what was coming next as soon as we heard Schindler flush the toilet.

Schindler opens the bathroom door and naturally walks toward the bar where we were talking and stops in his tracks to see that I had left the barstools.

Schindler then looks up at both Mamma-san and me, pauses and asks sternly, "What are you doing with my boyfriend!?"

My body froze and I became speechless. Mamma-san however, replied, "Witte-san promised me last night that he was going to eat Ramen with me tonight."

Schindler seemed upset and disappointed from his expression and actions as he grabbed his wallet from the bar and hastily walked towards the entrance to the bar. Schindler then pushed the bar door open and slammed shut the door without saying a word. No, "see you later" or "take care".

I was very relieved that I was able to get out of that situation however, I wasn't sure what Schindler was going to say about me when he got back to the ship. The thought of Schindler telling his shipmates that I was playing "hard to catch" or explaining his experience and conversation with me bothered me. This thought was briefly inter-rupted by Mamma-san who said, "Let me close down some things first and then we will go eat Ramen together."

As I waited for Mamma-san, I began to think of what I should do to prevent Schindler from spreading any rumors about our conver-sation and drinking together. Obviously, I could not tell just anyone about this as I too would be accused of homosexuality just talking to Schindler. If I were to report Schindler of his homosexuality, the Navy could also accuse me of associating with a homosexual which would land me an other-than-honorable Discharge.

If any of those "Gay Hating" shipmates who Schindler told me about found out about me talking to Schindler, I too could be a target for harassment. I needed to protect myself and my reputation before things got bad. I simply knew of no one would I could tell this story to except Szerlag, Knight and J.R.. And those f**kers didn't meet me at the bar tonight. If they had met me, Schindler would not have had talked to me.

"Ikimashouka"?, ("Let's go?" in Japanese), and so we went to the shopping plaza to find a mediocre Ramen shop to end the night.

## Where The F**K Were You Guys!?

The next morning, I awoke with excitement knowing that the USS Belleau Wood was going to the Philippines. Many of those who have been to the Philippines shared all of their stories about how much fun and entertainment you could have for $20 a night which included sex, a cooked meal, a long massage and a stay over. They mentioned that we would find these beautiful and exotic women in bars littering the streets of a city called "Olongapo".

But this excitement was suddenly replaced with the experience that I had last night drinking with Schindler. Unsure what kind of rumor Schindler could start on the ship sent fear inside of me. I needed to talk to Szerlag and Knight.

Knowing that both Szerlag and Knight were working today, I did my morning routine, got dressed and headed straight down 3 decks to the barber shop. I heard Metalica play from outside of the barber shop which was a clear indication that Knight was there. Walking closer to the glass door into the shop, I also saw Szerlag cleaning up hair clippings.

Knight turned down the music and said, "Hey Witte! What's up?"

I began to spill out the story that happened last night and when I mentioned, "Schindler said to Mamma-san and me 'What are you doing with my boyfriend'", Knight said, "Hold on…".

Knight walked over to the barber shop door, flipped the "Yes! We are open" sign to "Sorry, We are Closed", pulled down the shade and locked the door. Knight's expression displayed strong concern as well as fear.

The first thing that Knight asked me was, "Schindler? As in Allen Schindler!?" Keep in mind that Knight was the barber and he knew everybody and everything that went on around the ship. He said he had already heard some scuttlebutt about Schindler and me. Then he advised me to stick to someone and don't get caught alone anywhere. I needed to find my senior (PO Martinez) and tell him what happened.

Szerlag went to go find Martinez and Knight continued to explain things to me. He said that One: you could get thrown off the ship when we are deployed. Two: You could get an other-than-honorable Discharge. Three: You could get your ass kicked.

Even though I wasn't gay, it didn't matter. Anyone could report you for being homosexual. And since Knight had already heard about this rumor, it's only a matter of time until it reaches the master chiefs. Then, they are obligated to report you and submit you to Captain's Mast.

## The Silence Before The Storm Brews

Szerlag returned and said that Martinez would be here in a few minutes. I continued with my story to Knight and Szerlag saying that I didn't know who Schindler was until we sat down and talked. He seemed like a cool guy, nice and friendly. I remembered seeing his face before, but I forgot who he was. I told him the whole story about how I felt like he was hitting on me and I was trying to figure a way to get out of the situation. I mentioned Helvey coming into the bar, looking for Vins. I really didn't know if it was Helvey or Schindler who had started the rumor.

They both said that I really needed to confront both Helvey and Schindler and find out what was being said. I needed to let both of them know that they can't be saying things about me that aren't true and could jeopardize my career in the Navy or worse, get thrown off

Now, I was even more scared and concerned for my wellbeing and my career in the Navy.

Knight and Szerlag had nothing personal against gays in the Navy. Up until homosexuals and bisexuals were allowed to serve after 1993, any speculation of being gay would grant Captain's Mast. As there wasn't any real evidence to prove one was homosexual, just simply being rumored to being gay was enough to be seen as homosexual. Basically, you could be known as being gay and be other-than-honorable Discharged. Proving that you were not homosexual or bisexual was very difficult to prove. Szerlag and Knight were my best buddies in the Navy and anyone who you hung out with was there to fight with you until death. Szerlag and Knight's intentions were not to harm anyone regardless of being homosexual, bisexual or straight, but to protect their shipmate who was falsely accused which could result in serious consequences – either being harmed or other-than-honorable Discharged, which was my situation. They wanted to help. Only by reporting the incident drinking with Schindler at Snack Shipmates on October 25 to our seniors would fall on deaf ears.

Knight went on to tell us about two small gangs on the ship, known as the "Fabulous Five" and the "Gay Bashers". Not knowing who exactly these people are, I needed to keep this to myself and be very aware of my surroundings until we could confront Schindler and Helvey, find out who started the rumor and set them straight.

Martinez came in and we brought him up to date. He didn't seem near as worried about it until it was brought up that if both Schindler AND Helvey said that I was gay, I could be brought up to Captain's Mast. Martinez is a great guy and likes everyone. He didn't really care if anyone was gay or not. But he was my senior. Any issues that I had, he was responsible for. It wasn't his obligation to take care of his shipmates, it was just the kind of person he is. He cared for a lot of people and didn't mind helping anyone out. He was one of the guys who would give you his last dollar to help.

We conclude that I shouldn't worry too much. Martinez is going to talk to a friend, who is an Ensign (a low-ranking officer), and he would know how to handle everything. He tells me to stay close and don't get out of his sight until he figures out what to do. If I go off the ship either he will go with me or Szerlag and Knight.

Witte: "Thank you, Martinez. What about drinking on our last day here?"
Martinez: "You have tomorrow off, right?
Witte: "Yes"

Martinez: "I'll go drinking with you. And if we see Schindler or Hevley, we will talk with them."

Witte: "Thank you, Martinez"

Martinez: "No problem. It will be fine, okay?"

Knight walks to the barber shop door and unlocks it again. He flips the "Sorry, We are Closed" sign back to "Yes, We are Open" as Martinez and I leave the barber shop. "Thanks, Knight", I said and Knight simply replies, "No problem, brother".

Martinez has me walk in front of me as he feels that I need someone to watch out for me. We walk back up 3 decks to the galley and go back to work. Every-so often, Martinez checks on me.

Martinez, Knight, Szerlag have my back to make sure nothing happens to me. It reminded me of my best friend Michael back in Irving who would fight my fights and protect me. Of course I can fight my own battles, but it's great knowing that I have good friends who would go up and beyond for me.

Friends are awesome! Or are they?

*The bleachers where Helvey, Vins and another group of sailors were drinking beer, Gin and Juice before Helvey and Vins went back to Sailor Town. Crime photos provided by the Sasebo Police Department given to NCIS and later in 2015, obtained through the FOIA (Freedom Of Information Act).*

*A more closer look at the leftovers of Helvey and Vins's drinking session. It is quite common and legal to drink in public in Japan. Crime photos provided by the Sasebo Police Department given to NCIS and later in 2015, obtained through the FOIA (Freedom Of Information Act).*

*Leftover drinks from Helvey and Vins's heavy drinking session. Crime photos provided by the Sasebo Police Department given to NCIS and later in 2015, obtained through the FOIA (Freedom Of Information Act).*

*The Orange Juice and Miller Beer which Helvey was drinking from. These items were purchased from the base store as it was cheaper to purchase than from the Japanese stores. Crime photos provided by the Sasebo Police Department given to NCIS and later in 2015, obtained through the FOIA (Freedom Of Information Act).*

000704

(#1) *The fisheye glass window where I saw the murder happen. (#2) Women's bathroom. (#3) water fountain. Going left was the common route we sailors took as a shortcut to get back to the Sasebo Naval Base. Going right was the direction to where Shore patrol, the bleachers where Helvey and Vins drank at Nimitz park and then across the Albuquerque Bridge and Sailor Town. All of us would use this public bathroom as it was the halfway point from Sailor Town and our ship. We all would stop here to urinate as it took forever to get to our ship to urinate. Crime photos provided by the Sasebo Police Department given to NCIS and later in 2015, obtained through the FOIA (Freedom Of Information Act).*

*The exact bathroom (with the fisheye brick wall) taken by me in 2009 to re-enact the position where I left PO3 Martinez at the bench to use the restroom. From this position, I watched Helvey stomp forcefully yet could not see a body on the ground from the outside. It appeared that Helvey was stomp-dancing as I heard him sing as he stomped on the floor. There is a lamppost within 50 feet to the right however during my taking of this picture, the lamppost light was off.*

*The exact position from the exact bathroom window where I finally saw what Helvey was stomping on as I reached the fisheye brick wall. The body was motionless (between the urinal and window on the floor). Picture was taken by me in 2009.*

An NCIS agent re-enacts the position which Helvey was when I saw him jumping up and down on top of Allen Schindler's body. A few more steps closer I approached when I realized that there was a motionless body. Crime photos provided by the Sasebo Police Department given to NCIS and later in 2015, obtained through the FOIA (Freedom Of Information Act).

An NCIS agent poses to show how clear the fisheye-brick glass is if approached closer than which I saw. Crime photos provided by the Sasebo Police Department given to NCIS and later in 2015, obtained through the FOIA (Freedom Of Information Act).

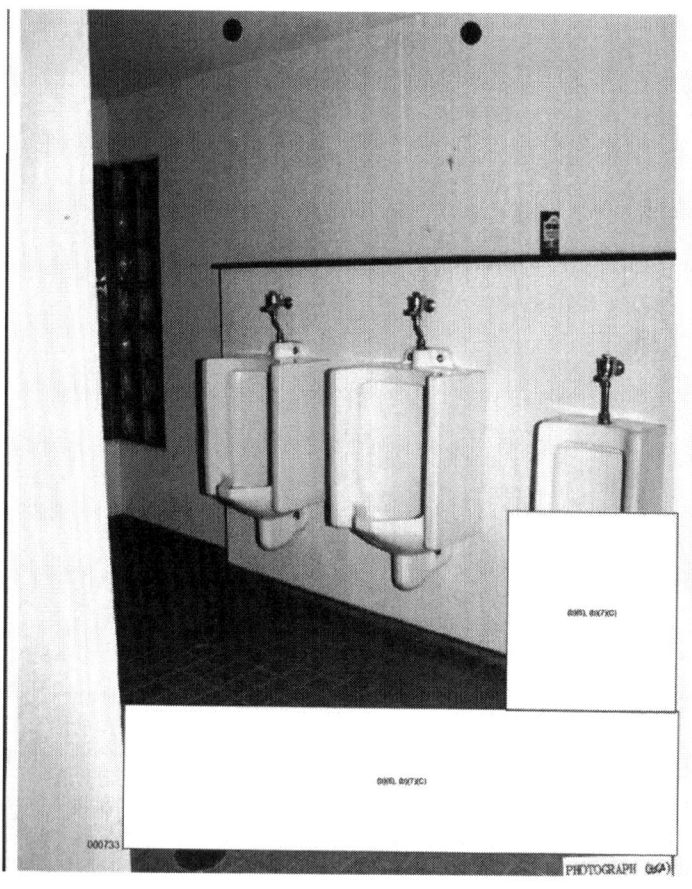

*The view of the urinals when entering the bathroom. The urinal to the left was being used by Allen Schindler. Helvey pretended to urinate in the urinal to the right. Crime photos provided by the Sasebo Police Department given to NCIS and later in 2015, obtained through the FOIA (Freedom Of Information Act).*

PHOTOGRAPH (209)

(#4) shows the urinal which Allen Schindler was using during his urinating. (#5) is the Georgia coffee can which Helvey was drinking from. Crime photos provided by the Sasebo Police Department given to NCIS and later in 2015, obtained through the FOIA (Freedom Of Information Act).

*Two NCIS agents showing the positions of how I (NCIS agent on the left) was standing when I saw Helvey (NCIS agent on the right) as he was jumping and stomping on Allen Schindler's body. Crime photos provided by the Sasebo Police Department given to NCIS and later in 2015, obtained through the FOIA (Freedom Of Information Act).*

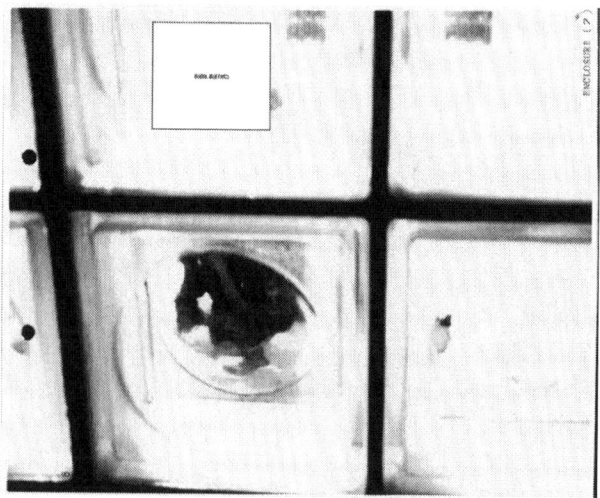

*An NCIS agent squats to show how clear I saw Allen Schindler's body as Helvey was stomping onto him. Crime photos provided by the Sasebo Police Department given to NCIS and later in 2015, obtained through the FOIA (Freedom Of Information Act).*

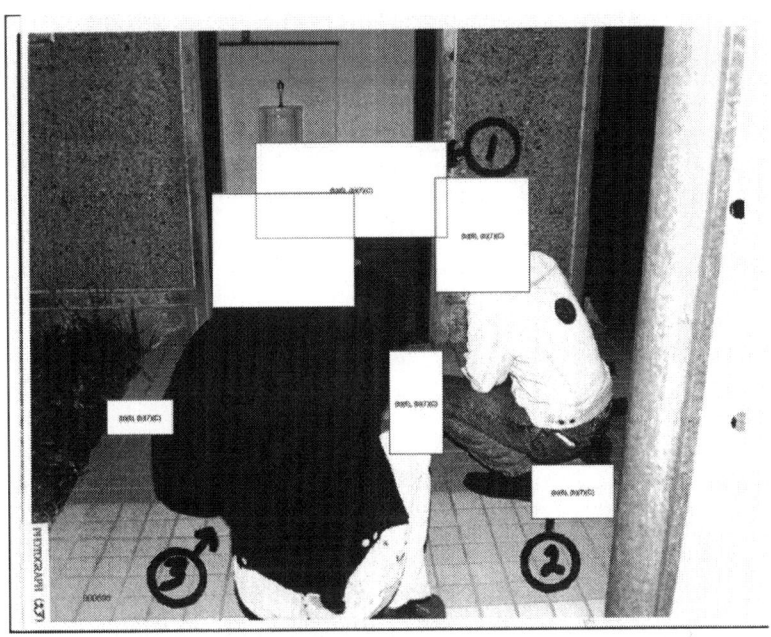

*PO Martinez (left) and I (right) pointing to where we saw Allen Schindler laying down, face-up, gurgling his own blood. He was motionless yet believed we had a chance to save him. I was the only one who did not enter the bathroom as there wasn't enough room. From this place where we are squatting, we carried him to the ground a few yards from here to get a better grip to further carry him. Crime photos provided by the Sasebo Police Department given to NCIS and later in 2015, obtained through the FOIA (Freedom Of Information Act).*

*The actual bathroom where Allen Schindler was brutally murdered. This picture was taken by me in 2009. Allen Schindler's head was lying to the right of the floor drain. His blood was splattered against the bottom part of the urinal and the wall to the right.*

*This is me pointing to where we saw Allen Schindler lying down. The black strips on the ground are tape to track sneaker marks and blood. Crime photos provided by the Sasebo Police Department given to NCIS and later in 2015, obtained through the FOIA (Freedom Of Information Act). (Freedom of Information Act)*

*PO Martinez (left) points from where he saw the murder take place. I (right) point into the direction where Shore Patrol were. Note: I took off from the fisheye glass window (#3). I was asked to point for investigation purposes. Crime photos provided by the Sasebo Police Department given to NCIS and later in 2015, obtained through the FOIA (Freedom Of Information Act).*

*Actual NCIS photo on 10/28/1992 of me pointing to where I had summoned the Shore Patrolmen. I clipped the photo and magnified it (left) to show the remaining dried blood after washing off with only water. Crime photos provided by the Sasebo Police Department given to NCIS and later in 2015, obtained through the FOIA (Freedom Of Information Act).*

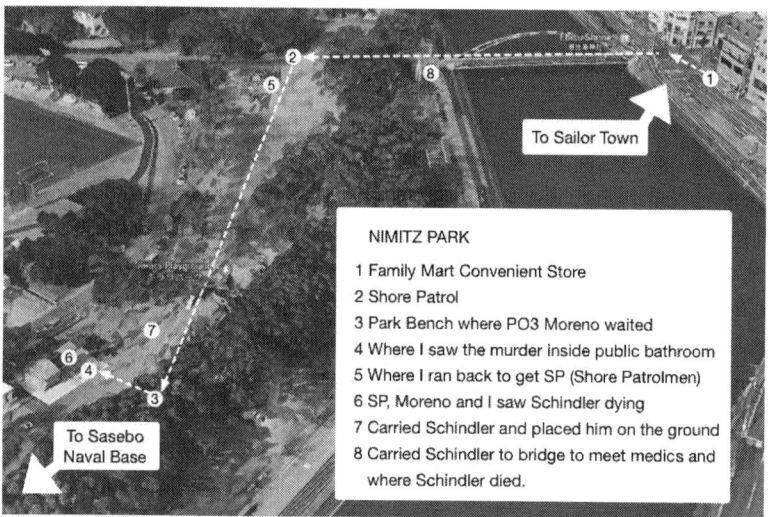

NIMITZ PARK

1 Family Mart Convenient Store
2 Shore Patrol
3 Park Bench where PO3 Moreno waited
4 Where I saw the murder inside public bathroom
5 Where I ran back to get SP (Shore Patrolmen)
6 SP, Moreno and I saw Schindler dying
7 Carried Schindler and placed him on the ground
8 Carried Schindler to bridge to meet medics and
   where Schindler died.

*The locations of the events and paths which happened from the bars, to the murder and to where Schindler died. Map provided by Google Earth.*

THE CHASE

A Where the murder took place
B Helvey & Vins washes blood off
C Helvey & Vins fight with Shore Patrolmen
D Helvey & Vins dump clothing evidence

E Create alibi visiting bars and shipmates
F Helvey & Vins looks for money exchange
   location but instead meet MA with a car
G MA drives Helvey & Vins back to base
H Helvey & Vins gets dropped off at back gate

*Map showing the most probable routes given by Helvey, Vins and NCIS testimonies. Map provided by Google Earth.*

*(#1) is where the murder took place. (#3) is where we placed Allen Schindler's body to get a better grip on him. (#4) was where PO Martinez was waiting for me on the picnic bench. (#5) is the direction to Sailor Town, to Albuquerque Bridge and where Shore Patrol were sitting. Crime photos provided by the Sasebo Police Department given to NCIS and later in 2015, obtained through the FOIA (Freedom Of Information Act).*

*After we placed Allen Schindler onto the ground for us to get a better grip to carry him to the bridge, a mix of Japanese and US coins (1,003 Yen) and American ($0.98) fell out of his fanny pack. Crime photos provided by the Sasebo Police Department given to NCIS and later in 2015, obtained through the FOIA (Freedom Of Information Act).*

*The Albuquerque Bridge where we carried Allen Schindler to and awaiting for the medics to arrive and to this point where we lost his pulse. The ambulance finally arrived on the other side of the bridge and brought the gurney across it. Picture was taken by me in 2009.*

*The fence to the Japanese Self Defense Force which Helvey and Vins jumped over after escaping Shore Patrol. Crime photos provided by the Sasebo Police Department given to NCIS and later in 2015, obtained through the FOIA (Freedom Of Information Act).*

ENCLOSURE ( 5 )

*The jean jacket which Helvey borrowed. The sleeves were torn off at the river as they contained blood. After fighting with Shore Patrol, Helvey dumped it at the Japanese Self Defense Force property. Crime photos provided by the Sasebo Police Department given to NCIS and later in 2015, obtained through the FOIA (Freedom Of Information Act).*

*XO R. Franklin. Current location and occupation unknown. Name changed and identity withheld as it could cause serious risk to other sailor's moral and security.*

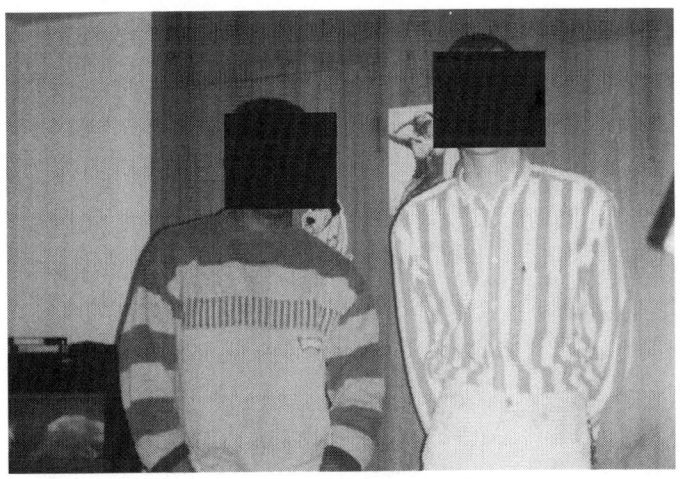

*Sims (left) and Eastman (right), two of the "Fabulous Five" members in the Yokokuska dormitory/barracks during the Court Martial "U.S. Versus Hevley" trial in 1993. Their visual identities intentionally concealed. I took this picture as a historic part of the so-called 'conspiracy'.*

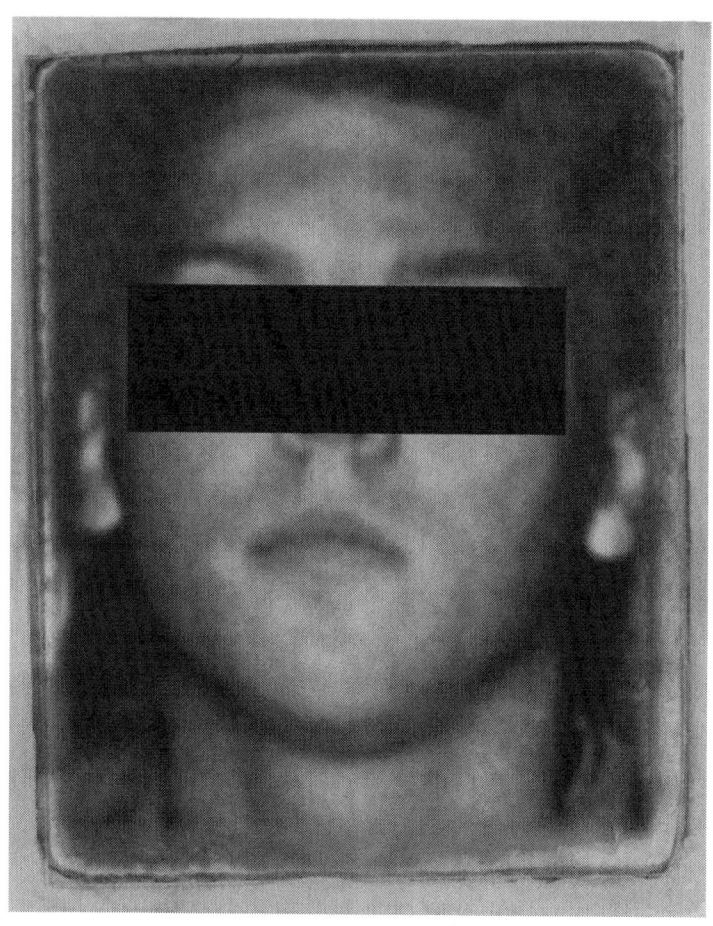

*Charles Vins's Ship photo ID obtained by a shipmate who I served with on the USS Belleau Wood. He is linked to the assault but not the punch/ kick/stomp the last blows that killed Allen Schindler and therefore have concealed his identity.*

*Helvey is being escorted out of the courtroom by his defense attorney, Lieutenant Smith*

# CHAPTER 10

# DARK LIBERTY

October 27, 1992

**NOTE:**

*The following were testimonies provided by Terry Helvey, Charles 'Chuck' Vins, PO3 Martinez, CPO Aptimes, BT Parsons, OS Johnson and myself, MS Witte. All testimonies were taken from a 900-page report provided by the Naval Criminal Investigative Services under the FOIA (Freedom of Information Act) and my own first-hand, witnessed accounts. The images shown and taken the night of the murder are both from the NCIS report as well as my own (taken 17 years afterwards). The images of the murder investigation have intentionally been censored by NCIS.*

*Any news reports since Allen Schindler's murder should be considered fabricated, exaggerated, misled, misinformed and/or out of context. I did not know who the killer(s) or the victim were until after the facts and/or incident in which I was involved. I have included their testimonies along with the times of the events to better describe the events which took place. The following are the true actual and detailed accounts that happened as I was there through it all.*

Yesterday was uneventful. No one came by to harass me. Martinez came by to wake me up and check on me to make sure that nothing had happened to me, "You good?", PO3 Martinez asked. "Yeah, all good, thank you".

"We only need to work for a few hours and then we can go out to do our food shopping and go grab our last drink before we get underway for the Philippines", Martinez reminded me.

"Sounds good! I'm going to do my four-S's (Sh*t, Shower, Shave and Smoke) and then I'll meet you in the galley", informing Martinez of my morning routine.

I headed out to the starboard side port window to smoke where I saw two of my shipmates smoking. They had just started to talk about another shipmate and one of the members of the "Fabulous Five":

Shipmate #1: "Whatever you do, don't tell the Filipinas (women from the Philippines) your real name"
Shipmate #2: "F**k no. I'd hate to get called by the OOD (Officer Of the Deck) saying that I had a new baby"

Knight walks out onto the smoking section and lights up his cigarette and says to the two shipmates, "What's up, shipmates?" however, Knight doesn't say anything to me except gives me a clandestine nod hoping that no one recognizes that he's associated with me. I kinda got the clue so I just leaned up against the bulkhead, smoked and continued to listen to the two shipmates talk.

Shipmate #1 and #2: "What's up, Knight"
Knight: "What's up, shipmates"
Shipmate #1: "(continues the conversation) No way you'd want that"

Shipmate #2: "I know. Well, there's too much sh*t happening on the ship that would not let us have Liberty in the Philippines"

Knight: "What are you guys talking about?"

Shipmate #2: "Someone got jumped last night"

Shipmate #1: "What do you mean, 'jumped'?"

Shipmate #2: "You know, all the sh*t going down with other shipmates getting punched while they slept"

Shipmate #1: "Huh? Who got punched?"

Shipmate #2: "Eastman, something"

Shipmate #1: "Why did Eastman get punched?"

Shipmate #2: "I'm not sure"

Shipmate #1: "Well, sh*t…then we won't get laid in paradise" (typically and depending on the nature of incidents, if one sailor causes a problem, the whole ship gets punished such as being restricted to the ship. For Eastman being hit, we would have most likely all been restricted from Liberty and Leave once we hit the port of the Philippines).

Knight doesn't even ask any further or add onto the discussion. He leans over the window and looks outward into the port and exhales a large quantity of smoke and then rests his head into his hands.

Shipmate #2: "Hey Knight, can you cut my hair tonight?"

Knight: "Yeah, sure. Come by in the evening"

Shipmate #1: "(talking to Shipmate #2) Let's go. We gotta go back to work."

Shipmate #2: "Take care, Knight. I'll see you later"

Knight: "alright, shipmate"

The two shipmates flicked their cigarettes into the Sasebo bay and walked into the ship. It was only Knight and I smoking.

Knight looks back into the ship to check if anyone was nearby. He then comes close to me and silently says:

Knight: "You see what I mean?"

Witte: "About what?"

Knight: "Eastman got punched"

Witte: "So? I've punched someone for not returning my cassette player"

Knight: "Eastman is one of the members of the 'Fabulous Five'"

Witte: "You mean, Schindler's friend?"

Knight: "Yup. You really need to watch your back"

Witte: "F**k"

Knight: "'F**k' is right. Where the f**k is Martinez?"

Witte: "He's just inside the galley"

Knight: "You need to stay close to him"

Witte: "huh? I am close. Martinez is just inside"

Knight: "Dude, you cannot afford to be smoking out hear alone"

Knight doesn't even finish his cigarette and flicks it into the bay outside of the starboard port window. He grabs mine from my hand and sparks go to the deck. He says sternly, "come with me". "What the f**k, Knight!?", I said as he flicks my cigarette into the bay.

Knight places his arm around my shoulders and walks me inside the ship and then into the galley.

"Martinez! Martinez! Where are you?", Knight shouts into the galley. Martinez answers, "Right here!".

Knight seemed very concerned and angry with Martinez even though Martinez is Knight's senior. Knight then tells Martinez, "don't let Witte out of your sight!" Martinez simply says, "okay" and Knight abruptly disappears out of the galley and into the ship.

For the rest of the afternoon, Martinez and I worked on the day's task until around 6:00pm when our shift ended. We both cleaned up our leftover mess and walked back to our division's berthing area. Martinez and my bunks were directly across from each other and we changed from our working Navy Dungarees and into civilian clothes.

Martinez sprayed on some Old Spice cologne and we headed out of the berthing area and to the hanger deck to check out with the OOD (Officer Of the Deck). We walked on the gangway and onto Sasebo Naval Base. As we were walking, Martinez recommends another place to drink, "Let's go to the Shooter's Bar. I don't think it would be a good idea to go to Snack Shipmates cause Schindler may go there looking for you". I agreed, "yeah, I agree. Also, I need a change of bars"

Knight and Szerlag was supposed to meet up with us but we had forgotten to tell them which bar we would meet up at. There were only a handful of bars in Sailor Town so we would surely meet up in one of them. We would try to meet up later to then look for Schindler or Helvey and confront them in hopes that they would retract the rumor that either of them had spread.

## Nimitz Park
OCTOBER 27, 1992 – 21:10

Martinez and I walked through Nimitz Park which was Sasebo City's public park. Anyone leaving the base for Sailor Town or the shops would cut through this park instead of walking all the way around it saving around 15 minutes. There was also a public bathroom conveniently located halfway on the path from the bars back to the base. All of us who would get drunk would finish our last sip of alcohol, walk through Nimitz Park, to the public bathroom to urinate, then continue on the path back to the base. There weren't any bathrooms on the way from the base's front gate until you got to the ship, so the Nimitz Park public bathroom was where we all frequented to urinate.

A lot happens in Nimitz park. Typically, this is the park where sailors who were pinching pennies couldn't afford 500-Yen drinks (USD$5) would buy drinks from the store and drink here. Sometimes, you would catch or hear sailors with bar-girls behind the bushes. A few fights would get out of hand or happy, drunk sailors would yell out jokes.

To keep the peace, the SP (Shore Patrolman who patrol places where sailors would frequent) would be assigned to the park to keep them at bay. The SP had batons for hitting sailors to have them yield, handcuffs and 2-way radios for communications.

As we came up to the end of the park which connects the park to Sailor Town, we ran into three SP from our ship that were patrolling Nimitz park; Chief Petty Officer Aptimes, Boilter Technician Parsons and Operation Specialist Johnson.

CPO Aptimes: "You guys stay out of trouble"

OS Johnson: "Don't be late getting back to the ship. We are shipping out tomorrow morning 10:00AM"
Martinez: "We are just going out for a few beers"
CPO Aptimes: "Aye, aye, have fun shipmates!"

The three SP sat down on the back support of the park bench with their feet on the bench seat and began talking about the fun time that they will have in the Philippines.

BT Parsons: "I wonder how many of these drunk bastards we will have to round up for deployment"
CPO Aptimes: "Nah, they will be back on board"
Martinez: "See you later"

Martinez and I continued our way out of Nimitz Park, over the Albuquerque Bridge that took us over a small inlet and into Sailor Town. I didn't feel that those SP were any of the "Fabulous Five" or the "Gay Bashers" which Knight told us about as they seemed nice and supportive of us sailors going out drinking before our deployment.

We were unaware that Helvey, Vins and two other shipmates were also in Nimitz Park less than 100 yards away by the bleachers mixing and drinking Vodka with Orange Juice. They had just finished watching "Single White Female" at the movie house on the base.

Public Intoxication is perfectly legal in Japan. You could walk with a liter of Vodka and take a swig of it in front of a Japanese cop, wave at him and nothing would happen except that the Japanese cop would simply wave back. Shore Patrol however, were there to ensure nothing got out of hand when we sailors drank more than we could handle.

## Shooters Bar
OCTOBER 27, 1992 – 21:30

Once we got to the Shooters Bar, the mood changed positively. We sat down with smiles on our faces, ordered an Asahi Beer and began laughing about other clumsy shipmates and our Filipino chief's bad English. The time that we had helped keep my mind off of the potential threats that I would go through.

Martinez wasn't much of a drinker so I paced my drinking with him. We only had a beer each as we needed to check the other three bars for Szerlag and Knight and possibly sit and drink there. By the time we drank at a total of 4 bars, we would be almost drunk.

Other drunken shipmates started to come into Shooters Bar which made it more difficult to talk. The bar owner turned up the music which made it less enjoyable and Martinez suggested that we go check out some other bars.

I gave Martinez a nod agreeing with his suggestions as I slammed the leftover beer in my bottle of Asahi.

We went to the Bunny Bar – no Szerlag or Knight. We headed over to Prime Bar – No Szerlag or Knight. We then headed over to Bar Sakura – no Szerlag or Knight. "Maybe they were looking for us too and then headed to Snack Shipmates", I informed Martinez. Martinez looks at me in doubt since that's where the trouble started. "Yeah, okay. Let's just drink one more beer and if no one else is there, let's just go back to the ship", Martinez agreed.

We walked about 10 minutes to Snack Shipmates Bar and poked our heads in. All of the seats were taken – a full bar! There were no seats available nor did we see Szerlag or Knight.

Martinez and I were exhausted walking around looking for our friends so Martinez said that he was tired from walking around and suggested that we just get a beer from the convenience store and drink it on our walk back to our ship. I agreed.

## 23:10

Helvy and Vins separated from the other two shipmates and went back into Sailor Town. Though they both had no money to buy any more drinks, they still poked their heads inside the bars looking for friends to borrow money from to drink more.

According to Charles Vins's (the accessory to the murder) testimony, both Vins and Helvey noticed Schindler walk by when they left the bar "Pub Eagle". They both began to follow Schindler after Helvey said, "Let's go f**k with him".

## 23:20 - Nimitz Park

Both Helvey and Vins continued to follow Schindler from Sailor Town, across Albuquerque Bridge, past the Shore Patrolmen and into the Nimitz Park.

About this time, Martinez and I had stopped at a convenience store before crossing Albuquerque Bridge.

## 23:20 - Albuquerque Bridge

Martinez and I walked into the "Family Mart", the last convenience store before Nimitz Park.

"I thought you were going to buy a beer?", I asked Martinez thinking that we could continue our laughing and drinking on our walk through Nimitz Park on the way back to our ship. Martinez instead bought a pint of orange juice. I still bought an Asahi and a box of chocolate "Pocky Sticks" (sweet sticks dipped in chocolate).

Martinez simply answered, "Nah, I'm good" and then we left the "Family Mart" towards Albuquerque Bridge.

## 23:30

Martinez and I crossed Albuquerque Bridge where we again met the three Shore Patrolmen; BT Parsons, CPO Aptimes, and OS Johnson who were all smoking cigarettes and sitting on the picnic bench at the entrance next to a Coca-cola vending machine as we walked by them.

> CPO Aptimes: "(talking to Martinez and I) Damn, you guys finished early!"
>
> PO3 Martinez: "Yeah, we're getting ready for tomorrow's deployment"
>
> OS Johnson: "Lucky bastards. We still have watch until 04:00 AM"
>
> PO3 Martinez: "(smiles) Well, get some rest when you get back to the ship"
>
> CPO Aptimes: "Okay, walk back safe!"

…and we thought we were…

As Helvey and Vins trail Schindler's path towards the US Naval Base Sasebo, Schindler enters the Nimitz Park public bathroom. Just as

Schindler entered, Helvey began to jog towards and into the restroom leaving Vins shortly behind.

Helvey and Vins were walking closely behind Schindler. The facts that it takes a grown man about a minute to urinate and that the area around the bathroom had enough light around to cover 50 feet a lamp post was within another 30-36 feet (10-12 yards) which align with the path that we take between Sailor Town and the US Naval Base Sasebo.

In Japan, typical Japanese public bathrooms do not have doors to enter inside, especially for the men. The reason for this is that traditionally, Japanese mothers do not work and take their children out to parks during the weekdays. When their little boys are old enough to use the bathrooms themselves, mothers need to be able to watch out for them from the outside.

There is plenty of daylight shining through the walls filled with "fisheye" bricks enabling mothers to see 50% inside the bathrooms. For this particular public bathroom, the foot-sized "fisheye" bricks were built 80% of the walls; 7 feet high and 5 feet wide, equaling 35, foot-sized, "Fisheye" transparent brick windows, 2 feet from the base/floor and ceiling. During the night, transcendent lights shine out of the bathroom clearly showing people inside using the bathroom but concealed by the urinals so there IS privacy. The women's restrooms were on the left and the men's on the right with a breezeway and a water fountain in the middle.

Helvey enters the bathroom and sees Schindler facing the 1st urinal on the far left against the wall and away from the entrance. Helvey already knows what Schindler looks like and recognizes him. Helvey steps between the 1st and 3rd urinal up to the 2nd one pretending to urinate next to where Schindler is urinating. This is typically an uncommon protocol for men when we urinate, but it happens sometimes.

Schindler notices Helvey to his right and says, "Hi!". This is when Vins steps into the bathroom and notices Helvey staring Schindler down. Helvey then lifts up his right hand preparing for a punch. Schindler confused, steps back from urinating with his pants zipper open. Before Schindler had the opportunity to return his penis back into his pants, the fight begins.

Helvey punches Schindler in the face several times and almost knocked Schindler out. Schindler loses his balance and falls to the ground. Helvey continues to punch Schindler as Schindler tries to regain his stance. They begin to wrestle with each other with one putting the other in a chokehold. Schindler bites Helvey on the arm at one point and Vins steps in to help Helvey kick Schindler several times. Both men continue to wrestle and punch each other until Schindler is lying on the floor, unconscious bleeding and defenseless. This was when I was approaching the restroom.

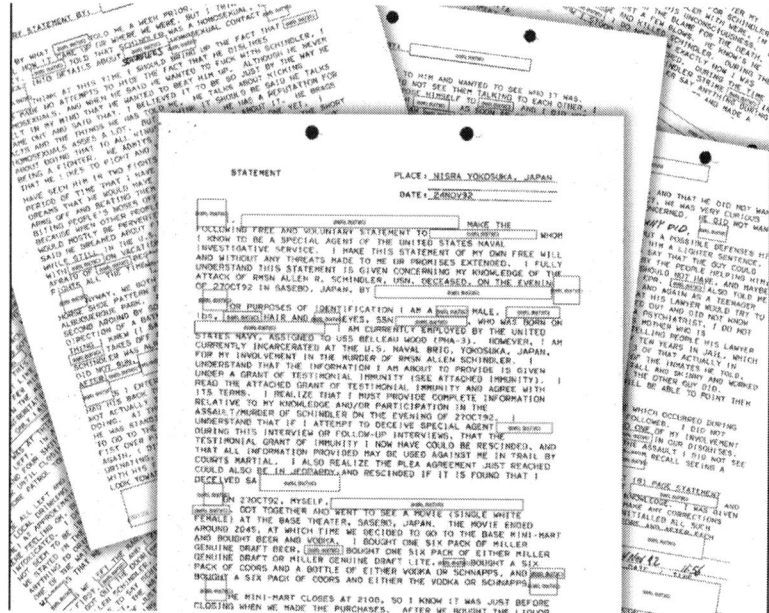

*Charles Vins' Testimony describing the accounts of what happened during the murder. Obtained through the FOIA (Freedom Of Information Act). Vins describes his assaulting in order to protect himself from Schindler rushing towards him however, it stopped as Helvey continued his assault on Schindler.*

## 23:45

Martinez was wearing a black jean jacket and I was wearing a dyed blue jean jacket with the music band RUSH logo centered on my back, which my sister gave me for my 18th birthday. Our jackets were enough to keep us comfortable in the partly-cloudy, 64-degree October night. The leaves had just begun to fall and scatter on the ground.

We walked slowly away from Sailor Town and away from the Shore Patrolmen sitting, smoking and chatting on the park bench.

We walked 350 feet (116 yards) from where the Shore Patrolmen were when I decided that I needed to relieve myself. Martinez didn't. So we walked over to a picnic bench where he would wait for me. I placed my beer and Pocky Sticks on the table. Martinez sat on the table with his feet on the seat while I made my way to the bathroom.

As I walk within 40 feet (13 yards), I hear some strong breathing noises which sounded as if I was overhearing a sailor and a Japanese bar-girl having sex in the bushes nearby. It was a faintly-lit area, but someone would be able to see another person clearly within 50 feet of the public bathroom.

I looked towards the restroom and see from the outside two large guys; one of the guys had just separated from the other and walked out of view, so he was blocked from my vision. The other large guy was jumping up and down violently as if he was at a thrash-metal mosh pit stomping up and down and up and down continuously with both feet. After every stomp, he would jump back up high into the air to where I could see both of his knees bending.

What was strange was that the guy stomping seemed very dedicated in stomping with such force that the other guy was still standing in the threshold.

Thinking that Martinez was seeing what I was seeing from his distance, I said, "Do you see this crazy f**ker dancing!?"

Martinez didn't answer but smirked. He was indeed seeing the guy in the bathroom stomping crazily.

When I got closer to the bathroom 20-feet (6 yards) away, I noticed that the guy was dancing unlike any type of dancing known at the time. He was concentrating only on one area of the floor which was right behind the "Fisheye" transparent brick windows. I was unable to see the floor but I was able to recognize the clothing he was wearing now; blue jean jacket, blue jeans and a dark-blue baseball cap. I was also able to see his white tennis shoes as he was jumping quite high. If it was some type of dancing, it was a weird one.

I really didn't want to go in there because this guy was obviously acting strange but didn't want to go in the bushes. I did not want to approach the couple f**king in the bushes. I rather preferred approaching the two strange guys dancing more as it would have been less awkward. Martinez would have given me a hard time about that. Since I was just about to the men's window, I thought that I should go ahead and commit to using the public bathroom.

## 23:47

I get within 10 feet, then to 3 feet (3 yards, then to 1 yard) and I hear grunts and the guy singing an unknown song as he's stomping.

Then I see the most horrific scene a human could ever see. During the next few seconds, I saw him stomping on another person, over and over, forcefully, repeatedly. Beneath each of his stomps, I could see a lifeless body bouncing back with the force; blood gushing out of the mouth and eyes; grunting; heavy breathing; unrecognizable face and so much blood – splattering all over the fisheye windows. I was so shocked and horrified, I couldn't move. It simply would not register in my brain. I froze.

A few seconds later, I managed to yell out to myself, "Oh sh*t!". It was loud enough for Martinez and the two guys in the restroom to hear and they were prompted to run out of the bathroom in the direction of the Base. I immediately launched and began to run towards the Shore Patrolmen that we had walked by earlier. I don't remember breathing or anything else. Just running. Faster than I had ever run in my life. The SP saw me and I just yelled that someone was getting really f\*\*ked up. Hurry.

All three of the Shore Patrolmen flicked their newly-lit cigarettes in different directions and jumped up from their butts off of the picnic table and ran towards me. From then, I started to run back to the bathroom with all three Shore Patrolmen trailing behind me.

I yelled at them to hurry. One of the Shore Patrolmen is yelling and asking me what's going on and I just yelled for them to hurry and follow me. I outran the Shore Patrolmen as I yelled back at them to pick up the pace.

I was so scared. My heart was already cold. My body cold.

In hindsight, perhaps I was having a heart attack or more adrenaline than a human could contain. As long as we all got back to the bathroom, I didn't care what would happen to me.

Just as the Shore Patrolmen and I got back to the front of the bathroom, I saw my senior PO3 Martinez standing close to the bathroom with a confused look.

Martinez says, "Witte, what the f\*\*k is going on!?". Martinez wasn't able to comprehend why I suddenly ran back to the direction of Sailor Town so fast and left him at the picnic bench. I had left and returned with the Shore Patrolmen so fast that I had only left Martinez for less than thirty seconds.

Of course upon my return with the three Shore Patrolmen, he knew something bad had happened.

## 23:48-ish

All three Shore Patrolmen looked inside the bathroom while I stood outside with Martinez to quickly brief him on why I ran.

CPO Aptimes: "Oh, my God! …Gotta call this in…"

OS Johnson: "Martinez, did you see anyone run from here?"

PO3 Martinez: "(pointing to the direction of the US Naval Base Sasebo) two guys ran that way"

OS Johnson: "Parsons, let's go!"

OS Johnson and BT Parsons give chase in the direction the two men went. As they left the other side of Nimitz Park towards the US Naval Base, they found a 20-something Japanese woman walking by herself in the direction of Nimitz Park.

OS Johnson asks the Japanese woman, "Did you see anyone run this way?" Confused and frightened by the sight of a Shore Patrolman approaching, she simply points and says "that way".

OS Johnson and BT Parsons continue with their foot-chase after the two men.

Back at the public bathroom, CPO Aptimes stayed with Martinez and I who were trying to grasp the situation.

Before Martinez, Aptimes and I look in, we can hear sounds of gurgling, choking, but no cry for help.

We look into the bathroom from the threshold of the entry to see the carnage which have been left for us. We are horrified by the sight of a body lying on the floor.

A 6-foot, 1-inch, 183-pound body clothed in a unzipped, brown leather jacket, a light-green turtleneck shirt, covered by a bloody, purple and black-stripped, long-sleeved shirt and a fanny pack around his waist, partially opened.

The body was surrounded in a pool of fresh blood gradually growing larger as it was gushing out of his mouth, making a gurgling noise. The bathroom walls were dotted with blood specks, some larger and dripping off of the two walls where they connected.

Then we see the pool of fresh blood grow larger and a stream of it reaches the bathroom's two-inch diameter floor drain that was meant for excess cleaning liquid, not blood. We could the blood draining into the pipe below it.

The sound of gargling and choking of blood continues to gush out of the mouth of a head that is disfigured. We could not tell if the body was that of a Japanese or any other nationality. We could only tell that it was a man as his black 'Bugle boy' trousers were opened and blood coming from his penis. We could only speculate that it was stomped on and cut from his zipper as he was urinating right as the attack happened.

He wasn't moving, but seemed to be trying to breathe around the large amount of blood gurgling and gushing out of his mouth more loudly. CPO Aptimes suggests, "We need to get him out of here."

He radios in for medic, "CPO Aptimes requesting an emergency medic, come in, over". Yet no one answers.

He tries again, "CPO Aptimes requesting a medic, come in, over!"

Still, no one replies.

## 23:55

With no time to wait, according to CPO Aptimes's body language and his tone of voice, he walks inside the bathroom and Martinez follows. Two other Shore Patrolmen arrive by Aptime's radioing in for help.

As the body was sprawled on the blood-filled floor and blocking the entrance, there wasn't enough room for me to enter inside with them. I was totally scared and didn't want to look anymore. Martinez, Aptimes and another Shore Patrolman enter the bathroom and grabbed the 183-pound body and placed him onto the outside patio which connected the men's and women's bathroom next to the water fountain. As they moved him, the gurgling continued left a trail of blood.

I examined the grotesque damage done to this human. His head was completely covered in blood. His eye sockets and nose were crushed which made the front of his face appear concave. It was as if he didn't have a nose or eye sockets.

His jaw was crushed and hanging loosely as his blood continued to gurgle and gush from where his mouth used to be. Only his lips were keeping his crushed upper and bottom jaw in place, yet loose.

There were several sneaker tread marks imprinted with blood on his cheek, forehead, chest and abdomen that were the results from all the repeated stomping and kicking.

Looking down at his chest, it was constricting and flat. With every gush, the body's chest would constrict. Otherwise, it would remain flat and the gurgling would commence.

Continued attempts with the radio, Aptimes requests emergency medical response, "CPO Aptimes requesting a medic, come in, over!" Still, no one replies.

Angry, Aptimes shouts, "What the f**k!" then reaches out to our Master-at-Arms, "CPO Aptimes requesting emergency assistance, come in, over!"

## 00:03

Finally, someone on the US Naval Base Sasebo answers:

MA Rodriguez: "Master-at-Arms Rodriguez, here. All others clear this frequency. CPO Aptimes, What's your emergency, over"

CPO Aptimes: "We have a badly injured man and need medic right away, over"

MA Rodriguez: "Roger. Contacting medical. Standby, over"

CPO Aptimes: "Can't standby, over. Requesting medic ETA, over"

(No one responds for 5 minutes, the body continues to gurgle blood)

## 00:08

MA Rodriguez: "What is your location, over"

CPO Aptimes: "Nimitz Park public bathroom, over"

MA Rodriguez: "Please provide precise location, over"

"Where are we!?", I said and we all looked in both directions; one back to Albuquerque Bridge which was 527-feet (175 yards) or closer access for medic to reach us only 360-feet (120 yards away) but we couldn't provide the name of the building that was in the Japanese language. During the heat of the moment, we decided to have medic meet us at the Albuquerque Bridge which farther away but everyone from the US Naval Base Sasebo knew where Albuquerque Bridge was.

CPO Aptimes: "ETA on Albuquerque Bridge, over"

(30 seconds pass)

MA Rodriguez: "ETA on Albuquerque Bridge 10-minutes, over"

CPO Aptimes: "Roger, over"

Just as we were preparing to carry the body to the bridge, the 20-something Japanese girl which guided OS Johnson and BT Parsons to the two men's direction, appeared right before the bathroom.

She startles us by her letting out a loud whimpering cry as she crouches down to the ground in fear of what she was seeing as the box of bakery goods and her purse fall to the ground.

"It's okay, He's going to live!", Aptimes says to her but we all knew that he wasn't going to make it.

CPO Aptimes, PO3 Martinez pulled up his pants to conceal his bloody penis and we began to carry him, but he was way too heavy for just four of us to carry a body covered in blood that was practically pouring out from many places of his body.

## 00:13

We got 57-feet (19-yards) when suddenly two other shipmates that we didn't know (perhaps from the USS Dubuque) came to our aid. We placed the body down gently and repositioned our grip to carry him further. CPO Aptimes gave him CPR again using only chest compressions as there was too much blood coming from the body's mouth and nose.

The two shipmates who were walking by joined in and grabbed each leg, Martinez and Aptimes carried each arm and by the opening of the unzipped, brown leather jacket. I volunteered to carry his badly disfigured head as no one else volunteered. I felt the back of his brownish, wet-with-blood hair warm against the back of his skull.

As we picked him up again, Japanese (1,003 Yen) and American ($0.98) coins fell from his fanny-pack. Obviously, we left it there. Though we now had five people carrying this 183-pound body, he was very heavy. We were still determined to make it to Albuquerque Bridge 470-feet (157-yards) more where we would meet the medics.

"We got you, brother. We got you...", Aptimes said. The rest of us began talking and cheering on, "You're going to make it. Don't worry. You're going to make it!" But we knew that he wasn't going to make it. We didn't need any medical professional to tell us that this man was probably not going to make it. It was difficult for all of us who were watching our fellow man dying and that there was nothing that we could do except to continue carrying and watching him drown and choke from his own blood.

As we carried the body to Albuquerque Bridge and according to testimonies by Helvey, Vins, BT Parsons and OS Johnson, their chase has become physical yet, unsuccessful.

According to Naval CIS, it appears that Helvey and Vins took a short rest running from the scene of the brutal assault to a few yards from outside the family resident buildings of the US Naval Base Sasebo. BT Parsons and OS Johnson stop running and begin to walk towards Helvey and Vins carefully to not scare them off.

BT Parsons approaches them confidently knowing that they were suspects as there were no one else around "Hey guys, were you at Nimitz Park a little while ago?"

"Yes", Helvey said calmly.

Just as BT Parsons finished asking both Helvey and Vins, Can you come into the light?" so that they could to get a better look at possible blood on their clothing, Helvey yells to Vins, "Run, Chuck!" and they both began to run.

BT Parsons was able to grab and hold onto Vins when Helvey stops to return to his shipmate and help him escape. BT Parsons pulls out his night stick and tries to hit Helvey who is a lot larger than BT Parsons. As Helvey turns, BT Parsons falls to the ground, Helvey throws the night stick back at BT Parsons and was able to free Vins.

Their escape continues into the night. Both BT Parsons and OS Johnson lick their wounds and call in for backup as Helvey and Vins jump over the barbed wire fence into the military housing.

Helvey and Vins both make their to Sailor Town together and during their walk back, Helvey bit and tore the sleeves off of a jean jacket that he borrowed from another shipmate and his pant legs to make them into shorts. He throws them into a public trash bin. Helvey takes off his sweater and shirt and throws them into two other separate public trash bins. Vins doesn't alter much of his clothing.

For the next three hours, they visit a few bars including the "Night Lounge" and "The Sailor Bar" in hopes of establishing alibis.

During their peeking in and out of bars penniless, they found no other shipmates that may know them. For the next few hours, Vins and Helvey search for an exchange shop to exchange their American dollars into Japanese Yen so that they can stay out later.

They coincidently end up at a police box where they meet a Navy Master-at-Arms stationed on-shore who was off-duty and on his way to utilize the laundry facilities on-base. He provided a ride for Helvey and Vins back to the base and entered the back entrance. From then, they both return to the USS Belleau Wood.

## 00:28 Sayonara Shipmate

We finally get to the Albuquerque Bridge but on the Nimitz Park side. The gurgling began to slow and we needed to try and resuscitate him again so we placed him on the ground and provided CPR using only chest compressions. CPO Aptimes uses his index and middle finger and places them into the mouth to try and clear the airflow. Still unsuccessful.

We were all wondering and complaining about how long it was taking the medics to arrive. From the request for an ambulance and our taking this badly beaten person to Albuquerque Bridge, it had been twenty minutes. It should have only taken ten minutes for an ambulance to get to us from calling for help and for them to arrive. Aptimes again provides chest compressions while we were catching our breath. The gurgling of blood reduces but is still present.

We couldn't determine if he was Japanese or American.

One of the two shipmates who assisted us went through the dark-brown fanny pack to look for an ID. I look down at the tattoos on the arms. I see a tiger on his inner, right forearm, Then I look at the other tattoo facing outwards. I lean over to see what tattoo it was and I see the USS Midway's "41" insignia with a dagger. I thought to myself, "I know those tattoos... oh sh*t! This is..." Before I could say the name, the shipmate going through the body's fanny pack, he was reading a military ID and tried his best to pronounce the name, "Schnidler, Shinder…"

"**SCHINDLER**!!", I yelled.

Everyone looks up to me and Aptimes asks as if I knew more than any of this incident, "You know this guy!?"

Indeed I did know who this man was – it was Allen Schindler, the guy that I met just two days ago and the Snack Shipmates bar who had confessed to me that he was gay. Since then, I had heard from my buddies that they had heard a rumor about my being Schindler's "boyfriend". I determined that it had to be either Schindler or Helvey (Helvey had seen me sitting in the bar talking to Schindler) that had said something so I was pissed at both of them. Preventing from complicating the situation at hand, I exchanged the answers that Aptimes wanted to know with, "Come on, Schindler. You can make it!"

The other shipmates joined in, "Come on! Don't die on us, Schindler" and "You're going to make it, Schindler!" as we looked at his disfigured face.

Aptimes again called the Master-at-arms, who he was communicating with via radio, "What is the ETA of the medic, over"

The Master-at-Arms replies, " They will arrive shortly, over"

By this time, a medic was with the Master-at-Arms and began to assist via radio as we waited for the ambulance to arrive.

Aptimes told the medic on the radio, "not looking good" and could not perform CPR, only chest compressions. He explained that there was too much blood is blocking the subjects airway and all of his ribs appeared to be crushed. The medic responded by telling him to stop chest compressions.

Schindler's gurgling of blood was slowly ceasing. I still held his head, never to let go as I kneel. Examining more of his face, it was clear that he had a disfigured and unrepairable face. The whole part of his face was flattened which forced his eyeballs where his eyebrows were. The top part of his bone which separates his eye socket bone, nose and top part of his teeth were smashed inwards and crushed. His jaw was disconnected and pushed back closely to his throat. Blood was coming out of both ears. Sneaker marks were on his forehead, cheek and throat. The smell of his blood was intense and all of us had blood on our clothing.

The ambulance finally arrives with no sirens. Two medics seemed to come flying out of the ambulance and onto the Albuquerque Bridge before it stopped. Both medics bring a gurney to the spot where we lay. A third medic driving the ambulance parks and runs over with a "Ambu-Bag" and places it on Schindler's mouth. He begins to squeeze the bag forcing air gently into Schindler's nose and mouth.

With every squeeze of the "Ambu-Bag", blood splatters everywhere out and onto my face. The three medics join us in praying and cheering Schindler to stay alive. We could hear the Master-at-Arms yelling on the radio for the status of the situation a few times however, no one answered.

The medic checks for Schindler's pulse and exclaims, "He's gone." Everyone who was touching and holding Schindler threw their hands back in amazement and shock, except for me.

I immediately began to feel bad about not being able to stop the fight in the bathroom.

"**Time of death; 00:43**", the medic confirms with the others. We then all helped the medics place Schindler onto the gurney and they drove him away.

## The Fiasco Begins

As Schindler is taken away by ambulance, everyone is looking at me. They all say nothing but look at my clothing that was bloodied. I looked down and was amazed to see so much blood on my clothing. The smell of Schindler's blood was intense.

I pulled out a cigarette and began to smoke.

No one said a word.

Some people passing by came to see what all the commotion was about and a few of the shipmates that met us halfway carrying Schindler explained what they saw, "not sure, but it looks like an accident." About five minutes passed as we three just stand around like zombies. We were confused, unsure and just numb.

The Master-at-Arms and medic called on the radio. Aptimes answers, "CPO Aptimes here, subject is dead, over".

A short pause and then the Master-at-Arms instructs Aptimes to bring witnesses with you to the CIS building, confirm. Talk to no one.

"Understood. ETA to CIS, 20 minutes, over", Aptimes replies on radio.

As we were walking back to the US Military Base Sasebo, we passed the murder scene. Other shore patrolmen (about five or six of them) who were aware of the situation had already secured the bathroom by simply standing there.

## 01:15

Upon our arrival to the main gate of the base, we were greeted by the Master-at-Arms who was on the radio with CPO Aptimes and an NIS agent named "Special Agent D. W." (name intentionally withheld) who asked, if we were both okay. We both answered in the affirmative.

Agent W. guided us in quickly into his office inside the CIS building which was right by the base gate.

He told us to immediately write down all the details of the two men that we saw in the bathroom. They were simple descriptions such as height, build and type of clothing. The descriptions were taken from us immediately to Shore Patrol

Martinez and I were then taken to another room and sat down on desks similar to those you would find in a high school where the wooden table was connected to a chair and was told to write out our statements, providing all possible details of the event, beginning to end.

I desperately needed to go to the bathroom and wash all the blood off but when I asked the NIS Special Agent W. said that we need you guys to write the events down quickly while it's still fresh in your minds. I really wanted to wash the blood that was drying on my face, arms, hands and skin. I could still smell the strong odor of blood.

Special Agent W. instructed us to hand-in our statements to the Lieutenant who was at the front of the office. My senior PO3 Martinez finished before me as he didn't have that much information that I had and he disappeared. I kept smelling the blood which distracted me while I was writing everything down.

I completed my testimony and headed over to the Lieutenant. He then told me to wait for NIS Agent W. to return. I told him that I needed to get back to my ship as we were leaving port for the Philippines later today. He tossed my statement on his desk as if it didn't mean anything to him and sternly accused me, "I don't think you're going anywhere, sailor. I think YOU killed the guy…and you know you did!"

**NOTE:**
To the Lieutenant who said this to me and who is reading this, "F**k you, a**hole"

I was really surprised that someone with such high ranking and without any evidence apart from the large amount of dried blood that was on me, would just out-right accuse me. This made me think that no one had found Helvey or Vins yet. If no one found Helvey or Vins, I started to worry that I would have been the only suspect. Martinez didn't see everything that I had witnessed. And if Helvey had seen me as I ran, he would have recognized me. That would mean that Helvey is most likely going to try to hunt me down and keep me from saying anything.

## 02:30

NIS Special Agent W. walks in the room with Martinez and says, "I know you guys don't want to spend any more time with this, but you both are requested to go back to the Nimitz Park bathroom at the scene of the crime for further investigation. Are you both willing to go back there with me?"

Martinez and I both answer, "sure". We too, wanted to do all we could to help find justice for our shipmate, Schindler. It was tragic for a sailor to be killed by the enemy but heinous to die by the hands of a fellow shipmate.

NIS Special Agent W. walked us to a white Toyota Corolla, where he got into the passenger seat and Martinez and I sat in the back seat. The driver was a Japanese police detective or an Inspector. Though everyone speculated that the suspects were not Japanese, the detective wore a worrisome expression, hoping to catch those who negatively impacted his Sasebo City with the fourth murder of 1992.

## 02:42

We drove off base and went back to the scene of the murder in Nimitz Park.

Once we got to the outside of Albuquerque Bridge by the Family Mart, we saw many Japanese police cars and vans with several other government vehicles. It looked like some sort of event with all of the emergency lights and yellow crime scene tape. There were crowds of people curious to see what had happened in the park.

We got out of the Toyota Corolla and walked towards the Albuquerque Bridge that was blocked off by Shore Patrol, Japanese police and local news reporters. Others that were around that area were sailors from both the USS Belleau Wood and the USS Dubuque as well as locals who worked and lived around the area.

The Japanese Inspector (who was driving us from the base), NCIS Special Agent W. , PO3 Martinez and I walked up to the yellow police tape.

Shore patrol loudly shouted at the news crews, civilians and sailors, "Make a hole" as the Japanese police raised the yellow crime scene police tape upward and said in Japanese "Please back away".

We continued walking towards the restroom. There were two Japanese policemen; one taking photographs of the Japanese and American coins that had fallen out of Schindler's fanny pack while we were taking him to the Albuquerque Bridge; another Japanese police officer was taking notes on the distance of how each coin was laid and a military officer taking notes of what the Japanese police officers were doing. It seemed like unnecessary work for them as they were just coins, but perhaps there was some science behind it.

The local police had set up two large lamps that shined on the surrounding areas of the public restroom. It was frightening to see that scene get so much attention. Unsure how Martinez felt, but I began feeling and wondering if I could have done something differently in order to save Schindler. Given the current circumstances, if I had entered the restroom to retrieve Schindler, my footprints would have been inside which would basically make me a one of the murderers...But my footprints were not inside however, my foot prints were everywhere outside on the patio that connected the women's and men's bathrooms.

The Japanese Inspector and NCIS Special Agent W. .asked us to reenact how we approached the bathroom, from what angle I saw Helvey dance and stomp on Schindler from the glass, fish-eye brick windows, where I saw Vins and which direction I ran to retrieve the Shore Patrolmen.

I could not endure the smell of the dried blood on my face. I got really pissed and frustrated at the situation that I just went into the women's restroom to pee and to wash the blood that was on my face. After relieving myself, I went to the sink to wash off the blood and looked into the mirror.

**From that point in my life, I began to unrecognized myself...**

My face was covered in blood specks. I was horrified. The front part of my jacket, shirt, hair, the skin on my eyelids, forearm, my jeans, my neck, hair and even my ears had blood specks and smears.

I began to stare into the mirror when all of a sudden, my feeling changed. It was a feeling of a falling on a roller coaster and fear (and a feeling that I still hold today for decades).

Trying to erase the feeling and the look that I saw in the mirror, I turned on the cold water and began splashing my face and arms. It was frustrating because Japanese public bathrooms do not have soap so regardless of all the washing I did, it was still there. With only water, it appeared that the blood just smeared. No towels in the restroom either! So the wet part of my skin would either have to dry in the cold wind or wipe them on my clothing. His blood just stayed there, the smears and the smell...the events continually played like a dream as my eyes remained opened looking at my reflection.

Unable to cope with it, I walked over to the Japanese Police Inspector who was smoking a cigarette and asked for one.

He struck-up a conversation not relating to all of the events. It was the best act of kindness that I had tonight after the murder.

The conversation continued about where we were from, what television shows we watched, school life, what countries and cities we had visited, and so on. It took my mind off of what was happening. It was similar to inserting a classical song into a mixed tape of heavy metal songs. It was a relaxing moment, too relaxing that I ended up smoking most of his cigarettes from his freshly, opened pack of Japanese Mild Seven cigarettes!

Then Martinez walks over to me with CPO Aptimes and told us that we needed to get back to the ship to talk with your captain.

Martinez and I look at each other with uncertainty but we were surprised to be called in by Captain Bradt who was the captain of our ship – a celebrity.

The only time that we met Captain Bradt was when we won our "Navy E Ribbon" for winning the battle efficiency competition in all of the Pacific Fleet. We each had our picture taken with Captain Bradt while receiving our award, but he never looked in our eyes. We had all stood in line together with hundreds of other sailors during the ceremony, but for this meeting, it will be with just Captain Bradt, Martinez and myself in his private quarters. We had no idea what to expect when we meet with the him, but I wanted to stop at a bathroom to wash Schindler's dried blood off of me this time using soap. Again, I was refused.

The strong smell of blood still wouldn't go away and I asked Martinez if he could smell it. He told me that I would need to throw my clothes away because it would never all wash out.

I was wondering what the Captain would say to us and Martinez knew he wouldn't be happy because he would lose the status of having an admiral aboard our ship in our deployment to the Philippines.

On our way back from Pearl Harbor, all of the ships in the Pacific Fleet were competing to win the "Battle E Ribbon" status that would win hosting an admiral aboard their ship. It was a captain's invitation for a promotion. Any ship participating for the "Battle E Ribbon" meant that there could be no mistakes, issues or mishaps. Unfortunately just before the Admiral came aboard our ship, Schindler was murdered by two of our own sailors.

Not only would this be a huge embarrassment for our captain and an admiral, but a complete embarrassment to our whole Pacific Fleet. Other ships who didn't win the "Battle E Ribbon" would question: "Why did the Belleau Wood get the status of "Flag Ship" (when an admiral is deployed on a ship) when their own shipmates killed another of their own shipmate?"

The "Battle E Ribbon" and "Flag Ship" status basically has lost its merit and purpose. So while deployed with an admiral aboard, things had to be kept secret until after we return back to our homeport in Sasebo, Japan.

## 03:55

Martinez, Aptimes and I finally get to our ship and Aptimes escorted us up to the OOD on the Quarterdeck Where we were met by the USS Belleau Wood's Master-at-Arms (whose name I have forgotten). CPO Aptimes surrendered us to the Belleau Wood's MA (Master-at-Arms) and Aptimes disappeared. This was the only time which the OOD did not record us coming aboard although it was strict protocol to record everyone that exited and entered the ship.

We were then secretly taken through passageways which were less accessible up into the stateroom which only officers were allowed. MA (Master-at-Arms) tells us to place our backs against the bulkhead at attention and knocks on the captain's door and says, "MA (Master-at-Arms) (name forgotten) reporting as requested. Permission to enter".

Silence for a good five minutes as we stood at attention when the door opens.

The Executive Officer Robert Franklin (XO Franklin, name is intentionally changed to conceal his identity) answers the door and tells us to have a seat. Both Martinez and I are nervous. The office is large, the floor is carpeted in a tacky 80's color, the walls are dark wood. Captain Bradt is sitting against the furthest wall in front of us in a tan-colored lounge chair smoking a fat cigar he had just lit. The only light in the room was a floor lamp that had a small circular table attached to it.

XO Franklin sat in a 1970's-looking, executive chair in the middle of the room. There were two standard military-looking chairs where Martinez and I were instructed to sit. Only a low, dark, wooden coffee table separated us from XO Franklin with his back against Captain Bradt. A fresh pot of coffee was brewed but we weren't offered any.

Captain Bradt says nothing, disconnecting himself from a snowballing, international conspiracy that was only getting larger and leaves it to XO Franklin to do all the talking about the murder. I could see them both looking at the abundance of blood that was drying on the front part of my body.

XO Franklin simply went straight for facts about the situation and cared less of what Martinez and I just went through:

XO Franklin: "Have either of you told anyone else about what happened tonight?"

Martinez: "No sir, we only told the Shore Patrol that were there at the scene"

Witte: "No sir, I haven't told anyone"

XO Franklin: "Do you know the guy who was killed tonight?"

Martinez: "Some guy, sir"

Witte: "Allen Schindler, sir"

XO Franklin: "(looking at me) How do you know Schindler?"

Witte: "The Shore Patrolmen pulled his DoD card out of his fanny pack, but I also met him two days ago, sir"

I regretted right then informing the XO that I knew Schindler but at that point, I couldn't control my thoughts.

XO Franklin: "What were you doing out with Schindler!?"

Witte: "Just talking about stuff, sir"

XO Franklin: "What were you two talking about!? What did Schindler tell you?"

Things began to connect as I remembered what Schindler told me about the captain and him being processed out for being a homosexual. I thought to myself, Uh oh. It seemed to me that XO Franklin and Captain Bradt were thinking that Schindler was murdered because of being gay. I thought that I probably knew more than anyone at this point about the situation. But it was apparent to me that XO Franklin and Captain Bradt were well aware who Allen Schindler was and knew that he was a homosexual.

Admittedly, I did say (and write) that I was going to confront Schindler (but did not mention Helvey) for spreading the rumor that I was his boyfriend. The reason for this was that there were a few people aboard the ship that wanted to harass and/or kill homosexuals. And rumors were if anyone was assumed to be homosexual, they would be harassed at the very least.

So in my defense, I was not homosexual yet the rumor had spread that I was because I coincidently met and had happened to have a drink with Schindler. Now it was also possible that Helvey thought I was gay when he poked his head through the Snack Shipmates bar seeing me with Schindler and that was why I sought advice from my crew Szerlag, Knight and Martinez.

Yes, we planned to confront either Schindler or Helvey as a group in order to protect the truth…and myself. I didn't want to be harassed or killed (according to the rumor on the ship) just because of a rumor. And I did not want to be other-than-honorably Discharged for just drinking with Schindler. I did nothing wrong. It was not fair. I felt that I needed to address the situation and clear everything up to protect myself.

As far as I knew, Helvey and Vins were still on the run and I was the only witness that could identify them. And I was sitting here with blood all over me, anyone would suspect that I would be prime suspect. If Helvey and Vins were to eliminate me, they would both be in the clear. Paranoia was kicking into high gear and I felt like my brain was on fire thinking about all that had transpired.

The conversation went something like this:

XO Franklin: "Do you know that there will be many people asking questions about the murder at Nimitz Park. Do both of you understand how bad this is going to get?"
Martinez: "No, sir"
Witte: "No, sir"
Martinez: "Are we in trouble, sir?"
XO Franklin: "I don't know…are you?"
Witte: "Sir, we didn't do anything wrong…"
XO Franklin: "Well, apparently our shipmate was murdered!"
Martinez: "We understand, sir, but we didn't kill Schindler, sir"
XO Franklin: "Well, as it is, that depends on the evidence, now, right?"

Confused, Martinez and I look at each other. We couldn't figure out if we were the prime suspects of Schindler's murder. We were the only ones closely connected to the murder at this time. If the murderers were not found or if they were found and cleaned the evidence they had on them, Martinez and I could be charged for the murder. Terrified, our hearts were racing as XO Franklin continued to instruct us:

XO Franklin: "You will not tell anyone about this. You won't tell your shipmates, your friends, don't even talk about this between yourselves. If anyone talks about it or asks you directly about it, you say that you 'don't know'.
Witte: "Yes, sir"
Martinez: "Yes, sir"

XO: "There may be the media that will ask you questions, you say nothing, understood?"

Witte: "Yes, sir"

Martinez: "Yes, sir"

XO Franklin: "Don't call your family and tell them about what happened. Don't tell them a thing about this. If they ask you about what happened, you say nothing and that you have nothing to do with this."

Witte: "Understood, sir"

Martinez: "Yes, sir"

XO Franklin: "If either one of you tell anyone about anything that happened tonight, you may not ever see your family and friends again."

Martinez and I look at each other in disbelief. We couldn't figure out if it was a threat or advice. We DID know that we needed to keep our mouths shut.

Captain Bradt neither confirms nor rejects what XO Franklin tells us as he seemed to not want to be connected to anything that happened tonight. The smell of Captain Bradt's cigar smelled sweet and delicious and temporarily hid the smell of Schindler's dried blood on my skin and clothes.

XO Franklin: "There may be other higher-ranking officers that will ask you for details about what happened tonight. You say nothing...nothing. Even you are NOT to tell your seniors in your division – no one!"

Silence as XO Franklin looks back behind him at Captain Bradt. No words nor nods were exchanged. The motion of Captain Bradt taking a puff from his sweet cigar is slightly concealed in the light that silhouettes.

> XO Franklin: "We don't want what happened to your shipmate tonight happen to you. You wouldn't want your parents and families miss you. You guys are just going to have to keep this to yourself. You both understand, right? (pauses), Understood!?", emphasizes with a strong annotation.
> Witte: "Understood, sir"
> Martinez: "Yes, sir"

XO Franklin leans over to the left of us and calls out for the MA (Master-at-Arms). He tells us to stand outside and the two have a short conversation of which we couldn't hear. I asked Martinez if he thought that we had just been threatened and he said that he took it that way too.

The door opens again and out comes the MA who tells Martinez to go back to his berthing division. He says I am to follow him and clean Schindler's locker out and return the contents to them

## 04:45 - Cleaning Out Schindler's Locker
### OCTOBER 28, 1992

Neither the MA (Master-at-Arms) or I spoke of anything once we got to Schindler's vertical, stand up locker. The berthing area was dark except for a few night lights that only lit up the floors.

He took the bolt cutters and cut the lock with a sound of a snap that was on Schindler's locker. He hands me a slightly, transparent trash bag and asks me to hold it as he empties out Schindler's locker.

I remove jeans, socks, tennis shoes, Japanese Camel cigarette coupons and a diary. Schindler's uniforms remained. What I found odd was that we only removed items from Schindler's standing vertical locker, but not the locker underneath Schindler's bunk. As I removed Schindler's 6" by 8" diary, which was a dark, green, almost like an olive-green color which looked like a government log book, the MA (Master-at-Arms) said to let him have the book and I placed everything else in the bag, which he ties in a knot at the top. The diary is under his arm.

The diary had disappeared from October 28, 1992, just 4 days until NCIS requested an investigation action to seize the diary on November 02, 1992 from the USS Belleau Wood's Master-at-Arms office. The most concerning diary log entries were written by Schindler on October 2, 1992 where he wrote:

> "...Other than that more people are finding out about me. It scares me a little. You never know who would want to injure me or end my existence. Still drawing, drinking sodas and smoking..."

Other entries in October 1992 only indicated that Schindler was attempting to process out of the US Navy in the near future.

The MA relieves me of my duty of the day and tells me that I should report to my senior as usual and if I just did what XO Franklin said, everything will be fine. I said, nor questioned anything as I just wanted to take a shower.

Looking back on the cleaning of Schindler's locker, I wonder why they instructed me to clean it out. Why me? Why not the MA instead or my senior, PO3 Martinez. Why me?

## 05:25

Upon returning to my berthing area, I removed my jean jacket, shirt and jean pants. There was no possible way that the blood which was practically soaked into my clothing would ever come out. So instead of putting my clothes into my wash bag, I simply threw them away a trash bin nearby and made my way to the head to wash the rest of the blood which penetrated my skin which had not been cleaned for several hours.

As I got into the shower, I felt relieved. I look down at the drain and saw blood again wet, make its way down the drain. There seemed to be no way that the smell of blood was coming out no matter how many times or how hard I scrubbed my skin. I had washed, rinsed, washed, rinsed, shampooed...still, the smell of blood was coming from somewhere. It was driving me crazy! Right before I went to sleep, I placed toothpaste in my nostrils however, the mint-flavored toothpaste only altered the smell of blood. But I was extremely tired and had to wake up in a few hours to work and prepare for our departure for the Philippines. Just as soon as I laid my head down on my pillow, I was out cold. Hopefully by the time I woke up, all that had happened will have been a bad dream...

## PART 4

# THE CONTRAST IN COLORFUL HUMANS

*"I became insane, with long intervals of horrible sanity.*
*During those fits of absolute unconsciousness, I drank."*
—Edgar Allan Poe (1885)

# CHAPTER 11

# PACIFIC BLOOD

October 28, 1992

The sound of AV-8B Harrier II jets taking off just a few decks above me are the sounds I hear when I up that next morning. Such a sexy and powerful sound muffled by the ship's steam engines. This indicated that we were already at sea heading to the Pacific to patrol the free trade routes.

I open my blue curtain that covers my bunk from the lights that shine bright in the berthing area. My analog clock reads 10:05 am. "Oh sh*t, I'm late. I'll be in so much trouble", I said to myself in my rack laying back down with my hand on my forehead. Oddly, even though I knew I had to get up, the restfulness that I needed had encompassed my body and I just sort of didn't care.

Then the scent of blood, mixed with the toothpaste I had put in my nose last night suddenly reminded me what had happened the night before. My heart began to thump rapidly which motivated me to get out of my bunk and get ready for being late for work. I was relieved that I had not been killed in my sleep by the murderers but that was they didn't know where I slept, right? Not knowing if they had been found, I was still reeling from the event. I wasn't sure if I was just worried or overly paranoid.

But before going to work, I felt that it was important for me to find Szerlag and Knight to tell them what had happened, regardless of XO Franklin told Martinez and me.

As I walked out of our division berthing area, I looked to the forward and aft directions in the passageway, looking out for the possible murderers.

My body was still cold. I could feel my chest pounding and felt very frightened about all what happened last night.

As I made my way to the barber shop where I hoped to meet Knight and Szerlag, the situation became more clear.

The speculations that I had in my head at that time were:

1. The murderers are still on the ship or on the USS Dubuque:
   a. If on the Belleau Wood, they would hunt me down to kill me to cover up their crime
   b. If on the USS Dubuque, they would certainly hunt for me down in the Philippines
2. Captain Bradt (though said nothing to me) and XO Franklin had made it very clear to Martinez and me that if we talked to anyone about the situation, it would have dire consequences. I was thinking my life was in jeopardy or I would go to prison.
3. The Lieutenant (a**hole) at the NCIS building on watch had accused me of the murder.
4. The "Gay Bashers" were still on the ship
5. If the murderers were not found, I would be the main suspect.

It was indeed a very scary time in my life.

Metallica's "Enter Sandman" was playing from the barber shop which pretty much indicated that Knight was there.

"Hey, Knight!", I announced as Knight looked at me and replied, "Good morning, Witte."

"Hey, Witte", Szerlag greeted me.

We three knew about our plan to stop the rumors that were spreading about me by confronting Shindler and/or Helvey. We hadn't had the opportunity because we were already at sea. A new plan would have to be made once we got to Okinawa to pick up the Marines or once we get to the Philippines. What Szerlag and Knight didn't know was that it was already taken care of in the most heinous way.

Knight turns the music down, puts up the closed sign and locks the door. I made them swear on their lives to not tell anyone what I was about to tell them. When I told them that Schindler was dead, the room was completely silent and they both just stared at me. They looked at each other remembering our conversation and plan to stop the rumor which we suspected Schindler of spreading. I told them that it wasn't me but I was there and the police were looking for the two guys. Plus, Martinez and I had been sternly warned that we were not to speak a word about it to anyone.

Knight: "You need to stop talking"
Szerlag: "Yeah, I think that would be a good idea"

It was upsetting that they couldn't hear the whole story but it's understandable considering what we had planned two days before by confronting Helvey or Schindler about spreading the rumor that I was Schindler's boyfriend, but it could have been anyone. Regardless, the rumor was out and I had to deal with things the best way possible.

Szerlag and Knight were both concerned for me, but they didn't want any part of this. We decided to stay low, say nothing more and move on. That's exactly what we did.

## Just Like Any Other Day

Returning to work and the weeks that followed after the murder and on our way to the Philippines, was just that – like clockwork. Every day, I would go back to my work station and did what I had always been doing aboard the ship. Everyone was doing their job just as we did when we sailed from San Diego and from Pearl Harbor.

Day after day and week after week. Everything just went on as nothing had happened. There were no announcements of Schindler's murder. There were no rumors nor any changes to what we had been doing when we worked tirelessly every day, eighteen hours a day. There wasn't even a ceremony for our shipmate's death! Nothing was different about our routine as if they wanted to erase the horrible event.

The only thing that had changed was my perspective on how I perceived everything. Colors were more bright, sounds were more clearer and I had apparently become acutely aware of my surroundings and people. If someone had a cup of coffee, I could predict where the person would place the coffee cup and where they would sit. If a person were to walk down the passageway, I could predict which route that they would take and who they would bump into. It was as if all of my senses had amplified.

If you were to actually witness a UFO or alien being by yourself, you would swear up and down that what you saw was in fact, real. Try and tell your family, friends and others that you saw an alien being and they would dismiss you and believe that you are a bit out of touch with reality.

As no one had discussed or announced anything about the murder that happened a few weeks ago, it felt like my own UFO. It made me feel very alone and as if I had imagined it. This became quite apparent with the only sense that I could not control – my olfaction.

Olfaction is a sense of smell that all mammals have. You most likely would remember the smell of your mother or father, or even your favorite meal.

Those who had traumatic events may for some unknown reason, remember the smell during the time of the traumatic event. This is known as "Phantosmia" or an olfactory hallucination. Those that had a terrible accident may remember the smell of metal, gas, oil, etc. For my Phantosmia, it's blood. The smell continued to stay with me for weeks after the murder and it was making me crazy.

To help put my Phantosmia at bay, I would not just take my typical morning shower, I would take two and sometimes three showers a day thinking that Schindler's blood was still on my skin somewhere. Little did I know about this phenomena that it was injected, embedded and locked into my brain and that the perfumes in the shampoo and soap temporarily overpowered the smell of blood.

When there were days where the smell of shampoo and body soap would sweat off my skin, the Phantosmia of blood would return. I would then think about the murder over and over again. I couldn't tell anyone about what I was enduring as I had never heard of Phantosmia, couldn't talk to anyone about the murder, there were no confirmations of the death of Schindler and the murderer was still on the loose. It was getting to a point where I felt like I was absolutely losing my mind.

With the constant stress of working eighteen hours a day, with my chief yelling at us, horrible re-creation of the scene in the bathroom and the Phantosmia of Schindler's blood that I couldn't wash off hours right after the murder, I couldn't hold back anymore…

## Kill The Meat

As if I was dreaming, my mind simply skipped taking the typical, daily routine and teleported directly from my sleep to becoming fully dressed for work, standing at the galley counter. Unsure of what just happened to my memory from the berthing area lounge to me standing in the kitchen with a big chunk of roast in front of me, there was a large chef's knife and I had just stood there for several minutes.

I become aware that Chief Cusaga continues to scold me for doing nothing, "Wat da gad damn mudda pukka, ju doin!? Ju just standin der! Pukking kut da gad damn pukkin meat…damn, man…"

Continuing to trim the raw roast beef, cutting little-by-little, the fat, the veins, the skin and to the bone until it looked like something that I remembered from that night…

For some strange reason, a feeling of rage overcomes me and I curse back at my senior Chief Cusaga.

Tossing the knife onto the counter, I took the largest breath in hopes of controlling this evil, foreign feeling inside my head and heart. As I exhaled strongly, I let out an even louder expletive.

Everyone in the kitchen looked our way to see what the commotion was about. They were mostly stunned but a few were laughing as they knew how the chief would be a dick every once in a while. My shipmates continued to watch and see how he was going to react to my breakdown. He, surprisingly, did nothing as if he understood the pressure of his subordinates were enduring.

The raw roast beef was still there and I wanted to destroy the feelings that I was experiencing, so I picked the chef's knife with my right hand but held it as if I was ready to stab. Suddenly and uncontrollably, I began stabbing the beef with the chef's knife yelling, "f**k you! F**k you!" and cried, cried and cried.

Chief Cusaga yells to everyone, "eberybody, out!" and out they went. It was only me in the kitchen trying to make sense of myself. Then I turned around and started stabbing the industrial fridge, only putting fifteen tiny, little dents. It was if I was blocked by something so strong and wanted to get to the other side. Though feeling a bit relieved, I was unsuccessful cutting my way out of the sick feelings, horrible thoughts and potential conclusion to this entire event. I wanted to vomit but instead nausea remained.

I then dropped the knife onto the deck, went into the back of the galley where the ten-count ovens were to hide from the world and cried. There was this heavy uncertainty hanging over me everywhere I went and every single minute.

Chief Cusaga comes to me as I dry my tears and tells me that it might be a good idea to go see the Chaplin. Wiping my snot away, I told him that I didn't know what to do, that I wasn't able to control myself right now. Again, he suggests that I go talk to the Chaplin. I didn't think there was anything in the Bible that could relate to what I was going through but it was worth a try.

I tell the Chief that I'm sorry and stand up. He puts his hand on my shoulder and escorts me out of the galley and says, "Ju need a gud taim in PI (Philippines). If da Chaplin suggest bacation in PI, I will applove it".

The Chaplin servers as many functions on a ship. Back in the early 1990's, there were no psychologists or psychiatrists on ships as all Navy personal had already been vetted and processed through MEPS (Military Entry Processing Service) and we all endured boot camp. It is also very expensive for stationing any psychologist on every ship out at sea. None of us were messed up in the head when we were aboard and deployed at sea. Majority of us were religious but rarely went to church on the ship as we would rather sleep, play games, work out in the gym and talk with our shipmates.

As there was only one Chaplin stationed aboard our ship, he was versed with mostly every religion; Catholic, Christianity, Jewish, Buddhist – you name it, he catered to all of the religions. It is an impressive MO (Military Occupation). Now, I hoped that he would be serving as a psychologist and help me figure out what was going on with me. Maybe he could shed some light on what was in my head and I could find the right path to take.

## Losing My Religion

The Chaplin was a Lieutenant, dressed smart and had a soon-to-be-starting bald on his mixed gray and brown hair. He wore the cloth of God over his beige, officer's uniform that appeared as if he spent hours ironing. He greeted me at the door and I told him that I needed help.

The small room of the church sat about thirty personnel on wooden benches lined up unevenly with prayer books on top of them. The scent of extinguished incense still lingered in the room. We entered his office where he has heard all of the sailors' confessions about raising hell, cheating and fighting. If anyone needed a Chaplin to talk to about anything, this was the man. He has heard it all... except for mine.

I began the conversation by telling him that something terrible had happened and I needed some guidance.

"Something really bad happened and I don't know where to turn", I began the conversation. I would first think of the sentence in my head, change the context and then speak it. "murder" would be changed to "horrible event". The date of "October 27" (the date of Schindler's murder) would be changed to "September 17". The phrase "been threatened to not speak of this by the XO and the Captain" would be changed to "unable to explain without getting in trouble or telling on someone". The Chaplin tried his best to understand what I was going through but understood that I could not fully explain most of the details due to my situation.

Somehow, I felt as if he already knew about the murder of Schindler but then he would talk about Bible verses I couldn't apply or it didn't help me. What the Chaplin did however, was recommend that I take a vacation in PI when we arrived in a few days to get my head together. It was only a 2-day vacation approval but that was more than I, or anyone else, could have expected.

Typically, those that are ranked from the bottom up (E1, E2 and E3 ranks) are not allowed to have cars overseas, live off base or be allowed to take vacations while deployed as we are inexperienced, immature or if we were demoted as a punishment. Anyone in those ranks are more apt getting in trouble, fighting or being found passed out drunk in the middle of the street (see previous chapters regarding Liberties).

Other than the Chaplin suggesting to my chief, Chief Cusaga and me to take a few days of vacation, there wasn't anything that he could help me with. Obviously, he couldn't resolve my issues, mostly because I really couldn't talk about what was really happening with me. He couldn't refer to anything in the Bible that would relate to my situation except that God will always wait for me when I was ready.

The Chaplin ended with "go with God" and so I went, without God.

As I returned back to Chief Cusaga's tiny office, he greets me, "Ju okay, Witte?"

"The Chaplin approves my 2-day vacation in PI", I replied.

"Alsou, ju will be poot on night watch apter we sail flom za Philippines", Chief Cusaga added. Apparently, he felt that I couldn't be around others in my current situation. So when Chief Cusaga suggested that I simply perform watches, ensuring that the boat, sailors and equipment was safe, it was like I had gotten promoted! I would still need to do work in the kitchen at night, but still, it was a lot better than cooking all day.

When I signed up for the military, I had a choice between being a cook or a Master-at-Arms (a police officer in the Navy). What the military was offering as a MS (Mess Specialist or cook) with an E3 pay rank ($878/month) compared to a Master-at-Arms with an E1 pay rank ($754/month). The idea was to enter as an MS and then transfer over as an MA at the E3 pay rank. By then, I would have made it to an E4 ($934/month) as the tests would coincide with the time expectancy of 2 years when every sailor is required to work on their promotion.

One of my shipmates who is ranked two higher ranks from me overhears our conversation and is shocked that someone under the rank of E4 was allowed to obtain a vacation while deployed.

"What the hell? Oh, Witte, you're lucky!", Petty Officer 2nd Class Daniels says.

PO2 Daniels follows with, "Then you and I can go to an awesome brothel!"

"Sure, I guess", I replied as I haven't got acquainted to PO2 Daniels as he worked in the Chief's Galley.

PO2 Daniels is an older man in his 30's. He's a chubby, jolly guy who has sailed many seas and visited many ports. He is the one, as many would say, "has a woman at every port". His hair is dark black, neatly combed and trimmed the way that he has since he first entered the Navy twenty years ago. A few others wouldn't want to associate with him as he is older and his sense of style is still reflecting twenty years ago. He makes no jokes about penises, poop, boogers or talks about the intricate details of a woman's body parts, but he does know his game and how to operate around the ports of the world – especially Olongapo. If anyone knew the inner workings of the town of Olongapo, PO2 Daniels is the man.

The majority of my shipmates and crew are E3 and below so they would have to return at the 12am curfew while I would be out so, it would be safe and wise to hang with PO2 Daniels during the 2-day Liberty. It was a long-overdue vacation and with the potential adventure of old-man PO2 Daniels who had visited PI several times and knew his way around the city, I imagined he could show me a time that I never forget in the Philippines! PO2 Daniels even provided a teaser to the excursion that gave me thirst for furthering beyond the city where we all were supposed to stay for our safety.

Daniels suggested that we go out to smoke because he wanted my help with something. We wait for a few marines and sailors to vacate the smoking section so that he could elaborate without anyone over-hearing. He tells me about a girl that is in PI that is being held against her will. He has promised to rescue her. I become very confused to what situation that PO2 Daniels is getting me into. It already sounds complicated and I don't really know PO2 Daniels that well, however I had failed saving Schindler, why not try to save someone to help balance it out?

PO2 Daniels continues to explain as I keep my doubts about his story. She used to be a working girl (prostitute) until someone bought her and now she's locked up until the second half of her payment is made (a doctor from California, he says). He tells me that he knows this girl's sister and she was the one telling him about this. The plan is to convince the mama-san to let me have her for one night ($500) and can get her out through a window. All he wanted me to do was distract the Madam (Queen Bee). For my help, he says he will pay for my girl and transportation. I told him that it sounded good and I was "in".

He said we would meet here in the smoking section and then will leave about 18:00 on November 21st, the day after we arrive. In passing, he said to find a place to hide your wallet – never in the back pocket. Then he walked away.

I couldn't understand what he meant about not keeping my wallet in my back pocket but it wasn't important at that time. The upcoming adventure involving saving a damsel in distress was exciting and I looked forward to screwing over someone who would think it's okay to buy a human being.

"This is going to be my chance to save someone", I thought for the next few days before our arrival to the Philippines which appeared to keep my Phantosmia at bay and distracted me from thinking about the murder. I needed something else to occupy my thoughts because I was making myself sick thinking about the murder over and over. It was a relief and I was looking forward to arriving in the Philippines.

# CHAPTER 12

# THE PHILIPPINE LIBERTY

## NOVEMBER 19, 1992

It was so freaking hot outside, a huge contrast from Sasebo from where we set sail from. We had yet to port our ship when we saw how gray everything was. There wasn't a speck of green as far as we could see.

Mount Pinatubo, located just twenty miles away from the US Naval Base Subic Bay, erupted just over a year before our arrival to Olongapo. With the lack of rain and city funds, they just dealt with the gray ash that made it part of the city's neon, bars and brothel neon lights that attract sailors who haven't drank a lick of alcohol or had the warm touch of a women for weeks and months.

Olongapo was a home for over 193,000 Filipino residents with frequent visitors from the farmland that come to Olongapo to prostitute themselves or have been asked by their family members to prostitute to make up the household finances which they lacked. Hustlers, scammers and thieves also joined in making their way from the farmlands to Olongapo to grab their chances at the drunken sailors' American dollars. Our seniors, who were mostly Filipino, told us stay with other sailors, especially those who had been to the Philippines before.

In one out of thousands of incidents where the locals would approach a sailor with a smile and say, "We welcome Americans, here, have a soda on the house to show our appreciation!" where one sailor said, "thanks!" It seemed harmless and such a nice gesture for the local to provide until he shouts, "Thief! Thief!" The sailor who is extremely nervous and doesn't want to cause any trouble hands over ten times the amount of the soda to the hustler.

The feeling of worry was overcome by the excitement in visiting a city so full of sin much more than a man could imagine. Any type of crime could easily be ignored in the Philippine's corrupt government with a few American dollars. The locals and business owners of run-down establishments knew just exactly what sailors wanted and they could get it dirt-cheap.

The USS Belleau Wood finally ports to the Naval Base Subic Bay pier. The men aboard our ship behaved as dogs in heat, howling out to the gray, ash-colored city. They saw the golden colors of cold, Filipino Red Horse and San Miguel Beer and smelled the delicious, candy-scented perfume of the petite and exotic women that awaited them with open arms.

The OOD (Officer Of the Deck) rings the Quarterdeck bell to let us know that Liberty has started and out of the 900 sailors with a friendly, yet repetitive reminder, "All sailors ranked E3 and below must return to the ship before curfew at 0:00 (midnight)".

All of us left on white prison-like busses that transported us to the inside gate that separated the United States and Olongapo. The busses stopped just a shy of the main gate and we began to walk to the base entrance like baseball patrons leaving at the eighth inning.

I look to my left to see a line of locals holding all sorts of buckets, none of which had the same color as if they had scavenged them from every corner of the city. Guarding them were a few rebels (of unknown political purposes or the militia, I couldn't confirm) which were hired by the mayor as the city lacked funding to hire its own police force to keep their people in line as well as drunken sailors who get out of hand.

There was a local agreement between the mayor and the commander of the Subic Bay Naval Base that allowed locals to take running water as the city of Olongapo had none. Obviously, such an under-the-table agreement would have only been understood locally; "scratch my back, and I'll scratch yours" type of agreement. As long as the rebels kept the locals well-behaved when they were on base, then there weren't any complaints. It was indeed sad to see this line as it went on for several blocks – definitely nothing an American tourist would ever experience there.

Szerlag, Knight and I finally get to the gate, which was at the right-side of the locals lining up for water. It appeared as the gate was similar to one you would see at the zoo. It was a metallic, turnstile type of door that would fit only one body at a time.

One-by-one, Szerlag, Knight and I walk through it to a threshold of gray, metallic bar-like sidewalk. It wouldn't let anyone get out of line but it was possible to jump over it. But this one, you most likely wouldn't jump over. This metallic-like sidewalk was lined with five rebels dressed in their own, customizable, Rambo-like uniform perhaps their wives made. Each of them were carrying an assortment of different types of automatic rifles. We felt intimidated by their custom-made uniform which had leather shoulder straps filled with a generous supply of .308 bullets ready to load. They all dressed in army-green uniforms, some stained while others looked as if they scavenged them off of their dead enemies or comrades. All of them had red bandanas, perhaps representing their platoon. A few of them were smoking both Lucky Strikes and Marlboro cigarettes out of a soft packs. The smell of body odor was quite apparent, their hair was long, wavy, black and uncombed, were all needed of a shave that they hadn't had since their last excursion.

It was a spitting image that one would see out of a military movie where heroes battled the rebellion except here in Olongapo, there were no heroes. The rebels (or militia, I couldn't confirm which) were simply here to enforce rule paid by the Olongapo city.

We continued along this walkway from Subic Bay Naval Base and onto the bridge over "Sh*t River" which led into the Olongapo wonderland when we abruptly heard in an aggressive and in a very perfect English accent, "You guys are going to keep your sh*t straight, right?"

We turned and saw that the largest of the group of rebels (or militia) was looking right at us with a stern expression on his face. His face was dotted with perspiration with large drops of sweat falling down to where he had a toothpick hanging out of his mouth. He held his rifle and shook it as he stared us down as if he was ready to shoot us.

We were quite surprised and scared at the same time. We just other bunch of horny sailors stepping off of the Subic Bay Naval Base with no weapons. As the metallic turnstile only went in one direction, out, we had to confront the conversation and reply with a simple, "yes". We were very thirsty for beer and would have said anything to get off the base and in the company of cold beer and hot women which we haven't touched in many weeks.

## American Occupation Of "Sh*T River"

We continue our walk out of the second checkpoint to the bridge which ran over "Sh*t River" and where we see a few sailors looking down into it. If any American were to jump into that river, they would end up in the hospital flushing out the bacteria whereas the street children and poor people would be completely immune. It is basically consisted of trash from the ocean, human waste, the city water runoffs, trash, discarded food, dead fish and dogs.

This river also caters to those who live by and above the waters for taking baths and for children to play in to relieve themselves from the year-long heat. It was also littered with squatters who had built "Stilts" above it, out of materials they scavenged from the ocean and trash dumps. Local builders will get their hammers and nails, large wooden posts and stick them in the dark and biohazardous river. Then, pallets and plywood are placed on the posts.

"Let's throw coins", says an old, chubby, salty sailor who had been here a few times. The children who lived in the "Stilts" above "Sh*t River" would then dive into this water, happily with large smiles in hopes of retrieving American pennies, nickels and dimes. Some of the sailors look down and laugh. Other sailors didn't like this either, but the children were happy for whatever they could find.

"Sh*t River" was actually a canal that was created in 1884 by the Spanish Navy that would make Subic Bay Naval Base practically a 262-square mile island, about the same size as Singapore. In June 1898, the American Navy defeated the Spanish Navy resulting in 167 deaths on the Spanish Navy side. The American Navy only suffered a few injuries.

The news of the "Treaty of Paris", signed in 1898, did not spread to the Philippines as fast as the US occupation and the end of Spanish Empire. And of course a $20 million dollar payment to Spain to shut down their religious empire in the Philippines,Cuba, Puerto Rico and Guam making these countries American Territories.

The very next year in 1899, the Filipino forces were upset and set up a few skirmishes around Olongapo to resist the American occupation as well as small arms deep within the city. It only took 90 soldiers from the 32nd to capture Olongapo. By December 10, 1899 the same year of the Philippine-American War, the Marines (of course with the assistance of the US Navy), the American flag was raised.

But, oh no...World War II came knocking on almost every Pacific country including the Philippines. A priest who had been helping Americans and Filipinos with their faith was also sharing information about US and Filipino operations to the Japanese Imperial Army. This ended with the priest taken behind his church and executed by a Marine firing squad. But it was too late as the Japanese Imperial Army was already occupying the majority of the Philippines and just a few days away from Olongapo. By the end of 1942, the Japanese Imperial Army ruled the Philippines. They built a few ships (that never launched) and housed both Filipino and American prisoners of war. By January 1945, the US ran the Japanese Imperial Army out of the Philippines except for Subic Bay. It had taken 175 tons of bombs to beat them.

Since the end of World War II, Subic Bay has been a very important strategic base for the Vietnam War, maintaining a peaceful passage for ships in the Pacific Trade Route to Singapore. Dependents of the US Military numbering around 20,000 were evacuated when the Pinatubo Eruption occurred in 1991 which pretty much ended the plan to keep Subic Bay Naval Base. It left over a foot of volcanic ash and mud and subsequent earthquakes destroyed the Subic Bay area.

Though the Philippines wanted us to maintain our military presence in Subic Bay with a $825 million per year lease for seven years, the American government only would provide $360 million per year. This resulted with Americans pulling out our military on September 13, 1991. By November 24, 1991, our ship the beloved USS Belleau Wood would be the last ship and the last of the military personnel to leave since our original and official occupation of the Philippines 46 years ago.

For the next five days until our last military withdrawal from the Philippines, we wanted to get a good taste of the life. The Filipinos had only five days to get as much American dollars as they could at any expense. Without knowing any of the history of the Philippines or how desperately corrupted Olongapo was, four of us simply walked across the canal that was created by the Spanish Empire, looking down not on the history, but on the locals as well.

Szerlag, Knight and I had finally crossed-over the bridge and past the river stench of chemicals and sewage water, we continued to walk down the ash-covered sidewalk off of Magasaysay Drive which is littered by small, family-owned stores and restaurants and bars and bars and more bars. These aren't the typical bars that only served beer. These bars served women – beautiful, soft exotic women who have come from the farmlands or other cities nearby hoping to get the American dollar from the American Sailors.

The roads are covered in volcanic ash that had fallen from another eruption over a year ago. The advertising signs that plaster every inch of every unprofessionally and unlicensed building are permanently rusted and dirty and possibly could fall loose from the make-shift support with old nuts and bolts. Electrical powerlines twisted that were improperly exposed and connected to anything and everything that needed power. The majority of the signs were in English and had some reference to some sort of American reference such as "Airwaves Club", "Carrier 7", "Grand Ole Opry Club", "Purple Haze", "AC/DC", and so on.

"Jeepneys" made from leftover jeeps after world war II converted into bus-like transportation where local commuters would enter and exit from the rear. Many of these dressed in tacky colors that were customized by their owners. Most of these vehicles had a small statue of Jesus, Mother Mary or a rosary. The drivers would casually drive by honking at other cars in the streets where there are no lanes nor lights.

Just as Remora fish that cling onto sharks, motorized "Trikes" or tricycles would drive one passenger to their precise location, carefully navigate around the Jeepneys. It was indeed a busy street yet pedestrians easily walk across the street weaving in and out of the traffic with no injuries or accidents.

As the sun was setting on Magasaysay Drive, we pass multiple bars filled with beautiful, petite and exotic women. They would call out to us to come talk to them. No one needed to be educated on what they knew what we wanted and they were there to provide it to us for a very reasonable price.

The Bar Girls (or women) wore these three-by-four laminated cards strapped by a shoelace string they wore around them as necklaces. No, it wasn't just their names that they were advertising around their necks – they were "health cards' showing that they were STD-free (Sexually Transmitted Disease). Who knew if the cards were updated on a frequent basis. We were told to stay out of the small bars and visit the larger ones that focused on their good reputations.

Knight, Szerlag and I were instead, super hungry. No McDonalds in sight – nothing western or appealing to our palates that would entice us to eat. Then Knight smells Yakitori, which is a Japanese appetizer of grilled chicken on a stick.

A vendor who was pushing a heavy cart with warm Yakitori that left a trail of its delicious smoke as the vendor walked slowly with it. Knight pays for three sticks and passes one to Szerlag and me. It looked very delicious with the juices running out of the dark, chicken meat and grilled to perfection.

We began to eat. Not one word was exchanged until we had just about finished eating until one of the old and experienced sailors who has been to the Philippines many times laughs and tells us that we were eating dog meat. We looked at our food and around the area and noticed an odd lack of street dogs.

Knight simply shrugged his shoulders and we threw our leftover Yakitori sticks into the street as we continued our way down the street in search of a suitable bar. We were very thirsty for beer. Cheap beer, very cheap beer.

## The AC/DC Bar

We continued further down Magasaysay Drive. Knight looks up and points to a bar called "AC/DC" which was several meters away but close enough to hear our other shipmates either stationed in Subic Bay Naval Base or from our ship (and Marines) yelling over the loud music with happiness and excitement. This was the bar that was recommended to us so we headed in that direction which was only a few minutes away until we hear a "ching-ching. Ching-ching",

All three of us look in the direction of an old 1960's bicycle and see a grandmother in her late 60's with whom we speculated was her granddaughter sitting behind her who appeared to be between five or seven years old dressed in a presumably cute yet very slutty attire.

"Sex with my baby? Sex with my baby?", the grandmother said as she stopped her bicycle and asked the three of us. All three of us spoke, replied, said nothing. It did not register in our brains that this woman was prostituting the little five or seven year old girl and it was her grandmother!

"Cheap, cheap sex with my baby. Free sample", she continues.

Disgusted, we turned back to the original direction of the AC/DC bar and walked away from the grandmother. She still continued to ask us, "Sex with my baby?" as we walked into the AC/DC bar.

It looked like a Tijuana bar, no walls, no windows, all neon and Christmas lights shine out from the bar and out of the patio-like bar. Dance music was blaring out of the bar. Large industrial fans blow out the cigarette smoke and humidity that was quickly replaced with cheap, sweet perfume which coated the women dancing on the stage wearing slutty yet classy bikinis or shorts with numbers taped to their stomachs. Turns out that if you see a girl on the stage, you pay the Mama-san a "Bar Fine" of $20 for her to sit with you. If you want to sleep with her, you discuss a price, which is typically another $20, but that payment again goes to the mamma-san directly. Then she takes you to her place, she will give you a meal, give you a massage and you can spend the night with her. This WAY better deal that in Tijuana and the women were beautiful and exotic.

Knight looks at us with a smile and his eyebrows flicker up and down. Szerlag and I too, were interested. Admittedly, the women were incredibly beautiful as if they stepped out of a Cosmopolitan Magazine with the perfume samples on the pages that came with it.

We had not even ordered a beer to my shipmates as two very cute women suddenly came from nowhere to each of our sides and grabbed onto our arms. I look over to Szerlag and he too, had two women at his side. We both smiled wickedly at each other knowing that something like this where beautiful women grabbed onto us, would never, ever happen to us in the United States. Though flattering and only an idiot would refuse having two beautiful women hanging onto their arms, we had "beer" on our minds. Okay, call me an idiot. Strangely after a month at sea without seeing a girl or even imagining being with a woman, one would think that when getting off a ship, one would head directly to a brothel. Not at all.

Working 18 hours a day, every day, being directed to do this and do that inside a large piece of iron, steel and metal floating across the Pacific with only men, there wasn't any time for even thinking about a woman. It is odd but if one were on a ship with the same scenario for a month and then presented with either a nice, cool glass of beer or a woman, one would chose the beer.

At least this was my case.

After sailing for a month and then getting off the ship, we wanted to drink beer first and before snuggling with a few ladies. But the ladies wouldn't let go of us – they wanted to party.

We told them that we just wanted to drink a beer, very politely. They did not reply. They continued to hold on strongly to my arms. Again I requested, "not now, ladies. I want to drink a beer first". Still, they said nothing. They slowed-down my walk to the bar. Frankly, it became more irritating as I wanted to drink a beer.

Szerlag and Knight already had their ladies dragging them away. We had to fend for ourselves. Both of them went into other directions and I lost my sight on them as I had to work on releasing myself from the two ladies who seemed to be permanently affixed to my arms.

"Ladies…", I said as I forced their hands away. They then returned to the same position, holding onto my arms firmly not letting go.

I then tried to peel the girl to my right's fingers off of my arm one finger at a time and just as she was going to return to grabbing my arms, I physically pushed her away. Then I worked on the girl to my left. She was a bit more stronger, holding my arm with both of her hands after witnessing how I got rid of the girl on my right.

"God damn it, woman! I want to drink a beer. Leave me the f**k alone!"

She still wouldn't let go, so I dragged her towards the bar as she continued to stumble catching up with me.

One would think, "What the heck is wrong with you pushing a woman away from you who was hot and then drag the other one with you like a doll going towards the bar?"

I really do not understand why I did this either, even to this day. But I remember that all I wanted to do was to get f**ked up off of beer as much as I could hold. In my defense, I asked the two women politely to let me go.

Finally making it to the bar to order my drink with a leech who was absolutely beautiful, soft and exotic grabbing onto my left arm as her life depended upon it. Unsure of what local beer was in Philippines, I ordered a "Red Horse" beer.

That drink went down into my throat before the bottle cap flew to the floor when the bartender opened the bottle. I wasn't able to taste what the "Red Horse" beer tasted like because it went down that fast.

I then grabbed another beer called San Miguel from the bartender, turned around (yup, with the girl still attached to my arm) and looked into the bar room looking for Knight and Szerlag. I should have stayed with them as they were already seated drinking beer that was served by a waitress. Both Szerlag and Knight had two women who seemed more well-mannered yet they were affixed to them, but sitting. They were with another fellow shipmate named J.R..

J.R. was a great guy who worked with the computers on the ship. We were all unsure exactly what he did in his office aboard the USS Belleau Wood, but he worked on some highly-advanced computers. Though he explained it to us before when we were in the smoking section on the ship, we still couldn't understand.

His hair was black, straightened as if he woke up gifted with straight, untangled hair. J.R. has super-white skin, perhaps from staying inside the ship, coding away. He seemed to hold himself to the best standard, perhaps of his high-level of intelligence. I hadn't really drank with him up until now and we were now getting to know each other on a drunken level.

Once I made it over to their table, we talked about everything and pretty much heard only fifty-percent as the dance music was blasting into the bar room. Once could probably hear the music all across the city, that they played it so loud. But we were there for the beer and letting out a month's worth of stress, working every day, seeing nothing but men high on testosterone, looking at iron, metal, steel and the endless horizon of where the skies kissed the Pacific Ocean all around us. The beer was amazingly, very delicious and we were having a wonderful time drinking, smoking, moving to the music in our chairs with hot women around us – we felt like men!

"Ya'll smell that!?", I said as I broke whatever, drunken conversation we were having.

"Smell what?", J.R. asked.

"Blood. Don't ya'll smell that?"

Knight looks at me as I had said something stupid and laughs, "Dude, shut the f**k up. Everything here stinks!"

Everyone starts laughing. A few of us recall the stench of "Sh*t River" and how it resembled the same smell as the other "Sh*t River" in Tijuana.

We were all pretty buzzed when all of a sudden, I started smelling blood. I asked them if they smelled it too and they all said to shut up, everything stinks in here. I chuckled but was a bit scared that no one else smelled blood. My expression went from having fun, to a dazed one.

The memory of Allen Schindler being murdered in Sasebo came rushing back to me.

The blood.

The motion Helvey (at this point in time, I still did not know it was Helvey) of stomping on a body.

The sound of Schindler gurgling, trying to breathe.

The look of Schindler's crushed, concaved face.

The smell.

The threat from XO Franklin and Captain Bradt's silent agreement.

Images in my head became questions that I couldn't answer...


"Witte! Witte! Hello?", Knight calls for my attention as he's snapping his fingers in front of me. "Anyone in there!?", J.R. asks.

Szerlag takes his bottle of beer and taps the bottom of his bottle on top of my bottle of beer which sends the head of the beer gushing out requiring me to drink the beer before any of it gushed out onto the table. It looked like the blood gushing out of Schindler's mouth when he was dying on the public bathroom floor in Sasebo, Japan.

I snapped-to and returned back from the memory of the murder to the bar that we were presently at and grabbed my beer which Szerlag made it gush and I began to drink the head of the beer as some of it already spilled onto the table.

It was as if I had time traveled. It felt very vivid and real as if I was just there at the murder again as my surroundings in the bar with J.R., Szerlag and Knight sitting at the table had all faded to black. I thought that this must be what having a flashback is like.

"heeeyyy...", I responded. "I'm just a bit tired", explaining for the reason why I had a flashback but didn't want to explain the real reason for my blacking out.

"dude, let's enjoy!", Szerlag enforces me to enjoy along with them at the table. I simply smiled at Szerlag. He knew what I was going through. Szerlag smiles back in confirmation.

As Knight leans to his right to look at the women dancing on the stage with numbers taped to their stomachs and says to me, "you just need to get laid".

Knight looks at me and again his eyebrows dance up and down signaling for me to look at what he was looking at on the stage.

"yea, I guess you're right", I replied.

"We all need to get laid", Szerlag adds as he too looks at the twenty beautiful and exotic women on the stage.

Then we all said nothing and watched the women dance on the stage. A new dance song begins at a slower 80 beats per minute and the twenty women change which synched their dancing very beautifully.

I wanted to rid the memory of Schindler dying and the smell of his blood that it had shaped my mind into a different being. I didn't care anymore. The more I thought about the murder, where the murderer was and how the rumors of people throwing others off of the ship because they were "different", I felt that I was going to die at any time.

Someone was out to kill me as well. I had seen more than I should have. XO Franklin and Captain Bradt also threatened to "get rid of me" or "have my family miss me" if I said anything, I thought it wasn't fair. There was too much fear and anxiety trying to take over my thoughts. I needed to enjoy whatever life I had left in me. My clock was ticking. If someone was going to kill me in the days to come, at least I should get laid for one last time.

My brain began making changes. The music, the women dancing, the lights and the alcohol continued to amplify my perspectives
and perceptions.

"I'm going to choose a girl, but I want the perfect one", I said to
myself as I continued hunting around the bar and on the stage for
the visually, perfect girl.

We continued to watch the beautiful and exotic women dance as
live art which entertained our eyes, brain, heart and penises. It did
help a lot watching beautiful women dancing that helped us forget
about work or being confined on a ship with men for weeks.

Though it's not politically correct, human instinct overtakes our
bodies and personal needs. Men were made to build, fight, protect,
defend and mate. 900 of us sailors aboard the USS Belleau Wood
were hunting and defending the international waters of the Pacific,
we instinctively thought

## Anna

The women dancing in front of us were going to reward us for protecting the ocean around them. We also have money to provide to make
them feel safe, feed themselves and their families. The women were
also sent by their families to Olongapo to prostitute themselves to get
that money to take care of their families. There was no other income
for to bring back to their families except non-growing farmlands
which were destroyed by the 1991 Mount Pinatubo volcanic eruption.
Their corrupted government wasn't going to pay the farmers money
and there was no international help which led to the farmers and
people of Olongapo to fend for themselves. Just one night of a woman
providing sexual favors to sailors would feed their whole family for

a month. This is supply and demand where political correctness is obsolete, regardless of what laws, arguments or protests. Everyone has to eat.

J.R. selected one of the girls dancing on the stage with a number "#19" taped to her stomach that he wanted for the night and I selected mine, "Girl #24". Szerlag and Knight however, decided to hit another bar so J.R. and I remained to talk to the girls that initially held onto our arms. We told the waitress which girls we wanted to come and sit with us and gave her $20 USD for each girl to sit with us.

By J.R. and I selecting girls from the stage to sit with us ended up pissing off the girls that grabbed onto our arms right when we had entered the AC/DC bar. Once the girls we chose came to our table, the "aggressively, clingy girls that held onto our arms left in a very rude way.

"Hi, I'm Anna", says Girl #24 as she sits on my left next to me and places her beautiful, soft, feminine hands on my thighs on my jeans.

"Hi, I'm Jasmine", says Girl #19 who sits next to J.R..

"Hi, I'm Jonathan," I said as I placed my left arm around her shoulder and Anna moves in closer to me with her incredibly petite body which as complementary to my body structure.

Her smell was as sweet as a tulip which quickly replaced the smell of blood that I kept smelling from somewhere and little-by-little, my thoughts of Schindler's murder, reduced.

"You buy me drink?", Anna says as she continues to rub my thigh with both of her hands.

My reply was of course, "sure!" and J.R. and I ordered drinks of their choice along with our perhaps, fifth beer.

Both Anna (Girl #24) and Jasmine (Girl #19) were very beautiful, clean, soft, exotic and polite. We were told that we had to pay for their glass of whiskey which cost $2 USD. Once their whiskey was placed on the table, they both slammed them into their mouths and asked for another. Once the second round came, I took a sip from it. It wasn't whiskey – it was tea. It was a smart yet deceitful way to run up our tabs.

As we had a 0:00 (midnight) curfew and it was 21:00, we told the girls that we wanted them to take us back to their place. We needed to speed things up, get laid, eat, get a massage and then get back to the ship before curfew. If either one of us (and sailors ranked E3 and below) were to show up to the OOD on the quarterdeck after 0:00, we would be restricted to the ship the following day. We wanted that day to do more adventuring out, shopping, drinking and getting laid again.

"So, what's next?", I asked Anna.

"You want to come to my place?", Anna asked me as she smiled beautifully.

Of course my reply was, "Yup!"

Anna turns to her friend Jasmine who was sitting and molesting J.R. with his perverted and happy expression and begins to speak the Filipino national language of Tagalog.

Both Anna and Jasmine kept talking in Tagalog as our entertainment hours was soon to expire in three hours before we needed to be back on the ship.

J.R. seemed irritated of that as the girls continued and asked the girls, "well? What's going on? Are we going or not?"

Jasmine turns to J.R. and simple says in a very calm, highly-pitched, feminine voice, "yes. Let's go. We can all go together"

"Great then, let's go to your place", J.R. adds.

Coincidently, both girls lived close to each other in the same apartments nearby so we paid the mamma-san the additional $20 USD for each girl and all walked out of the AC/DC bar and headed to their place.

My heart was racing. I couldn't believe that we could "sort-of legally" go to a bar, choose a girl and go back to their place for a mere $40 USD! I loved that system of supply and demand!

We continued walking down Magsaysay Drive and then off through some alleys that appeared pretty sketchy. There were no lights except those glowing out from homes tucked closely next to each other. Some Filipino men were outside sharing and drinking Tanduay Rum, which was a Filipino rum that was cheaper than milk for children. The men were taking drags from their cigarettes as they watched us without speaking to each other as the four of us walked back without saying a word.

The music and sounds that were blasting out from the bars off of Magsasay Drive became muffled. The further we walked into the dirty alleys, the softer the music from the bars became. And more my heart raced. Of course we could have taken on the fear of us rich, American GI Sailors being murdered by desperate thugs but we wanted to continue to inch our way through the rough-looking neighborhood to reach the girls' apartment to blow off steam.

Anna says quietly as she turns left on a foyer with Jasmine,

J.R. and I both look at the building where the girls lived. It was a building that would have been condemned in the United States as pieces of the building were brittle and falling apart. Both J.R. and I would have ran away thinking that there was a gang that were going to murder us in a vacant, deteriorating building however, there were several lights on inside this so-called apartment building.

An old lady walks out of the entrance and onto the foyer to greet her neighbors Jasmine and Anna a good evening.

"Seems legit", I said to J.R. thinking that we endured the fear of being mugged or harmed and made it this far. It was only in a matter of minutes before we were getting a massage, a meal and laid, so we continued to follow both Anna and Jasmine inside.

We all reach the third floor of the apartment building. J.R. and Jasmine stopped off in the apartment two doors before ours. J.R. pokes his head out and says, "Dude, meet you back at the ship?"

"Sure, see you back then. Take care, brother", I replied and both of the apartment room doors closed.

Anna's apartment was a one-bedroom apartment. The paint on the walls somewhat peeling off were light-blue in color to bring a lightness into the rooms.

Anna recommends, "let's go wash up" to get rid of the stench that we had accumulated from the bar and sweat. I look around and didn't see any other room. There was no bathroom or shower in her apartment!

Anna picks up a bucket filled with a bar of soap, a washrag and a towel.

"Come with me", she says as she carries the bucket and opens her apartment door.

"Where are we going?", I asked.

"Going to wash up, silly", Anna said laughing as I was some type of idiot.

I follow Anna down a different hallway going deeper into the apartment building leading up to the corner where a large shower with no curtains was. In the middle of the shower was a water pump that none of any Americans have ever used in their life (unless you were a baby boomer or lived way out in the country of the United States).

Anna steps into the shower and beings to pump the old water pump and to my surprise, it actually worked! I honestly wouldn't know how to use such an old water pump that pumped water out of the ground as I had been spoiled in the United States with simply twisting a nob and I could choose between hot, cold and warm water!

"Do the all the residents use the same shower!?", I asked Anna.

"Of course, silly", Anna replies again as if I were stupid.

She was surprisingly successful in washing her whole body without taking her bra or panties off. Spoiled-American-me would have to be completely nude to take a shower.

The bathrooms were the same, they were shared by all of the residents of the apartment building. Back in the 1990s, Americans weren't so anal-retentive about clean toilets as we are in the current age. Though the toilet area looked old, it had a hole to sh*t and pee into. I relieved myself there but I did not dare to take a shower the way that Anna was able to with her clothes on.

"No shower, it's okay. I like your smell", Anna says as she dries herself off. I simply watched her beautiful, exotic and petite body as it was in slow motion. It was a show that I didn't have to pay for!

Anna then gathers her toiletries and guides me back to her apartment.

"Have a seat", Anna says and pulls out a chair from her dining table for me to sit in. She goes to her tiny fridge and pulls out a bottle of Coca-Cola. She retrieves a transparent gold-colored drinking glass from out of her roughly-painted white cabinet and places it onto the dining table that's covered in cheap lace.

She pours the Coca-Cola into the glass and hands the drink to me and says, "I'll be right back. I need to go get dinner" and then she leaves me alone in her apartment.

I take a sip and scan her apartment. Majority of the items she's used for decorating seems to have come from the Dollar Store yet she decorated it the best that she could.

There is a picture of her family back at her home, wherever that may be but seems happy and signs of love. Right next to that is a crucifix and a religious candle for praying. Other small items were carefully and meticulously arranged around her apartment to make it seem like her home. Expecting Anna to take a little longer getting our dinner, she returns in less than ten minutes.

"I've got dinner", she says as she takes out Styrofoam to-go containers filled with rice, meat and vegetables. She then retrieves another glass for herself to drink from and a few plastic plates and empties the food onto them. The rice had small specs of insects and the meat was at room temperature. Definitely food that I would not eat and would complain about back in the states however, I was a guest and just grabbed a spoon that she gave me and began eating. The food had no taste to it at all but still filled my stomach with substance in preparation for the activity that I'd perform at the end of the night.

Once we had finished eating, she placed an ashtray on the dining table and i smoked. Before I was able to finish my cigarette, Anna says, "Come with me" and leads me into her bedroom.

Anna then turns on the radio which plays a Lionel Richie song "Hello" sung in Tagalog by a cover band. It sounded pretty good for being a cover. Anna moves behind me and sits me onto her bed. Both of Anna's hands touch my shoulders and she begins to massage me. It felt very good however, I wanted to proceed with the award and take her under the sheets.

I turned around to face her and pick her up and threw her onto her bed. She reaches over to turn on a side table lamp that was dimmed-red from a handkerchief she had used to cover the dried volcanic ash that still lingered in the air from the wind and got into the sheets.

We fooled around a bit until the reward was rendered. It was indeed an enjoyable evening.

Afterwards, we napped for a little. Thinking that she thought I was asleep, she checked on me to confirm this. I was not asleep. I was pretending to sleep to calculate her moves. I didn't know this girl and who knows, she may had wanted to kill me and take my military ID and the last $20 USD I had in my wallet.

"I knew it!", I exclaimed in my head as I saw her reach for my wallet from my jeans and looked through it. Anna didn't take my money but did get a good look at my Military DOD ID card. I was unsure for what reason she needed to look at my card, so I just let her fulfill her curiosity.

She then placed it back into my jeans and laid back down next to me. She placed her head and arm over my chest and then I pretended to wake up from a nap. I told her that I needed to get back to my ship. It was nearly midnight.

Anna agreed and called for a trike to take me back to the Base. I paid 5 Pesos (about $1 USD) to get back to the ship.

"5.00 Peso" (about $1 USD) read the sticker-like sign displaying the cost for the ride. I reconfirmed, "5 Peso?" where he replied, "yes, only 5 Peso". This "trike" was basically a motorcycle with a sidecar that could hold two people and it sounded like a lawnmower.

It was a nice evening after the sun set and at this time of night, not too many people were in the way for the motorized tricycle to navigate around. It was also a great way to see the neighborhoods and see how others in Olongapo lived. It was an enjoyable evening until…

We were just about in front of the Naval base when the driver of the motorized tricycle reaches down to where the sticker-like sign read "5.00 Peso" and removes the "." (dot) from the "5.00 Peso" (about $1 USD) to make it now read "500 Peso" (about $9 USD).

"Son of a bitch is scamming me", I said to myself.

"Ha!?", the motorized tricycle driver said.

I then said more loudly so that he could hear me, "What the f**k, man. Are you kidding me!?"

The motorized tricycle slowed down and turned the corner in another direction than we were headed toward the base.

"Ju hab a ploblem!?", the motorized tricycle asked.

"Dude, you said it was 5.00 Peso. I just f**king saw you remove the dot to make it 500 Peso. You're f**king ripping me off, mother-f**ker!", I scolded the motorized tricycle driver as I was preparing to knock the sh*t out of him and run like hell back to the base. But as the motorized tricycle made another right turn into a much darker alley where it ended with three other motorized tricycle drivers were resting looking in our direction.

The other three drivers didn't look like they were waiting to be hired. They appeared as if they rotated this scam so that no one would recognize their faces and report them to the militia that was hired by the mayor of Olongapo. It was a no-win for my situation so I had to yield.

I said, "okay, okay...I'll pay". I had no choice. I could fight-off one of the drivers, but four drivers? I couldn't take my chances.

I was safe as I had $20 USD in my wallet but the guy was charging me for $9. It would have been funny if I had asked him for change but knew that joke would have cost me my whole $20. I lied to him (sucker) and said I had no money so he looks at a watch that I had won from a $0.25 gumball machine when I lived in Irving, Texas and asks, "what about dat watch?".

Yeah, I played with him for a little on the watch by saying, "Oh, no. this watch is worth way too much than 500 Peso".

"Ju gib me jour watch and I take you right at da base gate, okay?", my motorized tricycle driver bartered.

"Okay...okay", I said acting as if I was honestly disappointed as slowly took my cheap-ass watch and handed it to him. The deal was sealed.

The motorized tricycle driver backed up away from his other motorized tricycle buddies, turned the tricycle around and headed to the base where he dropped me off.

I hurried through the military gates and was safely back onto the Subic Bay Naval Base and laughed on my way back on the bus which took us drunk sailors back to the ship.

Once aboard the ship, I headed straight to my division berthing area, climbed into my rack, laid down onto my bunk and went to sleep.

## Body In A Tubed Television Nightmares

In my sleep, I saw a tubed television sitting in a 1960s-looking living room. It looked something like a movie set created by Tim Burton – strange, uniformed and unforeseen happenings. The television was dark-brown with thin, vertical speakers of a tan color. The tube was that of old television colors when the power was off, a tinted, worn, green colored glass.

It turned on by itself and began to flicker. Nothing was coming on the screen, no shows at all. It needed to be hit on the sides to work so that I could see a television show. I walked over to it slowly and hit it several times on the top and sides. This began to make sounds unlike any television or electrical device.

The sounds were natural like a gurgling and repetitive dripping sound. Though I thought it could be blood, I was hoping that it was just a water leak coming from the television box. I then began to hear it breath and cry the most horrendous sound, much like a monster from a movie.

Curiosity instructed me to take a look in the back but there was a panel. There was a piece of the back panel that I could get a grasp onto and I began to force it open to see from where the noise was coming.

Once I opened the back, a huge gush of warm air came out as if it had been generating the heat inside. As there wasn't enough light to see what was inside, I could see something unlike any electrical matter, it was organic.

I continued to force the back panel open until it came completely off the back of the television box. To my surprise, I saw a mangled-up body with bones, blood, muscle, guts and eyeballs all mushed-up inside the television box. There was no skin present.

Strangely, I did not run away but instead, went around to the front of the television to see if I had fixed it. What I saw was the other side of mangled-up body parts of what I saw from the back of the television where I had pulled the back panel off. The mangled body parts were rotating, slithering, smacking against each other in a slow motion. Blood began to seep from the television screen and the cracks of where the other parts of the television box met.

I went to the channel dial to switch the channel but as I did that, the mangled-up body parts would jerk quite a bit each time I switch the dial. I continued to switch the dial to the other stations faster and faster and faster as the same time the mangled-up body parts would move along with my switching the dial faster and faster and faster.

Then, I began hitting and pounding the television box because it was disturbing to see the motion of the body parts move while I was controlling it. From then, I tried to scream. I was then motionless and restricted from moving freely.

The nightmare faded to black and I started to choke which woke me up. There was a huge puddle of my sweat on my bunk. I was very, very cold yet my hair, face, torso and thighs were covered in sweat. I was breathing too fast; my chest hurt a lot along with my head, hands and knuckles.

I look at my knuckles and they are red with a few cuts of blood. But what irritated me the most was that I was sweating and smelling blood a lot. I needed a shower very badly. Whatever was on my skin and in my nose needed to be scrubbed away quickly.

I took my shower bag, headed into the showers and scrubbed the sh*t out of my skin. By twisting the washcloth, I was able to scrub the inside of my nose to rid the scent of blood. The smell of blood did not disappear regardless of how much I scrubbed off the outer layer of my skin but was covered by the perfumes from the bar of soap.

"This will do", I comforted myself as I returned to the berthing area to get dressed into civilian clothing, preparing for another day in the Philippines.

I then got dressed and left the berthing area out into the galley. No one was there. It had already closed as it was 14:00.Unsure of what happened to the time but apparently I had slept for almost fourteen hours!

I thought I should feel good after sleeping for so long, but I felt quite irritated. The shell that my body was inside felt broken and injured. The more aggressive I felt, the more I was able to shed the twisted emotions. Thinking that by leaving the ship and heading into a different world, things would get better and my feelings would subdue.

Not thinking about looking for my shipmates Szerlag, Knight or J.R. to go out together into Olongapo, I just left by myself. Honestly, I didn't really want to be with anyone that day. Though we were told to hang with a fellow shipmate by our Filipino seniors, I instead headed to the base shuttle bus that would take drive me to Subic Bay Naval Base alone.

As the bus was aligning to the curb at the front gate, I again looked to the left to see the Filipino locals lining up again to pump clean water off of the base and into their mismatched buckets. The militia was there again holding their rifles on our base to ensure that the locals didn't get out of hand.

Again, I go through the gate which leads into Olongapo but today, there were no militia greeting any of us into Olongapo today so the other shipmates who rode with me from the ship and I walked calmly through the barrier and into Olongapo.

Crossing the bridge over "Sh*t River", I look down at the children playing in the toxic waste water screaming happily, playing some sort of game similar to Marco Polo. I light a cigarette and watch them play. They had nothing really to worry about except from where their next meal comes. another commodity that Americans take for granted.

I continue walking into the city staying on the Magsaysay Drive, not to venture into the alleys in case the motorized tricycle driver whom I had hilariously duped for 10 Peso ($0.25 USD) were to come back and collect the leftover 490 Peso ($9.15 USD) nor to be confronted by another dangerous situation.

Curious to see how far I would go, I walked for hours down the Magsaysay Drive until I had reached the Central Luzon.

Central Luzon was the exact downtown location of Olongapo. The main and popular stores were aligned directly around a round-about with cars, motorized tricycles, mopeds, humans and Jeepneys whirling around the 3-5-storied buildings. The locals in this area seemed to be more genuine than the sketchy folks back next to the base. They were kind and well-mannered.

There was a Mister Donut, dough-nut shop which was very popular in Japan. It was once an American company which later was bought by an international company. This gave Mister Donuts the opportunity to change their name to Dunkin' Donuts. By then, Mister Donuts became a popular donut store across Japan. Upon entering Mister Donuts, I purchased several donuts, a cup of coffee, grabbed an ashtray and sat down in a booth close to the back of the seating area. I hadn't had a donut since I was living at Dougy's place in Irving, Texas. It had reminded me of all the donuts I ate from the trash and the struggles that I had gone through to get into the Navy however, now I had found myself in another and worse struggle.

My symptoms of smelling blood, anger, frustration, nightmares, stress, irritation and chest pains continued, but I was counting on getting past that. I was going through options and trying to clear my head with the murder and the sh*t that followed shortly thereafter. There was no one to turn to or talk to about what major situation I was in and if I did, the captain and XO would make me "disappear". I couldn't even tell the Chaplin about what I was going through. None of my friends wanted to hear the whole story as it was too complicated and too close to being indicted for the murder investigation (I do not blame them for that) as the murderer had yet to be caught as far as I knew. Then of course, I had been keeping my eye out for anyone from the Navy who might be the actual killer who was looking for me to kill so that there were no more witnesses.

There were too many things way above my head though I was certain that I could overcome all of this…but how and when?

By the time my donuts were all gobbled-up, I had gone through a whole pack of cigarettes. The sky was getting dark and the city lights were turning on, building-by-building, so I decided to head back toward the Subic Bay Naval Base and go drink more. By drinking, perhaps some sort of solution will come to my head which will help me sort things out better.

As I returned from the Central Luzon in downtown Olongapo, I looked for the AC/DC bar off of Magsaysay Drive and made certain not to be seen by anyone there as Anna would most likely be looking for me. I didn't want to play with her tonight, I only wanted to drink and think more. Instead, I went from bar to bar, drinking a beer at each and picking up a go-go dancing girl to sit with me, just to be close to something soft, kind and hopefully calm my anger at the same time. I didn't need sex, I needed a conversation from beautiful girls who had a high-pitch, soothing voice to calm the angry voices in my head. It worked well! It was enjoyable and laughter was all around me.

By the time I had reached the last bar for the night, each of the names of the bars lost its name. I only remembered the girls in them and the fun that we had. The last bar of the night for me became more than I could handle. My eyes were becoming heavy. The two women at my table whom I paid for and their drinks were propositioning me to go back to their place for sleep and a massage, but I didn't want to go through that same issue I had last night with the scam artist that drove the motorized tricycle again. I was too tired and didn't want to fight anyone. One of the girls got closer to me who had large breasts and moved my head to her cleavage and petted my head. Just that alone was very relaxing.

Just as my head was going to fall into the girl with the large breasts' lap, we suddenly hear, "F**k you, a**hole!" from a few tables away and then a bottle crash. That woke me up and I lifted my head up fast which hit the girl's chin and made her yelp. I look around to see from where the commotion was. It didn't take that long to see five guys aggressively pushing each other at the back of the bar. The Marines seemed to have started an altercation with a few Sailors. They appeared outnumbered based on their size, but their size could be underestimated.

"Marines…", I said to myself which one of the girls heard me say to myself. The pushing between the Marines and the Sailors continue with additional heated curse words. It was easy to tell the difference between a marine and a sailor. Marines have much shorter hair, especially on the sides and a small patch of a bit longer hair on top of their head. Sailors typically have more hair on the side and let the top grow out to an inch and a half more.

What both Marines and Sailors had in common besides working together was fighting. All it took was something like "that girl is mine, not yours" and "I was ordering my beer first before you" type of things that started fights. Neither Marine nor Navy never back down as we are taught to well, not back down from confrontation. Neither give in nor give up which we were all taught in boot camp.

As Sailors and Marines typically consist of three or more in a crew or pack (just as Knight, Szerlag and sometimes J.R.), we protect our crew or packs. So once either throws a punch, they all go in for the fight. Yes, it hurts however, it feels nice to get that stress off our chests. We will get in trouble but we would never report our wounds from brawls. Once we get back on the ship, we work together as usual. It's simply how we worked and lived together. Not all Marines or Sailors fight, but it happens quite a bit.

Lots of shouting going on and the bar's mamma-san yells to the two crews to stop and that she was going to get Shore Patrol. No one listened. We hear what sounded like their senior who was older, chubbier yell out, "guys, knock it off or I'm going to give you sh*t when we get back to the ship". Neither of the crews heard. Others started to step in to separate them but that seemed to have started a larger altercation. The Marines weren't listening to anyone. Even the Sailors who they were arguing with kept telling them to chill out. And then a half-filled bottle of San Miguel beer goes flying across the bar room with the leftover beer trailing from the person who threw it directly hits the Marines. Then everyone stands up and goes to the two groups.

The two girls I was with get close to me as one of the guys who stood up after the initial altercation gets pushed and falls onto me. He says nothing but uses me as a handrail and pushes himself up from me, which really made me mad.

I yelled at him as I stood up and pushed him from behind. Then out of nowhere, I suppose his buddy, slugs me on the side of my right head and I fall to the floor which is sticky with old beer and spit. It hurt like hell and I almost blacked out but managed to pick myself up and search for that the jerk who slugged me.

As I continued to look around for the guy who got away with a nice hit to my head, I saw about thirty guys just kicking each other's' asses. Everyone almost looked the same except the differentiating Marines from Sailors so I jumped into the brawl to help my shipmates. Everyone was getting hit and punched, including me but apparently it didn't hurt us that much.

One of the shipmates poked his head up and yelled at another one of our shipmates who was fighting, but fighting the wall of the bar and yells, "Dude, what the f**k are you doing!? Get over here and help us!", however, our shipmate continues to punch the wall.

Momma-san joins in the brawl and pulls a few of us out by pulling onto our ears. I don't think any of us could take a pull to the ear, but a punch – yes. Then Shore Patrol starts coming in with their night sticks and uses them to pull several of us off.

The majority of others including myself, were able to jump out of the bar (which is like a patio, with no windows) and head toward another bar and hide. Unfortunately, a lot of us lost our girls that we were with, but by the time we got to another bar, there were more beautiful women there to help lick our wounds.

The night goes on like nothing happened. Those who were apprehended by the Shore Patrol will get into trouble. Though those who got caught will never report those who escaped as we live by an unspoken creed where we do not tell on each other regardless if they assaulted us or not. Shore Patrol will see those who return to the ship with cuts and bruises. They will ask us who had hit us, but we will simply reply that we fell or hit ourselves on a door. We were government property so any damage done to ourselves would make us responsible. To rat-out our fellow shipmate meant we were not teammates which would result in other shipmates not relying on us. If we got into a fight and there were visible wounds, we would not report this.

In Schindler's case, he was being harassed and received a few pushes himself by his own shipmates (according to the NCIS Investigation reports, Schindler's diary and my first-hand accounts) but he honored and respected his fellow shipmates regardless, apparently, Helvey and Vins did not.

# CHAPTER 13

# SAVING A DAMSEL IN DISTRESS

## NOVEMBER 21, 1992

November 21st was the first day of my 3-day/2-night vacation which was only granted to those who are ranked E4 and above however given my unique situation after discussing with the Chaplin, I was able to get a vacation while deployed.

It was also the day that PO2 Daniels and I were going off deeper out of the Subic Bay area to the rural area to rescue a girl that was supposedly being locked away against her will. PO2 Daniels story of an American making final payment in the months to come to have her shipped to him didn't really seem realistic. Sure. What the hell. I'm curious and adventurous. I'm going to die anyways so if one of the militia men give me sh*t, I'm going down fighting!

Even though it was my 3-day weekend, I had nothing planned except the excursion with Daniels.

Daniels appears with excitement as he entered the portside port smoking section where I had waited for him for thirty minutes. He dressed in a very touristy way with his brown cargo pants, fanny pack, loafers, white socks , you know, the clothing that you wouldn't be caught dead in and looks like your dad. I ALMOST didn't want to go now that I saw his attire but I had committed.

PO2 Daniels and I left the smoking section on the ship and headed to the hanger deck which leads to the Quarterdeck for us to exit the ship for our adventure.

We heard Captain Bradt and XO Franklin scolding a lot of our shipmates about behaving properly in the city. I had forgotten what he said but you could hear the tone and a few words coming out of his mouth such as "misbehaving in the city" and "fighting" and "You embarrassed…something". My mind was more set on getting off the ship and checking out stuff to get my mind off of things for a while.

PO2 Daniels and I snuck over to the Quarterdeck and showed our Liberty card (a card that allows us to leave the ship) and…

The OOD (Officer Of the Deck) instructs me, "Seaman Witte, you are not allowed to leave the ship due to your rank.

"What? Why?", I asked surprisingly.

The OOD Calmly tells me that something had happened back in Japan and that those ranked E3 and below were restricted to the ship.

"I am already on my 3-day vacation!", I exclaimed yet the OOD denied my permission to leave off the ship. I was stunned and pissed.

To my relief, the Chaplin was in the hanger deck listening to Captain Bradt and XO Franklin scolding the ranks. The Chaplin who had his arms crossed while listening to the scolding saw me as I was tried to flag him for his attention.

The Chaplin seemed confused and asked, "What's wrong, Witte?"

Which I replied, "The OOD has denied my permission to leave the ship though I am currently on a 3-day Liberty" The Chaplin seemed determined and tells me, "Stand fast" (Navy terminology request for "wait") to get me my permission to leave the ship. The

Chaplin then walks over to the OOD and guides the him to the side to chat a little in privacy.

PO2 Daniels is patiently waiting and a bit confused on how I was able to operate two senior officers to debate my exclusive permission to leave the ship. While the Chaplin explains the situation (whatever it may be) to the OOD, the both look my way. The OOD then raises his eyebrows and opens his mouth.

The Chaplin then walks back to me and says, "You're good to go!" My curiosity called me to ask him, "What did you tell the OOD?" The Chaplin smiles and simply says, "He knows who you are".

"What do you mean, sir?", I asked the Chaplin. He just looks at me and says, "Don't worry about it. Just don't come back to the ship until the restriction is lifted and all those ranked E3 and below can leave the ship".

I smiled at the Chaplin and thanked him.

PO2 Daniels was still waiting for me and was quite surprised that I was able to get off the ship regardless of my being in the ranks where we couldn't leave the ship however, now it put me in the situation where me being part of the Schindler murder investigation on the radar by others.

Before I thought any more about how the so-called "Key Witness" would have my face on it, PO2 Daniels impatiently said, "Dude, hurry the hell up!"

Once out of the Subic Bay Naval Base gate, PO2 Daniels hired a motorized tricycle (which I felt hesitant in riding from my previous experience) and we rode off to a Jeepney depot where the majority of the vehicles met to take its people in various locations around Olongapo. From there, we casually walked to the nearby bus depot that would take us to New Cabalan. He reminds me to take my wallet out of my back pocket and move it to a front one. There was no way that anyone could possibly grab my wallet out of my front pocket.

PO2 Daniels seemed comfortable walking and navigating through the swarms of local Filipino transients and food vendors as if he had been here many times. He told me that he was once stationed here for 3 years.

As we make our way to the most-center point of the bus terminal in the sea of Jeepneys, vendors, motorized tricycles and locals, we were approached by five small Filipino boys ranging in ages six to twelve each holding a handkerchief in their hand. Two of the children first approach Daniels and he begins poking the lit part of the cigarette towards the eyes of the children as if he was trying to poke them in their eyes.

I couldn't imagine what he was doing but the next second, three of the five children come towards me. Two of the boys start Karate-chopping my stomach asking, "You want massage? You want massage, mister?" Dumbfounded, I couldn't reply to these two children touching me that way which distracted my attention from the fifth boy who walked around behind me. I see his right hand leaving my front-right pocket with his blue handkerchief. I did not feel his hand at all going into my front-right pocket.

Quickly, I grabbed his hand that had just left my front-right pocket and pulled him towards me and began kicking him away. Success! Not only did I get my wallet back, but I was also able to grab the pick-pocket's handkerchief. The boy begins to cry and asks in a humiliated way, "can I get my handkerchief back?". I then threw his handkerchief back at him and the three children who were unsuccessful in stealing my wallet ran away into the sea of the locals.

I see embers flying everywhere near Daniels who is still struggling fighting off the other two children that were trying to reach for Daniels' wallet yelping from being burnt by his cigarette. The other two children were also unsuccessful in getting Daniels' wallet and ran after the three boys who were pickpocketing me.

There wasn't much to see outside the windowless windows of the bus except for a few locals walking from house to house. Occasionally passing by three or four compounds shared by family members. Their houses made of tin, wood and concrete where paint fades from the humidity. No electricity, just lanterns and from the moonlight.

I try looking inside their homes as the bus zooms by quickly to see families smiling, living life without the difficulties of technology or outside influences of other countries. Their children playing with metal, wood, rocks and tin. No television. No technology. Just the simplest materials created from the earth. They seemed happy, more happy than I was.

As I'm watching the locals live amongst themselves, I say to PO2 Daniels, "Man, we sure are going way into the country". PO2 Daniels turns to me and says, "It's worth it. Jasmine, the girl that we are going to rescue is being held against her will"

"Are you sh*tting me, man?", I asked in disbelief.

PO2 Daniels tells me that it's worth the trip to try and get Jasmine, the girl that we were going to find and rescue. He further explains that Jasmine was being bought for $2,000 USD from a doctor in Los Angeles, California. He had made a deposit of $1,000 USD to make sure that Jasmine would not have any sexual relations with any other customer until he made the final payment of another $2,000 USD and take her back with him to Los Angeles, California.

We continued discussing how Mount Pinatubo volcanic disaster had pressured families to send their wives, daughters, nieces, mothers – any female relative that looked attractive to the cities such as Olongapo and New Cabalan to sell themselves. The families had no choice as there were no more crops that had been damaged by the volcanic eruption. There was no help from the corrupted government nor any aid. Everybody needs to eat.

## New Cabalan

PO2 Daniels and I finally reach the bus terminal of New Cabalan, the only bus to arrive in a very rural village which is a province of Olongapo. There were swarms of motorized and analog tricycle drivers (also known as pedi-cabs) awaiting the bus riders who had just arrived. Other vendors selling towels, belts, food and snacks advertising their items by their voices which started off with, "Hey friend, hey friend!" And there were street children placing their hands together in a cup-shape begging for anything, mostly food – not money, but of course money would be appreciated. There had to have been ten or twelve of these children begging. All I had was a $20 bill which would have been useless as no one in that area had change for that amount.

"Keep walking. Don't look into their eyes or their way", PO2 Daniels advised me. So as arrogant as we walk, it was hard to ignore the children cry.

"Crocodile tears, that's all they are", Daniels concludes as we walk away from the children following us one-by-one.

We continue down a dirt road, again lined with rural houses with paint fading, stripping away from their outside walls exposing the dark-gray concrete. As the majority of the locals in New Cabalan had no televisions, let alone electricity, all they watched was the locals and visitors walking by in front of their compounds which family members shared. When non-locals and especially non-Filipinos such as us walk by, we become celebrities. All that we would hear was "hello!", "Hi G.I." and a few "Yankee!" but PO2 Daniels and I would looks straight down the dirt road as I followed.

House after house, we pass ignoring the locals calling out to us in hopes of making friends with rich Americans. If you glance their way into their eyes, then they will try to talk to you more. Sure, it's okay to talk to locals, but there were so many of them. If we stopped to chat with them, then we would never make it to our destination. It was hard to ignore them. Most of them just want to have a chance to talk to an American. Others want to scam or try to pickpocket you and we already experienced that back at the bus terminal in Olongapo City. Not wanting to be rude or arrogant, I'd glance at them and smile a bit. Daniels repeatedly told me to stop looking at them.

"Free sample suck, suck", a little girl about 10-years old and dressed in a white blouse and pink shorts comes directly up to us from our right. She was alone in the night running to catch up with our fast-paced walking.

"Wha?", I exclaimed in shock

"Watch out", PO Daniels says, "That's a scam"

The 10-year old girl then runs away ahead of us then stops, turns around and lifts her blouse up exposing her right nipple and says, "Free sample suck, suck, any okay."

I slow down and walk behind PO Daniels who also is trying to dart past her. "Dude, this is f**king weird", I say to Daniels who just laughs it off.

He then explains, "It's not weird, it's sad. Her family is probably starving as they have no jobs, no crops from the volcanic eruption, no jobs...They are lucky to have a cent to their name. Her mother probably is ugly, prostituting herself off as her husband drinks heavily to escape all the pain. Perhaps the mother just gave up and left them and all the income that they have to survive with is from his daughter selling herself so they can eat. Without her getting someone to molest her will send her family to their graves from starvation."

Of course, these assumptions are simply hypothetical but from hearing stories and seeing these events, at least one of those scenarios which PO Daniels was speaking of were true.

I had no expression on my face from PO2 Daniels' explanation of Filipinos in poverty except a deep exhale of disbelief and as the little, 10-year old girl walks slowly away from us in disappointment and appears to cry softly. PO2 Daniels continues to share his opinion, "In south America, they have a chance to jump over the border and into the United States for a chance. Americans in poverty have government assistance. In the Philippines, there's absolutely nothing, nowhere to go for help. All they have is their religion, but from the sins that they are forced into, they feel helpless and desperate. It is very sad, but you need to think about yourself in countries and situations like this."

## The Imrpisoned Girl Under The Staircase

"So what about this girl that we are going to rescue?", I say asserting that PO2 Daniels was a bit hypocritical and bias.

"You can help as many people as you can however, you cannot save everyone", he explains. I deeply understood this as I tried to save Schindler to the best of my abilities. Maybe Schindler was supposed to die, but for what reason? Was God planning something for the future and beyond my understanding by taking away a good soul as Schindler's?

Then, I began to think about Schindler's murder, the abundance of blood, his gurgling cry for help. "I have failed", I thought to myself. My eyes began to water and my chest began to rage however it was stopped short when a young Filipino boy about 11-years old came up to PO Daniels and began talking to him, "long time, no see", he says.

"Hey, Anthony!", PO2 Daniels replies to the boy. The boy was upset and says, "Call me 'Tony'"

"Hey, Little-boy Tony!", PO2 Daniels corrects himself as he chuckles.

From my impression, both PO2 Daniels and Tony knew each other. PO2 Daniels explains that he had been there two years ago and was a frequent visitor in this area and to the place where we were going to rescue this girl – at a brothel.

Little-boy Tony and PO2 Daniels continues small chit-chat, some of it in Tagalog with me in tow. Unaware to where they were heading to, Little-boy Tony begins walking next to me and says, "You need a girl? My sister is beautiful. She will do anything for you! I give you discount"

"Is that so?", I asked in hopes to deter the proposition. How could a younger brother pimp his sister? My thinking about the murder was mostly occupying my mind rather than getting laid or serviced by his older sister. Little-boy Tony continues to talk about what sexual services his sister can do for me as we finally make it up to the point of extraction where we were going to so-called "rescue the damsel in distress".

The building looked like a brothel right out of the movies; a large patio with pillars, opened windows with red, glowing curtains, concrete siding where paint was peeling off and prostitutes sitting on the window seal showing their legs and fanning themselves to rid the still heat in the night.

We walk in with Little-boy Tony who darts off to get his sister in hopes of enticing me. PO2 Daniels leans over to my ear and whispers, "Don't say anything" as if he was hinting that there would be some conversations that he had planned to convince the momma-san to see the girl who was locked up.

The bar is quite empty for a large so-called brothel and appeared to be more as a make-shift bar within a luxurious hotel built around the early 1920s. All of the walls were concrete, smaller pillars line the passageway to a large, curving staircase which led to the rooms. To our right which probably used as a fancy restaurant to cater to the elites now sits a bar with around twenty, loosely-dressed and depressed-looking women waiting for their customers.

PO2 Daniels walks in confidently as I follow. We sit right at the bar and are greeted by the mamma-san who's wiping the bar of dust and glass rings left by previous patrons who are now upstairs with women. Behind the bar are mostly empty or almost empty bottles of wine, a mirrored wall beautifully decorated with wooden trim. There are some photographs of their favorite moments with their customers, parties and soldiers who had visited them during the Vietnam war. To the right, there is a staircase, perhaps for servants or the workers to utilize as the curving staircase in the passageway and foyer were used for their customers.

The straight staircase behind the bar was also decorated with banners and a few posters of beautiful models holding alcohol. Underneath the staircase was a door and a Master Lock padlock, locking the contents behind it. It appeared as if it was temporarily made with plywood which didn't match the rest of the décor of the beautiful, and antique hotel/brothel.

PO2 Daniels orders our beer from a waitress as he looks at me, winks to hint at me to keep my mouth closed and calls out to the mamma-san. "Mamma-san, you know why I'm here.", PO2 Daniels says as if they had this conversation by phone before visiting.

Mamma-san appears as if she's seen a lot in her sixty-plus years of life. She's perfected the attitude but not her makeup which shows bright red on her cheeks, lips and purple on her eyelids. Her hair is black, wavy and shoulder-length with a few hairclips with cute, yellow butterflies. We didn't take her appearance for granted as she's also a hefty and plump woman who has probably thrown a lot of misbehaving soldiers out of her bar with her mighty strong-looking arms. She could probably kick PO2 Daniels' ass and mine at the same time while serving beer and a smile. She didn't need a gun.

She had attitude that would make any strong men run away if they crossed her the wrong way yet would give a beautiful smile if she favored you. Mamma-san's appearance and attitude was supported by a thick, light-brown stick known as a "Bunal Stick" (a stick for spanking children or men). Whenever she got mad, she would slam the "Bunal Stick" on the bar counter. The noise that it made frightened children and men. If the misbehaving of children or men didn't take that noise seriously, it would be used more effectively.

"No, I say No to ju already", Mamma-san says with her broken English as she slams the "Bunal Stick" onto the bar counter.

PO2 Daniels says, "this is the last time I'll ever get to see her. She and I have history. All I want to do is say 'good-bye'. That's all".

Mamma-san looks up from the corner of her eye and says, "Ju know I can't. She already paid by her husband".

"I know, mamma-san, but all I want to do is say good-bye. Just one more time", PO2 Daniels says in hopes of convincing Mamma-san.

"Ju don't hab to come here. Many beautipul girls in Subic Bay", Mamma-san replies.

PO2 Daniels then pulls a wad of $20 USD in two rubber bands which looked to be around $500 USD and says to Mammamma-san, "You see, she means a lot to me. Let me see her. Just one time and I go."

Mamma-san looks irritated however the wad of American $20s seemed to have changed her mind. Mamma-san reaches into her bra holding her sagging double-D breasts and pulls out a Master Lock key that sticks to her breasts from the sweat and walks to the closet made with plywood that's underneath the staircase behind the bar.

Mamma-san says, "Okay. Jus wan time, ok? Wan time only, ok?" as she grabs the lock with one hand, inserts the key that she grabbed out of her bra, turns the key, removes the Master Lock padlock and out comes a beautiful Filipino woman in her early 20's who appeared dazed and confused to what was happening. It was as if she had stepped out of a Playboy magazine; beautiful figure, beautifully natural face, perfect perky breasts (via a man's x-ray vision), nice, golden skin and eyes which you could stare into for hours.

The room, or I should say closet, which Jasmine came out of was decorated with Christmas lights, hearts made from construction paper, a mattress, blanket, a fan and two buckets; one for consumption and the other for sh*tting or peeing in.

"Jasmine!" PO2 Daniels shouts in happiness and holds out his arms for her. "Greg!" shouts Jasmine as she enters into his open arms. Her smile was very beautiful that could be seen for miles. They hug and whisper a short conversation which I could not hear, but suspect that they are confirmations of love.

Human-trafficking was quite bad during this time. Pedophiles, sex traffickers, human smuggling and sex tourism was quite strong in the south pacific – especially Thailand and Philippines. For the local villages, the sex industry was what kept them alive. Especially after the Mount Pinatubo volcanic eruption just a year ago, the families had no more crops which villages and families depended upon. With no more crops or opportunities, all that was left was scams, hustling and prostitution. For a fair price, human-traffickers would come from South Korea, China, Australia, Europe and the United States.

As for Jasmine, she intentionally came to the brothel for work to help send money back to her family who lived on the outskirts of New Cabalan. She didn't expect to be held prisoner in the sex-trafficking industry. Though her family suspected that she was leaving her family's farmland and going to the village to find work as a prostitute, they still supported her in hopes of finding a job.

Jasmine never returned home nor wrote them to tell them she's captured in the sex trade. Jasmine was left with only two decisions;

either go back home in shame or become the wife of a doctor in Los Angeles whom she did not love. Certainly, Jasmine could send money back to her family as a wife of the doctor, but she strongly preferred being with her family.

PO2 Daniels paid Mamma-san $500 USD just to have one more night with Jasmine but, Mamma-san didn't know our actual intentions of visiting her brothel. Mamma-san did break a verbal contract with the doctor in Los Angeles by pimping Jasmine out to PO2 Daniels, but who would ever find out? Mamma-san only needed to keep her locked up in the closet underneath the staircase where Jasmine lived for the past three months. Jasmine would have been simply happy to have seen anyone. Seeing her dear friend PO2 Daniels (and perhaps more of a friend) was an emotional encounter for her. One could tell by her grabbing tightly onto PO2 Daniels hugging him instead of what bar girls in Philippines do, touching us sexually.

"Okay, okay, jus go upstair", Mamma-san says as she hides her witnessing a happy, lovable moment.

Greg (PO2 Daniels) and Jasmine hurriedly go upstairs for a romantic moment that has been delayed too long. I sit alone trying to figure out what just happened and why a human would lock up another human in a closet with just a few buckets and Christmas lights but for the Philippines…life is unfortunately very cheap for some.

I continued to drink my beer and wait for PO2 Daniels to finish his business upstairs when I'm approached by little-boy Tony and another beautiful woman who was also in her early 20s'.

"Dis is my sista. Her name iz Erika.", little-boy Tony says as Erika smiles and sits next to me. Little-boy Tony runs away down the hall outside the bar and Erika just sits and touches me as I try to finish my beer.

"well sh*t, since I'm here…why not", I said as I finished the last chug of my beer and take Erika upstairs. Not knowing where I was going, I still guided her upstairs looking for an empty room.

Before we enter the room, we meet Little-boy Tony hands his sister a bowl of ice cubes and says, "$20 USD, okay?". I give him my last $20 and he again darts off into the hallway.

Erika takes me by the hand while holding the bowl of ice cubes and sits on the side of the bed, which was next to an open window with white curtains that flowed in the hot wind from outside. It was quite a large room for just two people.

"I don't think the ice cubes are going to help cool down this room", I said to Erika as she was stupid.

Erika smiles and says, "They not for air" as she unzips me and places an ice cube inside her mouth.

"Oh!", I replied.

## Run

Several hours later, the thoughts of Schindler's murder returns to my head and heart. Pondering questions to why he was murdered, a very high pitched noise begins to ring in my ears and a strange feeling inside my chest begins. I walked over to the window as the white curtains gently flow inward into the room. I light up a cigarette and take a drag. I looked out the window of the room to the street just outside to keep my mind off the strange feeling that was growing inside my body. The buildings I saw outside the Filipino brothel begin to leak blood from the cracks of the roofs and walls. A few locals walk around in the dirt street below as their bodies begin to walk awkwardly. Their faces begin to melt exposing their inner flesh. Blood leaks from their bodies. A few fall to the ground and begin to decompose in a grotesque way. The ground and dirt road begin to fill with blood. The intense smell of blood returns to my nose. My heart begins to pound as my breath becomes heavy and more frequent. At least I'm aware that I am hallucinating but it seemed very, very realistic.

I close my eyes trying to think of something better, but I can't. I look over to Erika who lays on the bed resting as we hear a knock on the door.

"Ju dun?", Little-boy Tony asks from the other side. "Greg luukin por ju".

Looking back outside, all of the blood and mutilated bodies that were in the road and grounds have all disappeared. A few of the locals that were decomposed are returned to their natural, lively figures and continue walking to where they originally were heading.

"Yea, yea..okay", I said as I tap my cigarette out into the ashtray.

Then I hear a loud whisper from outside in the street, "Witte! Witte! Let's go!" I look outside the window and see PO2 Daniels hiding across the street from the brothel with Jasmine hiding behind his shadow next to a stack of used tires and a shed. They both are looking to their right and their left making sure that Mamma-san doesn't see them.

Till this day, I don't know how they got out of the second floor room window, but they managed.

I give PO2 Daniels an 'okay' sign with my fingers and began to clean myself. Erika awakens and sees that I'm leaving in the middle of the night.

"It pibe tirty in da mouning", Erika says as I look at my watch to confirm the time of 05:30.

I make up an excuse to leave, "Yeah, we have to get back to our ship to check in". scrambling for my pants, Little-boy Tony knocks on the door and says through the beautiful, wooden door, "Mamma need tauk to ju".

"Yea, okay", I say as I begin to remember why we came to this brothel. Little-boy Tony becomes more angry like some bad-ass boss. "Ju come noaw!".

"God damn it, Tony! I'm coming. Sh*t...", I reply.

Erika sits up in the bed and simply gives me a smile and a cute wave. I return the gesture, open the door and head out to downstairs.

Mamma-san is standing in the foyer, looking really upset and asks as I'm walking down the spiral staircase, "Where Jasmine?".

As I get to the bottom of the stairs I lie, "Jasmine is still upstairs with Greg.

Mamma-san was on pins and needles and replies with a nagging, "Ha!?"

Changing the topic and deterring Mamma-san's paranoia that Jasmine was escaping, I ask, "Do you have any coffee?"

Mamma-san still looking frustrated simply says, "come" and we walk over to the bar where she begins to brew coffee in an old coffee percolator that appears to have outlived the second World War. It still smelled good!

Daybreak is coming soon as the skies become dark-blue and the background silence is interrupted by the crowing of neighborhood roosters which are used for cock-fighting. Soon, the neighbors will awake and see a chubby white sailor with a beautiful, frightened Filipino woman suspiciously hiding behind a stack of old, used tires. I needed to come up with a plan to escape with Jasmine and PO2 Daniels.

"Let me go see what's taking Greg (PO2 Daniels) and Jasmine so long", I say to Mamma-san who returns my statement with a simple "tisk" sound.

She goes to the end of the bar and away from her viewing of the foyer. As Mamma-san is occupied in cleaning up and replenishing the bar, I walk to the foyer and turn right pretending as if I was going upstairs. I look back and Mamma-san is out of sight allowing me the chance to go left instead, out of the brothel.

As I opened the door, a draft enters and signals the Mamma-san who says from her distance, "Welcome!" and walks back behind the bar in preparations for this ghost visitor. She doesn't know it's me until she sees me from behind the bar.

My only word to that situation was "sh*t!" and I ran out of the brothel without closing the door and into the street. Quickly, I looked left and right for PO2 Daniels and Jasmine and then hear a "Witte! Over here!" to my right, the direction which we should run back to the busses that will take us back to Olongapo City.

"Run, Daniels! Run!", I yelled at both Jasmine and PO2 Daniels who were still hiding behind a stack of old tires in an alley as I ran past them. Jasmine who was barefoot started running and caught up with me just about the same speed as I was running however, poor

PO2 Daniels had a lot more weight to run with and was straggling behind us.

I continue to yell to him behind us. Right behind PO2 Daniels, I see Mamma-san running after us with what looks like the thick, light-brown stick, the "Bunal Stick", up in the air yelling something in Tagalog. Unsure what Mamma-san was yelling at us, but it sure didn't sound like anything welcoming.

We continued to run for what seemed like half a mile until we got up close to the bus terminal where food vendors were setting up their stands to sell breakfast and lunch to arriving and departing patrons that use the bus terminal. Jasmine looks back and says, "no Mamma-san". I too look behind us and only see PO2 Daniels finally catching up to us. He appeared as if he had ran for miles, sweating and seemingly exhausted.

Breathing heavily after coming to a stop where Jasmine and I stopped, PO2 Daniels catches up with us. The three of us continue our way to the bus ticket booth to purchase tickets back to Olongapo City.

PO2 Daniels paid for our tickets; two tickets to Olongapo City and one for Jasmine who was headed back home to Santo Nino where her family awaits her return.

Jasmine and PO2 Daniels again exchange warm-looking hugs. Jasmine sheds tears and says to the both of us, "Thank you. God has brought you to help me. May he forever thank you for what you have done". Jasmine comes to me and hugs me warmly and then returns to PO2 Daniels. They exchange a few whispers and hugs. Jasmine then gets onto her bus. PO2 Daniels and I smoke a cigarette while we wait for her bus to depart. And so it did as Jasmine waves as the bus drives off to the city of Santo Nino.

"Thanks, Witte", PO2 Daniels says with a very accomplished expression.

"Dude, that was fun! We should do it again!", I replied as we both laughed our way to our bus which departs New Cabalan for Olongapo City. We both got onto the bus and took a seat for ourselves and napped all the way back.

Though there are hundreds of thousands of human-trafficking and in the sex trade, we only saved one victim. Jasmine's experience in the sex trade may go unnoticed in the world, but at least it's one less victim. Still, Schindler is dead. I felt unsuccessful saving his life. Thinking that saving Jasmine would help cure my guilt from not saving Schindler's life, the guilt remained.

## The Final Withdrawal Of The Us Forces From The Philippines
### NOVEMBER 24, 1992

Since 1944 and after the American military beat the hell out of the Japanese Imperial forces, today, the United States was finally pulling their military of the Philippines for the last time.

The "Military Bases Agreement" which allowed the US government to own the base was created in 1947. In 1979, it expired and from that date, both the Philippine and US government agreed to start leasing the base instead of owning it for $500 million USD.

By 1988, neither the Philippine government nor the United States could come to an agreement on the leasing costs to maintain a US military presence, which was currently $500 million USD per year from 1979.

When Mount Pinatubo Erupted and destroyed practically everything, farmers' crops, villages, homes, businesses and even the Subic Naval Base, the Philippine government requested a 7-year lease of the Subic Bay Naval Base (and Clark Air Base) of $825 million USD per year yet the US government could only budget $360 million USD per year. They simply couldn't continue to agree with the additional $500 million USD.

With the amount of damage that Mount Pinatubo left behind, there was too much cost in repairing and rebuilding the Subic Bay Naval Base. The Olongapo city needed much money to repair their city and perhaps thought, "Well, let's try to get more money from the US government and siphon that out to repair the city!" As the US government knew that the city government was suspected of being corrupted, how were they certain that money invested to the city of Olongapo would actually go to the locals?

By December 27, 1991, the Philippine government told us to pack up and move along. For the remaining months following up to November 24, 1992, the military had just been doing that. Ship-by-ship, plane-by-plane, all military dependents and personnel departed the Subic Bay Naval Base.

Today ,November 24, 1992, was the day that the United States was going to lower the American Flag on the Subic Bay Naval Base and raise the Philippines national flag. All personnel aboard the USS Belleau Wood had to return to the ship yesterday by a 22:00 curfew. Once all were aboard and accounted for, the United States was now ready to say 'farewell' to a very important base that lived through the Spanish War, two world wars, the Vietnam war and the Mount Pinatubo volcanic eruption.

The last military personnel were now on the USS Belleau Wood except for a few senior officers and marines left at the base where the American flag that remained flying on the Subic Bay Naval Base which needed to be lowered and taken with us.

The news on the ship was that masses of Filipino locals were just outside of the base preparing to rush the Subic Bay Naval Base once the American flag was lowered. A lot of us wanted to see this but as our ship was ported far from the base entrance, we needed to use the high-powered binoculars. These high-powered binoculars were huge and quite powerful. These high-powered binoculars allowed us to view threat or friendlies. From our current location where the ship was ported yet prepared to launch instantly in a hurry, we were able to see the Subic Bay Naval Base and the 2-mile stretch of road that leads up to our ship.

I rushed up to island of the ship (the big metal part of the ship that sticks out of an aircraft carrier or an amphibious assault ship, where the navigation equipment and where the captain controls the ship in the bridge) to one of the several high-powered binoculars were.

"Take a number, shipmate", one of the sailors said to another who were taking turns with the high-powered binoculars.

"One, Mississippi. Two Mississippi….Ten Mississippi, Next!" says one of the shipmates monitoring sailors one-by-one to view part of history through the high-powered binoculars.

"They're moving! They're moving!", yells one of my shipmates who is currently viewing the high-powered binoculars. "You can see them moving!", he continued.

My turn was next. I was able to see the caravan of jeeps make their way back but I wasn't able to see the Filipino locals rush onto the base as told to us after the Marines returned from the flag-lowering ceremony.

The caravan which carried the Marines and Navy (both from the USS Belleau Wood and those who were the last to be stationed at Subic Bay) performing the ceremony were speeding as fast as they could back to the ship. The caravan had less hope for the militia that was hired by the Olongapo City mayor as the militia had mistakenly opened the gate right when the flag was lowered. This indicated to the local Olongapo citizens that the land was now theirs. The citizens outnumbered the militia's bullets which they wore on their chests and therefore wasn't able to hold back the rush of their citizens from getting onto the now ex-base of the United States.

There was over $3 billion USD worth of facilities and equipment which the US military left behind for grabs. Not only did the US military leave this behind but they also left 3,500 fatherless children. Some of these children rushed onto the now ex-military base with their mothers hoping that their fathers stayed behind however, they were only left with deserted facilities, memories and hope. Unfortunately, their fathers have now become ghosts leaving them behind.

The caravan finally makes it to our ship and board. They left the vehicles which they traveled and the gangway which assisted them to board. Just as ships depart in wartime and disasters, we launched quickly from the pier and slowly sailed away from the Philippines for the last time.

THIS CERTIFIES THAT

JONATHAN WITTE

was a member of the "Last Ship from Subic Bay" which participated in the last phase of the final withdrawal of the U.S. Forces from the Philippines and the subsequent turnover of the U.S. Facility to the Philippine government.

Witnessed by my hand and seal this 24th day of November 1992, aboard the USS BELLEAU WOOD (LHA-3) on her departure from Subic, Bay, Republic of the Philippines.

D. J. BRADT
CAPT.   USN

The Last Ship from Subic Bay

One of the most memorable achievements for the crew aboard the USS Belleau Wood is the closing of the Subic Bay Naval Base and U.S. Forces in the Philippines.

# CHAPTER 14

# FINDING AND HIDING THE SAILORS

## NOVEMBER 27, 1992

After sailing from the Philippines for the last time, the ambience of the ship was quiet and somber. A lot of us got away with way too much stuff. Now that we were back on our ship and out to sea, there is no more trouble which we sailors could get into. No alcohol and no temptations. We were back in international waters, patrolling the seas of pirates, enemies and aiding friend or foe stranded in the Pacific ocean.

The Marines who we picked up from Subic Bay were kicking back and getting acquainted to living on a ship. Some had never been on a ship before. When Marines are transported on a ship, all that they do are sleep, exercise, play dominoes, cards, write letters and eat. They also get in our way. Since we were transporting almost 2,000 Marines, it was a lot more difficult to get our work done. More people to feed, more people to walk around and more people to keep safe.

Thankfully, with the suggestions that my supervisor Chief Cusaga suggested and with a few of his connections on the ship, I was reported to watch duty at night. My sole job was to make sure none of the Marines fell overboard and keep a look out for any vessels or aircraft from entering our surroundings. I was also given a clipboard and a booklet of aircraft and vessels known to sail in the Pacific and report any and all to the supervisor of the watch.

This job was what I wanted to do rather than working as a cook. Though boring for many to stand watch, I thought it was an opportunity to become save someone.

At times during my night watches, there would be nothing to do but watch the ocean and hope to find an enemy, or a sea turtle or whale. Other than that, I'd only walk around the ship to ensure its safety. Though thinking this would give me opportunity to do good performing these watches, it did nothing to keep very busy as most of the Marines and sailors were asleep during my night watches, it would be quite boring and would have nothing to do but think about home and back in Japan. When I would think about Japan, I would think about Schindler being murdered.

One night, the smell of Schindler's blood that was so much a part of my thoughts that it would make me hallucinate. When this happened, I didn't know that it was a hallucination. I thought I was travelling back to the scene of the murder, watching it happen again. The details of his mutilated face, his gurgling of blood, the taste and smell of his blood, how I was accused by the lieutenant at the NCIS office, how XO Franklin and Captain Bradt threatened my freedom and life to not speak about the murder and that the murderer was still on the ship somewhere.

The smell of Schindler's blood and the memory that's still heavily intact in my brain was killing me slowly and wouldn't go away. I felt that the last smell of the salt in the Pacific, the last virgin ocean breeze and the grand display of the Milky Way were the last things that I'd like to feel, think, smell and see before I died. My sense of reality and self no longer existed. It was more beautiful to end my life in the ocean with the Milky Way above rather than suffer the constant thoughts, day after day.

At night, the "smoking lamp" was out, meaning that we were not allowed to smoke. A phrase that has been used on ships since the 1500s to ensure that enemies cannot see sailors smoking at night from a distance and to protect the hazardous cargo which ships carried from igniting. The majority of us didn't care as we were too far away from the missiles and gas tanks and smoked at night anyways

## Dropping Jarheads
December 5, 1992

Before we made a "port call" (land at a pier and take Liberty) in Okinawa, Japan, which is the most southern part of the Japanese mainland and where eight Marine bases are located, our ship again was heading straight for a typhoon. Our ship was bottlenecked between Taiwan and China (which is a free trade route which our Pacific Fleet protected from the Chinese military occupying). There was no way around this typhoon. If we had sailed on the eastside of Taiwan to divert the typhoon, we would have wasted a week and thousands of dollars, which was not in our military budget. As we found out from Hurricane Iniki in Hawaii, we knew that our ship could handle this typhoon.

As we left the bottleneck route north between China and Taiwan, we met the Typhoon. The Marines who were used to land and unfamiliar with rough seas were mixed with excitement and fear. As the boat swayed up and down then left and right, we saw some of the Marines' expressions go from a solid poker face to a frightened little child as if they were riding a roller coaster. There were a few heavy rolls of the ship which again, forced those walking on the deck to push against the bulkheads preventing them from falling onto the walls.

"The ship is sinking! Argh!!", one of the Marines cried, we heard him run down through the passageway. The other marines laugh with a few of US sailors. We couldn't blame him for being afraid or maybe he was going to throw up. The USS Belleau Wood was a huge ship and anyone who has seen how large they are would not think that they would sway, but place them in a typhoon and a hurricane and they become like little toy boats in a water park. The USS Belleau Wood continues to ride with the typhoon which was heading north along the path which we were taking to Okinawa.

My night watch had ended and I was heading off to bed around 09:00 in the morning. It was quite noisy with all the other men getting ready for the day's work. The ship gently rocks when it's out at sea and typically puts everyone to sleep once they hit their bunks, but today was a bit harder to sleep. I instead listened to my portable cassette tape player and began writing a letter to my parents.

"Away the SNOOPIE Team! Away the SNOOPIE Team! Starboard-side", a call comes out ship-wide on the 1MC from the OOD on the bridge. Calling the 'S.N.O.O.P.I.E. Team' (Ship's Nautical or Otherwise Photographic Intelligence Exploitation) meant that there was an unidentified aircraft or vessel nearby which could be a potential threat.

We hadn't had any issues with other vessels from other countries that entered our vicinity. Once we saw any vessels in the horizon, we would make contact with their ship to confirm our passages, country and status. Then we would bully them away from our path in which we were headed. The call for the SNOOPIE Team was a first since our voyages in the Pacific which got everyone curious to see what was headed our way.

As the other men started to rush up to look at the unidentified vessel or aircraft, I followed up to the starboard side port window. We look out and see a red and light-blue-colored, civilian sailboat drifting fast towards our direction and path about a half mile away without its sail deployed. As we hadn't received any feedback from radio nor visual, we deployed a UH-1N Twin Huey helicopter to get a closer look and take photographs.

After a few flybys, the helicopter returns. The sailboat is still headed our way. All of us could see if there was anyone on the boat from the outside but not inside. There were some clothing drying on the boom of the sailboat, but nothing else.

"Maybe the passengers are sleeping hard? Got knocked out from the typhoon?", a Marine says.

"I don't know. Maybe it got loose from the typhoon? They would have woken up by now from our helicopter flying over it.", says a sailor.

Then without warning, we hear several blasts from one of the four 25mm, MK-38 Guns that are mounted on our ship and controlled from inside the ship.

The sailboat gets closer and then we hear, "Pow! Pow! Pow! Pow! Pow! Pow! Pow! Pow! Pow!" Our gun begins its wrath splattering the water around it from the bullets missing the target and then blows onto the sailboat. The gun continues to hit the sailboat as parts of its wood begins to chip away from the holes that the 25mm bullets make.

"Oh man, that's crazy!", says one of the sailors as the rest of us awe at the destruction of the boat.

It was sad to think as the bullets were pounding the sailboat that there could have been someone who felt afraid and hid deep inside it. Maybe a family was inside and decided to hide from the American forces out of fear? Unfortunately, these are the rules of engagement at sea for all vessels when small, fast-moving boats head straight towards larger vessels that are unable to out-maneuver in time.

"Pow! Pow! Pow! Pow! Pow! Pow! Pow! Pow! Pow!", again the MK-38 shoots-off its large 25mm bullets as the rest of us look-on in awe and concern.

The shooting stops after what sounded like fifty rounds and the boat slowly begins to sink. Within 20 minutes, the sailboat slowly makes its way to the bottom of the Pacific ocean leaving the clothing that were drying on the boom of the sailboat, now wet floating next to the unsecured buoyant items that were once on it.

Death. Another murder associated with the USS Belleau Wood. The feeling of fear again wrapped around my soul and I began to relapse to the brutal murder scenario that I witnessed of Allen Schindler however, the smell of blood didn't return. Once I realized that I couldn't smell his blood that had permeated for months inside my head, I began to feel relieved.

Was it stimulation which helped? Perhaps the distraction helped keep my mind off of Schindler's murder? As I had been bottling the murder's effects without seeking professional help in organizing it, I was able to focus on things outside of myself rather than inside of me. The similar situation where I didn't think about Schindler's murder or the smell of his blood when we were in New Cabalan in the Philippines rescuing Jasmine from the sex slave trade.

I could not understand why but it was working. Regardless of understanding how I could keep my PTSD symptoms at bay, I was getting awfully sleepy and headed back to my bunk. Without having these terrible feelings and haunting memories of the murder, I slept quite well until my night watch began.

## Okinawa, Japan
December 15, 1992

As we continued on our journey towards Okinawa, we had forgotten all about our naughty adventures in the Philippines. The smelling of Schindler's blood was gone and I was feeling quite well. There were no more thoughts about jumping off the ship and I was looking forward to getting back to Japan.

It had been quite some time since I had spoken to either Szerlag and Knight, so I went down to the barber shop where they worked to get a recap on their own adventures and potential ones in Okinawa. We talked for a while about what we should do.

Knight recommends going to something called the 'Quarter Show' in the red light district. Neither Szerlag or I knew what he was talking about but we were curious. Then, we started talking about the events in PI. We all agreed to meet up in the hanger deck once we pulled into port. I smiled a bit more that day.

## Find The Witness
December 17, 1992

We launched from the White Beach Naval Base in Okinawa and headed back to our homeport in Sasebo, Japan. Things began to get strange as we had several officers and a few civilians walking in the enlisted berthing areas asking questions. Typically, officers do not roam around the enlisted berthing areas – especially civilians. We could not understand why they were here.

To myself, I suspected that they were here to arrest some of us for fighting in the bars. I didn't think that they were here to question people about Allen Schindler's murder. If they were, they would have spoken with me, but they didn't.

After I had received the 900-page NCIS investigation report in 2018 of Allen Schindler's murder (almost 30 years later), they were interviewing and creating 26 testimonies of those who worked or known Allen Schindler, Charles Vins and Terry Helvey. They never asked me. The NCIS only took my 2-page statement. That's it, nothing more. They never asked me about the conversation which Allen Schindler and I had right before he was murdered.

Some of the six questions that were asked of those who had worked or lived with either Allen Schindler or Terry Helvey were questions such as:

Q. have you ever heard Helvey talk about Schindler, gays or homosexuals in general?
3 out of 20 circled 'yes'. Those that circled 'yes' only mentioned Helvey said that he hated gays. Out of the 20 that circled 'no', most wrote-in 'N/A'
Q. How long have you worked with or shared the same berthing area as Helvey?
12 shared the same berthing area with Helvey and 7 worked with Helvey.

Q. How long have you worked with or shared the same berthing area as Allen Schindler?

14 shared the same berthing area with Schindler and 13 worked with Schindler.

Q. Is there any additional information that you may have initially withheld during your first interview with an NCIS agent?

0 answered 'yes' and 24 answered 'no'.

Q. Do you have any additional information that may help us in this investigation?

2 answered 'yes' while 22 others answered 'no'.

Of those 2 that answered 'yes', one mentioned that Helvey said that he 'hated gays' and that he wished that 'gays would die'. The other who answered 'yes' simply referred NCIS investigators to those who knew Schindler on his previous ship, the USS Midway.

Whoever the civilians and officers were interviewing people on the ship (those who worked or shared the same berthing area as Schindler and Helvey), we felt that they were here for something important. None of us had seen them until we left the White Beach Naval Base in Okinawa as we would have noticed them going through the passageways looking for people.

When our ship finally ported back in Sasebo, Japan (our home-port), Szerlag, Knight, J.R. and I headed to our favorite bar and where I had the conversation with Allen Schindler, Snack Shipmates Bar. Nothing had changed. It was an eerie feeling as my buddies and I had amazing and interesting adventures on Liberty while being deployed.

In the weeks that followed, my drinking increased from two beers and a Rum and Coke to four beers and two Rum and Coke. My behavior became more irritating, impatient and was overwhelmed by nightmares and drowsy days due to the lack of sleep. I also found it difficult to urinate in standing stalls in bathrooms thinking that the murderer was still out there and planning his attack on me which diverted me using the sitting toilet stalls where I could lock the door. Especially with those civilians and officers on board asking people questions. For me to urinate, I would usually go in the bathroom toilet stalls.

The frequency of my taking showers had increased from once a day to two or sometimes three times a day. Even the slightest sweat that dried on my skin resulting in a fraction of "stickiness" of my skin would drive me insane resulting in another shower to get it off. Subconsciously, it was the blood which had dried on my skin several hours after the murder which I could not wash off. In reality, it was only sweat that dried on my skin. To the present day, I would forever take two to three showers a day otherwise, I would become cranky, frustrated and extremely uncomfortable until I took a shower.

On more stressful days, the smell of blood would return and I would see my shipmates faces peel off exposing the meat and see puddles of blood replacing the puddles of water from the rain that collected on the streets and sidewalks. Szerlag and Knight slowly distanced themselves from me when I became irritated or angered but they would sometimes still go drinking with me – especially Szerlag who I believe had an understanding of what I was going through.

Weeks went by and there was only a few people who had heard about the murder and that they speculated that Schindler was killed because he was gay.

Days moved onto weeks and the Allen Schindler murder slowly became something of the past. The nightmare that I witnessed on October 27 became part of a nightmare during the day and night. Awake, asleep, eyes opened or closed, it didn't matter. They all seemed the same as I was having problems with nightmares and reality.

## We Found You!

The thoughts and questions that had been swimming inside my head was met by more frequent drinking. I was using alcohol to self-medicate the PTSD symptoms that I was enduring but also attempting to get a different perspective to why no one from the Navy was reaching out to me. It just seemed to me that if there was an investigation that someone would have more questions for me. Maybe the Captain was trying to protect Martinez and myself. There wasn't even an "All-clear" from anyone. I was simply left in the dark. Not only was I left in the dark, but the rest of the world had no idea of the motive for the murder. I wondered what his family thought had happened. The incident simply, disappeared.

As time moved on, my shipmates had forgotten all about the murder. There weren't any news articles following up with the murder. There was no formal ceremony for Allen Schindler's funeral. Nothing. It was as if Allen Schindler had simply disappeared and his murder became a legend. The only thing that was left was my PTSD symptoms, swirling questions and the scent of his blood that remained in my nose and brain. This was followed by with nights filled with drunkenness and heightened paranoia.

I had finished my night watch and was walking through Nimitz Park on my way to Sailor Town and Szerlag meets up with me. We decided to go to a bar that we had previously been to where I was involved in a fight with a guy with 6 fingers – 3 on each hand. Rumored that he was a member of the Japanese Mafia or Yakuza. His girlfriend was the bar's mama-san and she was the one who had put a stop to the fight.

To Szerlag and my surprise, the Yakuza mafia member with six fingers wasn't there. We sat at the bar and ordered Asahis. There were only a few sailors at the black-lacquered bar with bottles of Japanese whiskey and sake surrounded by glass shelving. There were two red, leather booths behind us, one was empty and another one had five sober-looking men who appeared to be officers sitting there. They were not drinking beer but rather orange juice, cola and tea. They did seem out of place, not from around here and definitely not drinking like all of us sailors do in Sailor Town. I briefly looked at them. All five of them look at me and say nothing.

Since the bar was quiet, I was able to overhear other bar patrons discuss things. Their conversation was mostly about sex, money, television, work and so on however, the five men, that looked like officers, sitting in the booth behind us were discussing something that I knew about.

I heard them saying things like it was important to find this guy, October 27 and bathroom at the park.

"Holy sh*t!", I thought to myself. I was quite sure that they were talking about me but I wasn't sure. I nudge Szerlag with my left elbow to call his attention to the five officer-looking guys sitting in the red-leather, crescent-shaped booth.

"Dude, listen", I whispered to Szerlag hinting to the men sitting at the booth. We overheard things like "October 27", "the Captain" and "witness"….

If they were looking for me, why not simply walk up to the USS Belleau Wood and ask for me? They also could have asked the NCIS agents for me but for some odd reason, they simply couldn't find me. This sparked my curiosity of why they were possibly looking for me so I grabbed my Asahi beer bottle, stood up from the bar and walked over.

I calmly started the conversation by asking them, "Are you guys looking for they guy who saw Allen Schindler's murder?"

One of the officer-looking men answered, "that depends on who you are".

It wasn't the answer that I was hoping for. I wasn't simply going to tell them that I was the guy that they were looking for because I had been warned to keep my mouth shut.

I had learned through the Stars and Stripes Newspaper that they had found the two murderers but as far as I knew, there hadn't been any kind of trial. I told them that I might know this person and asked who they were. One said that they were a special team sent by the Pacific Fleet Activities headquarters from Yokuska to conduct a separate investigation into the murder of a shipmate that took place in the public park nearby. We are looking for the key witness who saw the murder.

Once one of them said that I could be in danger staying on the USS Belleau Wood, I instantly relapsed into fear and paranoia. According to the Stars and Stripes, the suspects Helvey and Vins had already been caught. I told them that I was the witness they were looking for and they asked me to join them.

Captain Maggio, prosecuting attorney appointed by the Judge Advocate General (JAG Officer) introduced himself. I knew that he was a marine based on his short haircut. His jaw was strong and held himself as a distinguished officer. He was fairly built and bulky regardless of his height.

Next were Major Wilson and Lieutenant Smith who were defense attorneys appointed by JAG. In addition, there was Lieutenant Commander Young, Psychiatrist at the Pacific Fleet Headquarters medical branch in Yokosuka and PO2 Fillmore.

After the four officers and petty officer introduced themselves and the reason for them traveling 700 miles to find the witness, I began to see that Allen Schindler's murder had not been swept under the rug. One of the men explained that the murder had gotten a lot of international attention and they had information that there was a witness on the USS Belleau Wood. They needed to find him before the trial would begin.

If anyone who has not lived in the Navy life during the 1990's, it was a serious offence to be known as a homosexual. Our working environment did not include females let alone homosexuals. The media, television shows and movies made in the 1990s poked fun at those who were homosexuals and in the general population, homosexuality was an alternate lifestyle and a disorder. Very little was known about homosexuality and in a rough, high-pressured environment in the Navy, identifying as a homosexual would have gotten you beat up by the wrong crowd. Others really didn't care as long as you weren't associated with a homosexual. If you were associated with a homosexual, that could bring you to a Captain's Mass and possibly suspected as being gay too. That could result in you being other than honorably discharged.

They told me that they did have the murderers in their custody but could get off with an easy sentence if they couldn't find any witnesses. They did have several statements, the shore patrol who caught Helvey and Vins, the Japanese girl who was walking by as Helvey and Vins were running away (900-page report provided by the NCIS released in 2015), but they didn't have anyone who could connect them from the actual action of stomping on Schindler. Both the prosecuting attorney and defense attorneys seemed very relieved that they had found me.

The next step, they said, was to get me off the ship and to Yokosuka as quickly as possible and without anyone knowing so that I could testify. I DID feel I needed to testify on behalf of Allen Schindler and the way that he died.

The plan to get me off the ship was when the ship stopped off at White Beach Naval Base in Okinawa. We were to be picking up several hundred Marines there which may distract the OOD (Officer Of the Deck). By the time the USS Belleau Wood loads and unloads Marines and the ship departs from Okinawa, they won't know realize that you're missing. This would be called AWOL I thought but they quickly told me that they would contact my ship. The ship would be informed that I had been transferred at the request of the JAG office which takes precedence over your captain. I was told not to tell anyone else about this, period – even your best buddies on the ship.

"So when I get to Okinawa, do I simply walk off the ship?", I asked.

"We will call for you from the Quartermaster in the hanger deck. We will send someone there to escort you off the ship and to an undisclosed berthing area on the base in Okinawa. We will then send you on a plane to Yokota Air Base where we then will drive you to the Yokosuka base. We will provide you with military orders once you report to either Major Wilson or Lieutenant Smith", the officer instructed me.

Lieutenant Commander Young jumps in the conversation and asks, "Were you sent to medical after the murder?"

"Nothing was wrong with me, no injuries", I replied not knowing why I would need to see medical.

"Oh my, that's unfortunate", he replied. I continued to look at him with a confused look. Though I had no obvious injuries, Lieutenant Commander explained that anyone experiencing such a traumatic event needed to seek medical attention.

"Do you feel or think that you are going to harm anyone or harm yourself?", Lieutenant Commander Young asks.

"Well…I kept smelling blood…even now. I can't get rid of the smell.", I explained.

"Yup, that is what we call PTSD or Post Traumatic Stress Disorder. The earlier we catch the symptoms, the better we can help you.", Lieutenant Commander Young explains. He explained symptoms, statistics and his experience working with people with PTSD. He seemed genuinely concerned and told me to come and see him, that he could help me with it.

The officers continued to explain the steps which we would take to get me from Okinawa and then to Yokosuka base. They would assign me to the base performing security and watch duties during the Court

Martial. No one from the Navy would ever know what happened to me except that I was temporarily to be stationed in Yokosuka.

Szerlag had left two hours ago but the time passed quickly as my beer that I had ordered still sat in front of me. All six of us reiterated several times on how to get me off the ship without anyone knowing. We wanted to make sure that things went quickly and smoothly without any mix-ups.

If I had missed that window of opportunity loading up Marines in Okinawa, I would not be able to get to Yokosuka for the Court Martial (initially set for February of 1993) as the USS Belleau Wood would have been deployed from January to March 1993. If I had not been at the Court Martial, the prosecuting attorney would have lost their only key witness connecting Helvey and Vins to the murder.

The four officers tells me that PO2 Fillmore will help with the processing from the USS Belleau Wood, to an undisclosed berthing room in Okinawa and then on a plane to Yokota Airbase near Yokosuka.

Walking back through Sailor Town, I came to the same Family Mart convenience store that PO3 Martinez and I visited before we walked up onto the murder. I grabbed a beer, paid the clerk, walked to the picnic bench where PO3 Martinez and I went to that horrible night and drank my beer. I stared into the Fisheye glass wall re-enacting the murder where I saw Helvey stomp on Allen Schindler repeatedly and began to cry.

And little did Dorothy (Allen Schindler's mother) and I know that from the events that took place on that mildly, cold October night of 1992 was the beginning of some interesting changes.

# CHAPTER 15

# MY NEW PRISONS

January 04, 1993

Szerlag and I never discussed what the five officers and I were discussing at the jazz bar that night before we shipped off from Sasebo to Okinawa. My mission was to keep quiet and completely off the radar on the ship. It would only take three days to sail from Sasebo to Okinawa. As long as I continued to conduct my rounds doing night watch and do as I was told, I should be okay and manage to find my way to get off the ship. I was concerned about my safety it would probably be a good idea to just get off of the ship, considering rumors were flying. Too much had happened and I didn't want any part of it.

Only three days passed since we sailed from Sasebo and the sailors aboard the USS Belleau Wood seemed to have kept things to themselves. Since we had NCIS agents on board our ship asking questions, all of the rumors about homosexuals on board had stopped. No one was talking to anyone in fear of getting caught up with the investigation.

The USS Belleau Wood was leaving for White Beach Naval Base in Okinawa again and that had me on edge. I was ordered to leave the ship without anyone knowing. Just the feeling of my home sailing off from me and nowhere to go had me feeling antsy, cold-footed about it. It was pretty scary thinking that if the five officers I had met three days before in Sasebo had pulled out of the plan of getting me off the ship without official orders to be relieved, I would be in serious trouble. Without orders (which i wasn't provided by the secret team), I would be arrested and given the death penalty for abandoning my post, according to Article 113 of the UCMJ. The last solider that was executed for the same crime was in 1945 however since then yet were only sent to jail. As i had been given direct orders from the Captain and the XO, who knows what they would do with me. The "gay bashers" were still on the ship looking for me to kill me to protect their comrades Helvey and Vins and as our ship was going to be en route to patrol the Pacific for the next three months, my chances of survival would be quite minimal.

I had to choose between being executed (or incarcerated) or being thrown off the ship in route for The Philippines as I hadn't heard of the murderers being caught, to my knowledge. I took the gamble and decided to move forward with the secret plan and meet the officers in Yokosuka therefore, I needed to escape the ship and meet one of the secret team members on the base at White Beach in Okinawa.

## Cat Leaves The Bag

The USS Belleau Wood reaches White Beach Naval Base and the gangway is connected to the ship from the pier. The Boatswain whistle blows informing us that the Marines were boarding our ship and replenishment of goods, ammunition and equipment needed to be loaded.

*Marines and equipment being loaded up onto the USS Belleau Wood*

I frantically and hurriedly began packing my gear into my sea bag which I would take and left the other things I wouldn't need. I couldn't fit everything that I owned. Damn.

Shortly, the Master-at-Arms of the ship greets me with his side-arm and police badge. He simply says, "It's time". I throw my sea bag over my shoulder, walk out of the berthing area and walk through the passageway with him walking behind me.

It made me feel more comfortable knowing that the plan which was discussed between the five officers and myself was in-play after all. It was completely operated outside of proper protocol and without official military orders. Things were working completely off the radar and only by word-of-mouth. It was so secret that only a handful of people knew what was happening. It was mandatory, protocol for the captain and my senior officers to know why and when any of their sailors leave the ship, but my reasons for leaving was something different.

As we are walking through the passageways, several of my shipmates see the sight of my being escorted by the Master-at-Arms asking, "Dude, what did you do!?" and "Oh man, did you kill Schindler!?"

The Master-at-Arms replies to them by getting in front of me to make room for our passage, "make a hole, shipmates!". Our shipmates eyes big and with their mouths opened. I couldn't reply them not only because the Master-at-Arms and I were walking quite fast, but that we couldn't let them know why I was being escorted.

The Master-at-Arms and I made it to the quarterdeck where we were met by the OOD (Officer Of the Deck) who typically requests my Liberty Card. The OOD simply looked the other way as if he was ignoring me. I was then met by two armed Marine Military police officers who saluted the Master-at-arms to exchange me.

We walked down the gangway as other Marines walked up toward the USS Belleau Wood for their deployment, eyeing my escorting. We then got onto the pier and walked halfway down and stopped for a moment for one of the MPs to radio-in my location. As he continued to provide the information to whoever was on the other end of the radio call, The USS Belleau Wood gave a loud blow from its horn and was shoved-off by the tugboats. I looked back at the ship leaving me behind.

It was a very lonesome feeling to see my adventures with my shipmates and buddies on the USS Belleau Wood end. I really wanted to go with them and continue my career in the Navy, but my bed has been made and must proceed with the plan and make my way to the Pacific Fleet Headquarters in Yokosuka, Japan.

My gaze at the ship was cut short as one of the MPs instructed me to head to a building to check in with PO2 Fillmore (who was part of the team of four other officers I met three nights ago) for the next steps. The MPs instructed me to meet PO2 Fillmore in the White Beach Naval Base Administration Office for my (finally) official orders and then left me alone and walked towards another direction for their next duty.

The overcast of the skies began to grow dark. Then it started to rain. I saw it as a sign from the heavens that my life was starting to clean. It was the right thing to do. If I had stayed on that ship, I would have either been killed or killed myself. Perhaps my PTSD symptoms would have eventually gone away and nothing would have happened. After being told that I was the only key witness to connect the actions by the murderers to the murdered, I had to show up for the trial. Though I felt as if I betrayed my shipmates, captain, the XO and the USS Belleau Wood gang, it was the right thing to do. Otherwise, the murderer would have gotten away and released back into the ranks of the Navy. If that were to have happened, who knows how many more homosexuals would have been murdered?

## Into The Witness Protection Program, I Go

As I entered the administration office, I was greeted by PO2 Fillmore and a chief petty officer. The moment when I saw the chief petty officer act extremely nervous and anxious, I realized that I had become famous by word-of-mouth. The chief petty officer was rambling in his words, moving around frantically trying to arrange for my stay in the berthing room on the base. PO2 Fillmore was cool as a cucumber. PO2 Fillmore says as he grabs a set of keys and takes me to another building nearby.

"You didn't tell anybody that you left, right?, PO Fillmore asks.

My reply was sharp and simple, "Nope".

PO Fillmore ends the conversation, "From now on, don't tell anyone who you are, what ship you're from or why you are traveling".

I said nothing as we both knew what was happening and how important it was to keep my mouth shut during these events. I was practically untouchable. A zombie in a sailor's uniform.

We continued to walk, down to a basement, down a long, narrow hallways lined with white, painted cinderblocks with brown doors. PO2 Fillmore opens up one of the random doors, unlocks it and he tells me to wait here.

*The exact room where I stayed. I took this picture after arriving in Okinawa in 1993 as I was scared thinking that USS Belleau Wood XO and Captain Bradt found out I told someone about the murder. I felt that I was going to be killed next and wanted to document things just as Allen Schindler did before he was murdered.*

I simply say 'thanks' and he closes the door. I dropped my sea bag onto the bed and began scanning the room. No window. No phone. Just a bed, a brown-colored desk and a standing closet. It looked like a nice prison cell. Then I wondered if the captain and the XO just found out that I was going to testify. Fear set in as I wondered if I fell asleep, would they lock me in the room? Was I duped into giving myself away to the senior officers of the USS Belleau Wood and walked right into a prison cell?

I jumped up and ran to the door to see if it was unlocked. It opened and I peered out into the white-painted cinder brick hallway where no one was there. The fast-paced packing and getting off of the ship had left me exhausted so I went to the shower and got ready for bed. Still paranoid, it remained cracked-open and kept watch for it to close and lock me in for the rest of the night.

At about 05:00 the next morning and without sleep, PO2 Fillmore knocks on the door and opens it. He hands me a manila envelope with my orders to take a shuttle to the Kaneda Air Base (an Airforce base which the navy shared for air flights) to Yokoto Air Base near Tokyo. No escort required. I didn't have time for a shower or anything and he apologized for the short notice. It was important that I get to the air base as fast as possible. He wished me luck and sent me on my way.

Once I reported at the Kaneda Air Base, three other high-ranking officers met me in the lobby and together we walked to a small Cessna plane. Again, no time for using the restroom. We boarded without any conversation and took off into the skies. I did not know if they were part of the trial who they were.

The plane begins to move about like a toy plane through a windy storm. The captain turns his head sideways, unable to turn completely around from his thick-ass neck and yells at us, "You gentlemen better hang on. We are flying through a small typhoon". The jolting of the plane trying to out-maneuver the gusts of the turbulence punched my bladder with such great force that I had to pee. In a Cessna, there are no toilets.

"Sir!", I yelled at the pilot that was muffled by the sound of the strong wind and the plane's engine, "I need to use the head. I can't hold my pee".

"Starboard side, there's a hole. Don't pee in my plane!", the pilot says while he smirks.

The other officers on the plane start to laugh. I unbuckled my seatbelt and headed to the Starboard side of the plane in the back. It was well hidden yet a plastic sign the size of a cigarette lighter showing above a triangular inset of the plane with a black plug. I unplugged it and a felt a strong gust of wind. This was the first and only time I can remember that I had ever peed while kneeling. It was almost embarrassing to think that any of the sudden gusts of wind and turbulence would knock me onto the deck of the plane with my penis sticking out urinating everywhere. Thankfully, it was a quick pee.

Finally relieved, I made my way back to my seat while the Cessna continued to fly through the typhoon for the rest of the 700 miles.

After landing at Yokota Air Base and taking a shuttle to the Yokosuka Naval Base near Tokyo, I had finally made it to the Command Fleet Activities Yokosuka, Japan – the main headquarters for the Navy's Pacific Fleet.

## Yokosuka, Japan

Yokosuka is a fairly large shipping city in Yokohama with a population of three-million Japanese, the second-most population in all of Japan and is bordered southwest of Tokyo. It was initially a fishing port during the Edo Period (1603-1868 AD) until Matthew Perry forced his way through with his American Navy Fleet of four warships in 1853 AD to impose the Peace and Amity Treaty under threat which ended the 220-yearlong Japanese national seclusion from the rest of the world. During this transition, the "Tokugawa Shogunate" had then fallen which ended the famous "Shogun" rule.

Due to Yokosuka's topography in catering to large vessels and easy access, the "Yokosuka Naval Yard" was completed in 1886. Until the end of World War II in 1945, it served as the Japanese Imperial Navy Base covering 280 acres and employed over 40,000 workers that built, produced and manufactured supplies, weaponry, ships and everything else that helped maintain a strong military presence for Japan. After the end of War World II, the base was peacefully transferred to the American military, renamed to "Yokosuka Naval Base" and was expanded to the current size of 568 acres. Since then, Yokosuka Naval Base has been one of the most important naval bases in the pacific during the Korean and Vietnam wars.

Today, the Yokosuka Naval Base supports all activities for the Seventh Fleet consisting a command ship, cruisers, an aircraft carrier and several destroyers to assist with logistical services and administration support for General Court Martials and various military discharges. The Yokosuka Naval Base is huge. It was like a small part of America inside an almost 600-acre base. There was a commissary (a grocery store), an exchange (think Walmart), a 32-lane AMF bowling center, two movie theatres, a gym, a swimming pool, five restaurants, a Burger King, a hotel, a library and a three-story club called "Club Alliance". There were even two places where they had slot machines that took and rewarded real American quarters! Public grade schools were available for dependents as well as college classes. This place had it all!

My travel orders contained a billet of money to use to bunk up in a dormitory which I shared with two other shipmates that were stationed on shore.

The night had just started around 20:00 in the evening and those on Liberty were walking up and down The Honch both bar-hopping and looking for girls. There were over twenty bars ranging from a country and western bar to another bar which I became fond of called, "Smashing Pumpkins".

Smashing Pumpkins was a dingy-looking bar plastered with military and party event pictures, paper currency from all over the world, beer posters and a 50-cent pool table. The music was loud and blared Nirvana music so loud that it could be heard outside in the street.

I found a seat at the bar and ordered my favorite Japanese Asahi Beer in a 20-ounce bottle. I lit a cigarette and began examining several jars of home-made saki made with snake venom called, "Habu-sake" or in English, "Snake Sake". It is more widely known as "Habushu" that is distilled in Okinawa, Japan. Curious to know the taste as it had a deadly snake inside, I requested one with a warning from a fellow shipmate stationed to the USS Independence air craft carrier, "Dude, careful with that drink there. Stand up slowly afterwards".

"I can handle my alcohol", I replied confidently which the sailor replied in a doubting laughter.

I went straight for the drink even before I finished my beer. Though it tasted strong, I continued to doubt what he said and slammed the rest of the Habu-Sake and finished nursing on my beer. Curious to visit the other bars, I pushed my empty bottle of beer and the small drinking glass that had the saki in it and stood up. For a brief moment, things went dark and I stumbled onto the bar stools next to me. I admit that it kicked my ass and had enough so I instead decided to head back to the base and my dormitory to sleep it off.

From the hard effects of the Habu-sake, I couldn't remembered how I got back to the Yokosuka base which was located just across a busy street from The Honch. The last I remembered was getting into my dormitory. It was dark and I crawled onto my top-bunk hoping that the spinning in my head would stop. I spent the rest of the next day nursing my hangover. Never again will I drink Habu-Sake, but I had to try it.

## Psych Eval

There were too many issues in my situation. One being the hangover I was trying to sleep off and the other was that I had to report to Lieutenant Commander Young for my psychological testing and then later report to the JAGS that I met at the jazz bar in Sasebo's Sailor Town.

After sleeping in from such a crazy night and healing from my hangover, I headed towards the Naval Hospital Yokosuka which was between the dormitory where I stayed and the main entrance of the base. I was greeted by the receptionist who seemed to be happy to see me and sent me directly to Lieutenant Commander Young's office.

We talked a bit more about PTSD, symptoms and how little was really known about the disorder. There was a basic test about 30-40 questions long that asked about how I saw the world. Though I thought that I was completely off the chart, the medical team found that I had about 10% of PTSD symptoms (out of 100% totally disabled) which means there is hope for improvement. Note to date as of 2014, I am 100% disabled, a misdiagnose of my initial symptoms and further evaluations.

Then, I discussed my other symptoms such as smelling blood, feeling calm in stressful situations, hallucinations, the ability to predict outcomes of objects and people, understanding others' intentions clearly, vivid senses and detailed, graphic nightmares. The doctors said that it was completely normal and that in time, the symptoms will go away (FYI, to this day, they have not).

Once the medical exam completed, my files were filed and I was prescribed some medicine to help me with my unknown feelings. Then they requested me to check back with them next week and the weeks afterwards.

## The Honch

After taking the medicine right after I left the hospital, I headed straight out of the base to walk around Yokosuka city. It was a bad idea. There were so many people here. So many people riding bicycles, too many loud advertisements, too much noise that it made me uncomfortable.

Again, there were too many people walking around which required me to move left, right, go fast, slow down, move left again and move right again. I got so angry that I stopped moving so much and bumped my shoulder into strangers. Anyone who had made a noise or said something, I would turn around and curse at them. Some of them had their faces peeled off exposing their tissue on their faces, which was one of the symptoms I had told the doctors about. It was frightening.

Thinking that the medicine that was prescribed to me would help with my symptoms, it didn't. Alcohol helped. I stopped by a Japanese liquor store and bought a cheap bottle of sake. Beer did help but I wanted try anything to rid the feelings and views that I had. After my purchase, I took the bottle of sake behind the stores and began to chug half the bottle. Instantly, I began to feel relieved. It made me feel quite happy! So happy that I wanted to celebrate with someone.

Knowing that there would be some people at "The Honch" (the street lined with western bars outside of Yokosuka Base were sailors frequent bars catering to sailors and Marines), I made my way there and began bar-hopping. Bar-by-bar, only a handful of sailors were there with their own friends. I felt isolated but at one of the bars I met a Japanese girl, Ayako, who had just come from a wedding. We spent an hour or so talking and drinking and ended up in a room at a nearby hotel.

I was awakened by both the sunrise and the feeling of needles stabbing my skin all over. It hurt badly. Every time I moved my fingers, arms, legs, it felt as if someone was stabbing me with sharp needles. I got out of the bed and slowly went to the bathroom to see what it was. Thinking that they were bedbugs and after turning on the lights, I saw that my whole body was all dark red. I thought I was hallucinating!

"I'm sorry Ayako, I need to leave", I said.

She thought that I was mad at her but it was the needle-stabbing feeling that I had. I quickly dressed, left the hotel room and made my way back to the Yokosuka Naval Base hospital to show my new condition. Upon entering the hospital, a nurse stationed during that time knew exactly what my symptoms were from and said that I shouldn't have drank any alcohol. She then prescribed me some cream to help the pain. I went back to my dormitory to sleep for the rest of the day.

## CHAPTER 16

# THE UNITED STATES VS A NEW CULTURE

february 21, 1993

A few days after my 19th birthday in February of 1993, I was to report to the attorneys who I met in Sasebo. All three attorneys were there; the prosecuting attorney Marine Captain Maggio, defense attorneys Major Wilson and Lieutenant Smith. All three appeared happy and relieved that I was there. Later, I found out that one of the two guys I had seen beating Schindler, Charles Vins, was going to be testifying against Helvey as well.

They all shook my hand, asked how I was doing with my PTSD conditions and went over my testimony. I had to re-enact the whole murder so that my memory coincided with the testimony that I wrote the night of the murder. They asked for further details, if I had any. I explained to them that I had met Schindler two days before he died and what we had discussed. I felt that I needed get some closure to this whole thing and asked them again, who killed Schindler. They would only tell me that they did have two people that were from my ship that would stand trial. They couldn't tell me who they were because "It's an ongoing investigation."

After returning to my room and getting dressed into my civilian clothing, I headed off to the base club called "Club Alliance" which is only available for service members although we can escort civilians to join us. Club Alliance has three stories with three different clubs; a dance club downstairs, a country and western club, restaurant with a few, real slot machines and the top floor where top-20 hits would play. There was a stage on the club on the top floor where local bands would play.

I bought a few beers and began to chug them fast. "How Soon Is Now" by The Smiths was playing over the speakers. As my feelings became relaxed after drinking the first of many beers, I listened to the words of the song that was blaring out of the speakers in the club:

*"You shut your mouth. How can you say, I go about things the wrong way? I am human and I need to be loved. Just like everybody else does...*

*You could meet somebody who really loves you. So you go and you stand on your own. And you leave on your own. And you go home and you cry and you want to die..."*

I was a bit drunk and dramatic so the song lyrics reminded me of Schindler. He was a nice guy. Kind, positive and seemed to express his own kind of happiness. He didn't deserve to be murdered, especially in the way he was left dying on the floor. I then thought to myself, "I need to get out of here."

I finished my beer and headed down to the second floor of the club Alliance to get something to eat. On the second floor was the country and western club as well as where we get food to dissolve all of the drinking which we sailors did heavily. After purchasing some Texas comfort food, Nachos and jalapenos. I sat down at a table to watch the "Sh*t Kickers" (as we called them) dancing with their cowboy boots.

Tonight however, there is a guy by himself in the middle of the floor bending over and grabbing onto the seat of a chair.

"Happy Birthday!", his shipmates are yelling. A line of twenty of his shipmates forms in front of him, the number of years of the sailors new age. The sailor celebrating his birthday holds on tightly to the chair with his butt facing the line of his shipmates. One-by-one, his shipmates remove their belts, folds them and extends the belt in their hands behind their backs as far as they can. The first one begins to run towards the birthday sailor's butt and you hear a loud snap. He yelps in excruciating pain yet tries to hold a smile. The other shipmates follow through one after the other until all twenty of his shipmates finish swatting his butt with their leather belts. The birthday sailor slowly tries to turn around and sit on the chair he had been holding but the pain prevents him from doing so. Everyone including me sings the Happy Birthday song while laughing. The birthday sailor says after the song while laughing, "Man, it would suck to be forty …"

Everyone else joins in laughing at his comment and they continue to drink in celebration.

That type of horsing-around, getting drunk and laughing with shipmates is what I missed with my buddies in Sasebo. Knight and Szerlag would have followed through with such a celebration without hesitation. There had been other days where I would miss hanging out with my brothers aboard the USS Belleau Wood. With minimal work requirements in Yokosuka and several days of vacation left, I requested permission to travel back to Sasebo. With no actual trial date set, there was plenty of time to hang with the crew back on the USS Belleau Wood.

With my travel request approved, I flew down to Sasebo and continued what Szerlag, Knight and my other buddies did before the murder, get drunk, laugh and share stories. I would then be stationed on the Sasebo Naval Base performing minimal tasks, doing watches, repairing buildings, painting, security watches, whatever was needed, I was there to do my duties. Until I was called again to fly up to Yokosuka for the trial and after my duties were done, Szerlag, Knight and our other buddies would drink. For me, it was heavy drinking. Every night was fun and had no ambition to go back to Yokosuka. I knew of no one in Yokosuka and hated the idea of going back. I was now back with the people that made me happy in Sasebo, supported me and the making fun of each other. I tried not to think about having to go back to Yokosuka or think about the murder for a little while.

I never discussed the details of the trial with Szerlag, Knight or any of my other friends about the upcoming case as I was instructed by the attorneys to not talk about it. Such topic would have only dampened our fun and laughter which we always had. I also did not know much about what was happening with the case at that time. They too, knew it was a heavy topic and sensitive in nature.

The fun drinking and laughing with my buddies soon quickly ended by the JAGs who sent a request (an actual one which I could hold in my hands) to report back up to the Yokosuka Naval Base for the U.S. Vs Helvey murder trial. As I had official orders in hand, it allowed me to say 'see you later, guys' instead of simply vanishing like I did last time. It also guarantees that I didn't go AWOL, which worried me for months as I had no documentation for being off of my ship.

Returning to my temporary dormitory on the Sasebo Naval Base, I packed the little gear I brought with me (as the majority of it was back in Yokosuka). I remembered that I had left so fast off the ship that I had forgotten some personal items in my bunk. Since I still had access to the USS Belleau Wood and had my ID to get aboard, I got a small, white trash bag and walked twenty minutes on foot to the ship.

"Permission to come aboard", I announced as I saluted to the ODD once I got onto my ship. It had been quite some time since I had been on the ship. Knowing that the murderer(s) were in Yokosuka, it felt a bit more safe than it did when I was last here. After the ODD examined my ship ID, he salutes back and says, "Permission granted".

"Hey, Witte!", one of my shipmates said as I made my way back to the S-2 Division berthing area where I once called home.

"Hey!", I simply replied. I had about four shipmates welcome me back home on the USS Belleau Wood. It was strange as it seemed as if the darkness of the ship had changed to light. Though the USS Belleau Wood was preparing for their deployment out to Korea, the sailors aboard seemed very happy, something which would be considered opposite as they would be deployed at sea for the next month.

Further down the passageway to my previous berthing area, I am met by my bunkmate. For his privacy, I will name him "Timmy" and will not be descriptive of his appearance. Timmy was not only my bunkmate, but he and I also worked together. Everyone liked Timmy. He was kind, nice, always had a smile and was always supportive of his shipmates.

This time, Timmy didn't have that typical, kind face. He looked pale when he saw me. Without greeting me from afar, he gets into my personal space and speaks quietly to me so that others couldn't hear. He says, "can you come with me?". He then walks in front of me as I followed to a passageway which is rarely used by sailors.

Timmy comes clean with many questions, "Where did you go? Why are you back? Can we 'come out'?"

Confused with his last question, I asked, "Come out? Come out of where!?"

Timmy further explaining, "Come out of the closet that we are gay. That's why you were taken off the ship, right?"

"Oh my, Timmy... I am not gay. I just happened to see Schindler get killed. I'm the key witness to the murder."

Timmy became more pale than he was when I saw him minutes ago to the point that he may have died. Still, homosexuality either being suspected or confessing to anyone will begin procedures for discharge from the military.

Timmy asked me intimately, "Please don't tell anyone I'm gay. I thought you were gay and I was going to ask you for help on how I can get help."

"Timmy, I will never tell anyone. And I'm not gay. It's no one's business if we are or aren't."

Timmy seemed relieved that I wouldn't tell anyone about his homosexuality. We knew each other well. Timmy continued in trust about others aboard the USS Belleau Wood who were gay. Apparently the so-called "Fabulous Five" wasn't the only five homosexuals on the ship. There were about twenty! Who knows, there could have been a lot more!

Timmy and the other homosexuals aboard the ship were becoming very scared after hearing about Allen Schindler's murder. They were in fear after hearing rumors that the command was searching for homosexuals on the ship, like a "gay cleansing". Timmy told me that a few other shipmates part of the "Fabulous Five" who were close to Schindler named Sims and Eastwood were found to be gay, they were immediately removed off the ship for their safety yet were on their way to be discharged for admitting their homosexuality. Not only were they removed from the ship for being gay but also had information about the "Gay Bashers" harassing them. They may have been sent up to Yokosuka to testify.

Timmy explained that after some of the Fabulous Five members were removed from the ship, Timmy and the others who were gay, remained on the ship were in great fear for their lives and careers. They too, heard about the murder of a gay sailor and thought that they were next. Since I was the only one who returned to the ship after being taken off the ship close to the same time as the other homosexuals were taken off, they presumed that I was gay. I further explained about the murder to my knowledge yet remained distant with what I was told to keep secret for the trial.

I ensured Timmy that as long as they didn't tell anyone that they were homosexual, they had nothing to worry about. My lack of helping Timmy and the others only left them further to ponder on how to deal with their fear of coming out, if they ever did. We both wished each other good luck and returned to our berthing area for me to get the rest of my personal items that I had left behind.

Thinking that I would be back on the USS Belleau Wood after the trial, I left a few of my military gear including my pea coat. It was one of the best of my gear as it was warm and looked cool. It was perhaps the warmest coat I have ever worn in the cold weather during my night watches. It was too large and since Spring and Summer were upon us, I left it in my footlocker.

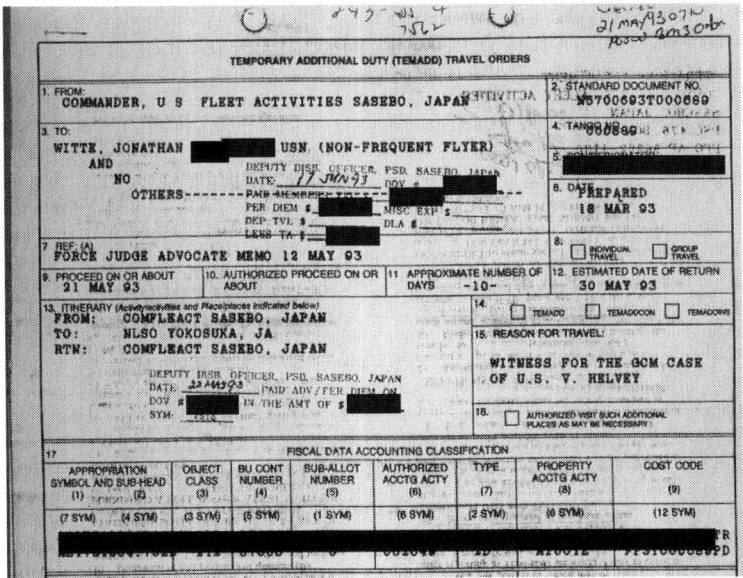

*This is one of the three orders which I received from the JAGs in Yokosuka for questioning and preparations for the trial however, this is the last one I received to actually testify in the trial with Helvey.*

I disembarked from the ship and gave the flag that separated the ship and pier a salute.

"See you soon!", I mumbled out of my mouth and walked off the ship and walked slowly back to the dormitory.

The next day, I boarded the shuttle to Nagasaki Airport which flew me on a medivac to Yokota Air Base and then a military bus to Yokosuka Naval Base. I returned to the same dormitory where the rest of my gear was and was again greeted by the previous roommates who I shared the room with. They were still playing some football game on the Super Nintendo game console. With nowhere to go and nothing to do, I attempted to write poetry, thinking it would help put my feelings into words. From the long travel and trying to come up with difficult yet colorful, poetic words, I passed out with my face on the paper and my pen in hand.

## The Fabulous Five

The Division Petty Officer comes by my dormitory room and wakes me up from my nap to say that there was someone who wanted to speak with me on the phone. Usually it's the lawyers that call me when they need to speak with me. This time, it was one of the members of the famous "Fabulous Five"!

"We need to talk", he says to me on the phone and requests that I speak to no one about our meeting. He suggests that I go to their dormitory room which was in the next building to mine. His request to meet and talk was more interesting to me than how he found me. I had been walking around the base with my USS Belleau Wood ball cap which could have tipped them off. Maybe the attorneys told them that I was on the base. Since the "Fabulous Five" knew Schindler very closely, I wanted to know who murdered Schindler and for why.

They wanted me to come to their room as soon as I got off the phone, so I hung up and checked in with the DPO in their dormitory building. I was then directed to walk to their room which was the last one to the left. After knocking on the door, I was greeted by two members of the Fabulous Five; Sims and Eastman.

They both appeared frightened, eyes wide open, straight faced and never took their eyes off of me. Sims from Illinois was a short, black guy, kind and quite vocal about how much he knew Schindler. Eastman from Kalamazoo, Michigan was a tall, slender, white fellow who most of the time remained quiet. He allowed Sims to do most of the talking except for the part where he experienced harassment.

They both made it clear that I not tell anyone that they are there in fear that other gay-bashers would find out that they were part of the "Fabulous Five".

Both Sims and Eastman had been taken off the ship in order to protect them from the other "Gay Bashers" who would have possibly taken action by further harassment or worse, killed. Just like me, we were hidden underneath the JAG's order and to testify in court for Allen Schindler's murder.

"Someone wanted me dead", Eastman said in a quiet, concerned voice. He explained the night before Allen Schindler was beaten to death that someone had come to his bunk and punched him in the face. After he had woken up from such a punch, he heard a voice saying, "You better leave the ship before you get killed". By the time he recuperated from the punch and opened the blue curtains that shaded the berthing area lights, the perpetrator had already gone.

Eastman did report the attack to his senior (which is protocol), the senior simply made the incident report "disappear". Such horseplay or brotherly-like teasing is common and expected on long deployments at sea.

Sims didn't disclose any harassment on his part as he was more concerned about the General Court Martial which was ongoing. He did agree with Eastman that harassment was going on around the ship and they were tired of it.

There weren't any women stationed on our ship so that basically threw, what we knew at the time as "Sexual Harassment", out the window. Anyone picking on another shipmate was basically "playing around" or "bullying". If you couldn't get backed up by your buddies on the ship or couldn't stand up for yourself, you became not-Navy-worthy.

If any seniors found out about their juniors being bullied, they would tell them to face them and stand up for themselves. We are soldiers, not civilians. We are government property, expendable. Our seniors are busy themselves and have their own problems to deal with. Unable to take care of your own problems as a soldier meant you would not be able to perform your own job. That was the working environment in the US Navy.

When Eastman reported the incidents of harassment, it fell on deaf ears. I remembered this incident right after I met Allen Schindler which sparked my fear. He was the shipmate that Seaman Knight told me about during the witch-hunt. Eastman had spoken to Schindler about him being bullied or harassed himself, Schindler replied to "bite your lip and take it" since Schindler was supposed to be discharged for being a homosexual. He was on his way home. He had already had a bad reputation with Captain Bradt and Captain Bradt was already pissed off with Schindler. Any further issues that were to come to light would only delay Schindler's discharge as he would have to serve more months on "ship restriction" (the confiscation of a sailor's Liberty Card and inability to leave a ship for a certain number of days, weeks or months).

"Do you know who murdered Schindler?", Sims asks me.

I smirked trying to not reply though I had suspected it was Helvey.

Sims took a deep breath and said quietly, "You know that Helvey was the one who murdered Schindler". Sims explained that Schindler, Helvey and Vins worked and lived close to each other. Schindler had bossy attitude however Schindler was one rank higher with authority.

Helvey didn't like to be bossed around, would get angry and throw fits when he was told to do minimal, administrative or cleaning tasks. After everyone had found out that Schindler was getting out for being gay (a rumor leaked from Schindler's open Captain's Mast), he endured constant harassment from a few others. They called him "faggot", "Queer" and physically pushed him by using their shoulders when they passed in the passageways. This information I learned from Sims is identical to the 900-page report provided by the NCIS from several others who knew Helvey and Schindler. The testimonies did not express or explain who pushed or called-out hate slurs toward Schindler.

"I drank with Schindler two days before he died. He too, said that he was pushed and shoved in the passageways", I said accurately confirming what Eastman and Sims already knew. I wasn't 100% certain that he was being harassed because of his sexuality. I couldn't connect the two. Schindler was a neat, kind, fun guy besides him hitting on me, which made me very uncomfortable. I had no understanding of why another person would push or shove him. If they did, Schindler was over 6-feet and 200 pounds and could protect himself. From my short time knowing Schindler, I would think that he would take punches before throwing them.

Sims defended Schindler's good nature and told me that Schindler would simply bite his tongue or let it slide. He didn't want to escalate the issue. He knew that he was going to be discharged. He was already on Captain Bradt's bad list for causing trouble, such as reporting his sexuality on the Pacific Fleet's secured airways and coming back to the ship drunk. The brass thought of him as a trouble-maker.

I had already knew about those two issues which Schindler caused. It did require Captain's Mass which resulted in Schindler losing his secret security clearance. Before the Captain's Mass, he confessed to Captain Bradt and the XO, Captain Franklin about his sexuality and requested a close hearing. But then a few days later during the Captain's Mast (which was opened for others to hear although Schindler requested a closed Captain's Mast), they acknowledge his homosexuality in front of several others. One of those officials informed this to another and then the rumor spread that Schindler was homosexual.

Sims repeats, "Helvey killed Schindler because he was gay".

Sim's face clearly showed that it affected him. He said that Schindler was a neat guy.

I then told Sims and Eastman that I was to testify a few days later. I had been on standby for quite some time anxious to have the trial end so that I could move on with my life and career in the Navy. Both Sims and Eastman continued to probe for more information, a lot which I did not know at the time or was unable to share with them.

They asked if I saw Helvey's face to which I replied that I was only able to see the type of clothing, build, height and the beating, kicking Helvey did to Schindler. Though Helvey's face was a bit disfigured from the fish-eye, brick wall, I could make out parts of his face. As for Charles Vins, I could not say that I saw him even touch Schindler. Though I wanted Vins to be the accessory to the murder, I wanted to be completely honest with the world and myself to only tell the court what I saw.

Sims and Eastman both said that they were the ones who contacted Rick Rodgers at the Stars and Stripes to sound the alarm about the "gay bashers" harassing them and Schindler. They handed me the newspaper with the article about it which they contributed to. My jaw dropped. The article dated December 13, 1992 wrote that Schindler was possibly murdered for being a homosexual titled "Slain Belleau Wood sailor was homosexual". In addition to that first article written in the Stars and Stripes of the Pacific, they presented other news articles from the LA Times and Chicago Tribune. All of the articles noted that there had been harassment aboard the USS Belleau Wood. The one's being harassed in the articles besides Schindler were Sims and Eastman.

Eastman says, "this case is being closely watched by the media back in the states. You have no idea how important this is back home".

In Japan (and for Americans living outside of America) received news days or even weeks behind. There obviously was no internet and any national newspapers were quickly taken by others on the base.

"Captain Bradt intentionally delayed Schindler's discharge", Sims added. I had my own theories, but Sims had a good point. Though being a homosexual in the Navy was not as extreme as taking drugs, but if anyone had taken drugs, they would not have remained on the ship. Both had equal punishments. They would have been sent to Yokosuka for discharge procedures. Remaining on the ship would have been trumped by being discharged. Since Schindler admitted to being gay, he should have been sent directly to Yokosuka for discharge – not remain on the ship for his earlier punishment by finishing up his "30-day Ship Restriction".

In Captain Bradt's defense, he was preparing for the USS Belleau Wood to leave for the Philippines the night that Schindler was murdered. Such preparations takes weeks. He had a ship and its crew to manage. Being honored to host an admiral added on the stress and limited time to deal with just one sailor complaining about being harassed for being gay. More was on Captain Bradt's radar than just one sailor.

This explanation, I did not share with either Sims or Eastman as they had their own problems: they were being discharged for being homosexual. Though they did not tell anyone of their sexual orientation, they were investigated by the NCIS having known Schindler. When probed and interrogated in connection with knowing Allen Schindler, they admitted being part of the "Fabulous Five" and practicing homosexuality. Entrusting the investigator to more concentrate on the facts of the murder case, their sexuality was included which resulted in their being discharged.

I knew that Schindler had his issues with other shipmates. All of us did. We horsed-around, hazing, getting in verbal disagreements, typical things that I had experienced before entering as well as during my time in the Navy. Schindler shared his same experiences on the USS Belleau Wood. He did hate being on that ship. I knew that he was getting picked on but I didn't know he was getting harassed for being homosexual. I personally couldn't grasp the concept of "being harassed for being gay". I thought he was being harassed because Helvey was simply teasing Schindler. We ended what seemed to be hours long on a friendly note and an agreement that we wanted justice for Allen Schindler. We would only provide facts from our knowledge and pass these onto the attorneys and investigators

## President Bill Clinton Knows

The day before my testifying in the trial for Helvey, the attorneys asked me if I knew Helvey. I explained the story when I was first stationed on the USS Belleau Wood and mistakenly walked on the newly-cleaned deck which Helvey had just swabbed and him yelling at me, threatening to tear-off my arms and slap me with it. He also said he would kill me but people say stuff like that all the time – they don't actually mean it.

One of the attorneys (whom I will intentionally not disclose) asked me if I had spoken to any reporters. Of course no one knew me or who I was. The attorney then tells me that this case has President Bill Clinton watching closely to the case. They then explained the "Don't Ask, Don't Tell" policy which Clinton was possibly considering enacting dependent upon the results of the US vs Helvey trial. I had not known about how important Schindler's death was. As far as I knew, only five people were gay in every branch of the military. Not being acquainted with homosexuals or their struggles, I had no idea that this murder was about to impact thousands of gay service members who were in hiding and hundreds of thousands more back in the United States. Regardless, this trial was to give Allen Schindler his justice.

"The gravity of this trial is very important", the attorney continues. "You should be honest and match that of the statements you made in your testimony. If there is anything else that you would like to add or change, let us know before your testifying tomorrow. Anything not shared with us could incriminate you"

I simply replied, "Understood". Regardless of what Eastman and Sims told me and whatever I felt had no impact with my testimony. I really hoped that they found Schindler's killer and that he would get what he deserved by the laws handed before him.

## Hello Helvey
MAY 21-37, 1993

"It was scary to see the two mothers together", I hear a woman speak on the other side of the wall in the attorney's office where I wait for my turn to testify. They were talking about Allen Schindler's mother, Dororthy Hajdys and Terry Helvey's mother Regina Helvey. The woman's voice behind the wall were discussing the tense moments that both mothers had walked together to get some snacks and cola. She mentioned that they did not say a word to each other but how the air they shared was extremely tense.

Two mothers who loved their sons, gave them birthday parties, loved them with all their hearts just as mothers did, now have mother issues which one of their sons has harmed the other. Just as young mothers who drop their children off at a day care, one has hurt the other and now they must exchange parenting lessons. The day care is now the United States Navy. They both spent years growing them up to be the best that they can be, but without their husbands' help.

"Witte, are you ready?", Marine Captain Maggio asks as he opens the door to his office where I was waiting in my dress, summer-white sailor uniform. I had spent a good hour ironing and preparing for my presence in court today. I double-checked my uniform to ensure its perfection as the whole world waits to witness me. I used the back of my hand to iron-out new, existing wrinkle and polish my left shoe with the back of my right leg and say, "I guess I'm ready".

*The day that I was to testify as the main witness to the murder in my 'summer-whites' uniform.*

Captain Maggio walks out the door as I follow down a decorated hallway to the courtroom. The hallway was decorated with military pictures, historic photographs of the history of the Navy and the Yokosuka Naval Base. Military flags and banners litter the hallway that led to two large, brown doors into the courtroom.

On my way to the large doors to the courtroom, I hear small conversations from a room on the left as large as a public high school and look in. There are rows of tables with civilians writing and recording two tubed-televisions affixed to the wall with their cameras. I look at their large, name plates that are placed in front of them on the table reading; BBC, ABC, NBC, CBS and other major news media. Seeing this confirmed what Sims and Eastman told me a few days ago where they were hiding in the dormitory room. It was indeed a major event. That made me even more nervous. I began to tremble yet I was confident with what I saw. All that I needed to do was answer the JAGs' questions and explain what I saw that night on October 27, 1992.

The doors open and we walk inside the courtroom. The courtroom was large and typical of that of any courtroom. There had to have been thirty people watching the trial. Some relatives of the defendant and Allen Schindler. Others were the media and some other military personnel that wanted to watch history in the making. The prosecutor to the right and the defense team to the left, however there were eight judges dressed in their summer white officer uniforms. I gathered that they had been in the Navy for quite some time noticing their gray hair and the many ribbons which they wore on their chests. Somber expressions from everyone. I looked down and continued to walk through the courtroom.

I reach the witness stand to the left and sat down on a wooden chair which creaked. Now the prosecutors were the furthest away from me and the defense team closer to me on the right. The eight JAG judges were on my left. There were windows lined on the wall behind me situated close to the ceiling rather than within an eye-level. All of the blinds were opened. It was super quiet. I look to the prosecutors and see them searching for papers. Then I look directly to my right where the defendant was sitting within a few arm-length of my chair. There he was – Terry Helvey.

Helvey was motionless. He had his hands in his lap and his head down. His eyes were looking down and rarely blinked. He too was wearing the identical, summer-white sailor uniform, the same ribbons of achievements that I was wearing on my chest. We appeared all the same on the outside yet completely different inside the uniforms we wore.

My heart began to pound hard and fast with both fear and anger. This man sitting within two arm-length had done something horrific. It changed who I was. He was the reason why I continue to smell blood and recall the memories of the murder. His actions woke me up from sleep, sweating profusely from the nightmares that have haunted me. I wanted to jump over the two shallow wall dividers that separate us and beat him. The fact that Dorothy Hajdys (Allen Schindler's mother) was present and thinking about what impact this had on her was heavy on my mind as well. It was very hard to imagine what she had been going through since she had lost her son.

Before I was able to try to prepare myself, the prosecuting attorney Captain Maggio calls out my name, "Witte, state your name, rank and ship for the court to recognize you…"

I looked away from Helvey and looked at Captain Maggio. I paused.

In a shallow, shaken voice I replied, "Seaman Witte, MSSN, USS Belleau Wood LHA-3".

Captain Maggio continues establishing by asking how long I was stationed on the USS Belleau Wood, what I did, where I was from and so on.

Captian Maggio then begins to ask questions about my relation the murder, "How do you know Helvey?"

Unsure of how to answer, I said, "I only know him when I saw him stomping on Schindler"

A few gasps from the spectators sound off. Captain Maggio comments in private to one of the eight JAGs in private on what I had said, then returns to say in a lowered voice, "We are jumping the gun here". He returns to his table to create another question which does not imply that I saw Helvey's face when he was jumping on Schindler.

Captain Maggio walks away from his table and towards me but not as close as Helvey was sitting from me, asks me, "Tell us from your story what were you doing before you walked to the restroom".

I explain that I was with PO3 Martinez that night for a few drinks before we headed back to the ship. I told the court that I had one beer at one of the bars and bought another beer at the convenience store and walked with the beer as I drank it to the park. Once my story reached the time that I walked up to the fish-eye brick wall, Captain Maggio's voice became softer and says, "In your own words, please tell us what happened...take your time".

I took a deep breath and began explaining the sounds I heard which sounded as if two people were having sex. Knowing that I have seen such things in that park before, it was ignored and proceeded to the bathroom. I recalled what I saw through the fish-eye brick wall which was a man dancing and jumping up and down with great force. Every time the man jumped back up, his arms were spread out to gain more momentum, more force.

Captain Maggio interrupts me and asks, "explain what the person was wearing". In every detail I could remember, I explained Helvey's clothing; jean jacket, blue jeans, tennis shoes, ball cap, over six feet and quite large. I did capture his face though it was distorted by the fish-eye brick wall. I was able to recognize his face as I had been a few feet from the wall on the other side.

Captain Maggio then asks, "Can you identify the man you saw though the clear, fish-eye, brick wall in the courtroom?"

My answer was simple. "This guy right here", I answered as I point directly to Helvey. Everyone in the courtroom looked at Helvey but he still remained in his exact position as he did when I entered the courtroom – hands in his lap, his head facing the slightly downwards and his eyes lowered.

The courtroom then became eerily quiet for a good thirty seconds. I continued to look at Helvey and my perception and calmness just lost it. I had monsters inside of me needing to release. All of these bad feelings bottled inside of me for months, all the paranoia, smell of blood, my emotions (sort of) pure as any 19-year old could have had and the loss of my religion was caused by Helvey were starting to come to the surface and straight out of my mouth.

I felt that I needed to tell Helvey in-person what I thought. He wasn't looking at me as I stared at him. Out of line and out of order, I verbally told him in a subtle voice only allowing a few people nearby Helvey to hear me say, "You know you did it. You know you killed Allen Schindler". Helvey still remained in his same position. He said nothing to my accusation.

"That is all", Captain Maggio ends his deliberation. Captain Maggio did ask me many detailed questions but not enough for me to remember and not anything new to what I wrote in this book. It was a fast questioning and answering, though. Still, throughout my standing trial, Helvey did not move at all.

"Witte, thank you for coming today. I will ask you some questions and I hope that you can accurately explain them", the defense team Lieutenant Jacques Smith says.

"Yes, sir.", I replied.

Back and forth, Lieutenant Smith asks questions about my personal history before joining the Navy. These types of questions didn't seem to have anything to do with this case. I could only think that he was trying to establish some type of leverage so that my being a witness might be less credible. Lieutenant Smith asking and probing for answers to my personal life generated anger inside of me. I felt that I was being accused. He too, could see that I was becoming agitated. He seemed to have liked that. I tried to answer his basic questions like the relationship that I had with my parents, my friends and so on. Every time he would ask a question, I would look around at the spectators watching the trial. Everyone had their eyes on Lieutenant Smith and me except for two people in the back of the courtroom. Allen Schindler's mother, Dorothy Hajdys and his sister Kathy Eickhoff were both sitting together at the furthest in the room crying and holding each other. I remembered seeing them in a photograph which Schindler showed me two nights before he was murdered where Schindler got mad at me when I asked if that girl in his photograph was his girlfriend. He missed them and now they will miss him forever.

## Allen Schindler's Autopsy Report
### (AUTOPSY REPORT TAKEN ON OCTOBER 29, 1992)

Allen Schindler's autopsy report had already been announced and his corpse was shown to the eight judges on the panel:

1. Contusions on forehead

2. Contusions on nose

3. Contusions on left cheek

4. Contusions on eyes

5. Dried blood on his entire facial area.

6. Both eyes were swollen shut.

7. Dried blood on and in both ears.

8. 2-inch laceration above eight eye, under right brow

9. Two 2-inch laceration above left eye, under left brow

10. 1-2 inch laceration no the bridge of nose

11. ¼-inch laceration on front right scalp area.

12. 1.5-inch laceration 4-inches above right ear with contusions.

13. Laceration and swelling of the bottom lip.

14. Lacerations and contusions on tip of tongue.

15. Sunken bridge of the nose, nose abrasion.

16. 1-2 inch abrasion with surrounding contusion on the throat and neck.

17. Abrasion located and surrounding contusion 22-inches from the top of head and 12-inches from his left shoulder and 4.5-inches from his mid line.

18. An inverted "Y" laceration 4-inches from right ear towards his rear scalp.

19. Liver pulverized from multiple lacerations.

20. Multiple front and rear contusions on right and left lungs.

21. 8 broken ribs (5 on right and 3 on left)

22. Heart's aorta was torn (examiner states that 20 G force needs to occur for this type of injury).

23. Bleeding in bladder

24. Hemorrhaging of neck muscles

25. Bruising of thyroid cartilage

26. Bleeding inside the trachea.

27. Factures of the bridge of the nose

28. Fractured eye orbits

29. Shattered maxilla (upper jaw, eye sockets and nose bridge)

30. Right and left temporal lobe contusions

31. Left occipital contusions

32. Lacerated penis

Allen Schindler's lacerated penis was caused by Helvey who had surprised Schindler as he was urinating. By the results of how we found his body, Apparently another area where Helvey stomped unlike what the media mentioning that his penis was intentionally cut by Helvey.

I continued to watch Dorothy and Kathy wipe their tears. Dorothy rubs Kathy's back comforting her with her left hand fighting to keep her composure. I thought that nothing in the world could ever break Dorothy. Through the largest part of her life, she had been through a lot and was trying her best to be strong through the trial. I was amazed at her courage.

I held back my own tears looking at Dorothy and Kathy wiping their tears hearing my story. The sight of them distracted me from answering the defense team. Lieutenant Smith got right to the point and asks me in a tone that perhaps I didn't see anything.

"Witte, what did you see when you looked into the bathroom?", he asks.

"Blood..a lot of blood", I answer.

Lieutenant Smith asked again as if he didn't like the answer I gave him, "What did you see!?", he says louder and angrily.

I look at Dorothy and Kathy again. They begin to cry harder. Lieutenant Smith yells out my name, "Witte, answer the question!" From that point, I lost my respect for those in authority. I couldn't understand why it was important to describe the horrible, embarrassing, graphic results of how Schindler appeared lying on the bathroom floor while his poor mother and Kathy cried more loudly.

"Witte!", Lieutenant Smith yells at me again. I was disappointed with Smith. He was one of the five officers looking for me in Sasebo and had promised to take care of me, but now he was ripping me apart, yelling at me, trying to destroy my demeanor and now further hurt Schindler's mother and sister. I then...had enough. I exploded. I simply had lost it.

"I just said there was a lot of blood!", I yelled back at Lieutenant Smith. Then I looked at Helvey and began yelling at him, "You f**king did it! You f**king killed Schindler, you piece of sh*t! You know you did it!"

Though Helvey had already confessed to killing Schindler, I just wanted to voice my feelings about it. He was either going to be in prison for life or executed. It would have been the last and only chance I would have the opportunity and I had to tell him how I felt.

Still, Helvey remained in the same position with his head down, his eyes further down with his hands in his lap. He obviously felt very badly. He never looked up. Never flinched.

I was ready to jump over to him and fight him. I briefly stood up with my hands on the arms of the wooden chair.

I then hear Dorothy and Kathy crying more and making whimpering sounds. It was enough. It was obvious that Helvey was guilty of murder. There was no reason to explain the graphic details as Schindler's mother and sister listen.

Without warning, I kicked the witness booth, stood up and said, "F**k you! I've had enough!"

I walked out of the witness booth, slammed-open the small doors that separate the JAGs and attorneys to the spectator booths and walked hastily between the two sides until I got to the doors that separated the court and the military-decorated hallways. I slammed open the brown wooden doors and headed out of the building.

The exit that I made from the courtroom was inappropriate and I should have been apprehended or even jailed for leaving abruptly and not excused by the court, I just couldn't take it anymore. My yelling at Helvey demanding him to admit it was too late. He had already confessed to murdering Schindler the day after he was killed. During all that time from the murder up until my testifying, I had no idea that he had already confessed. With all of the stress that I had been under for months and for me to detail how Schindler laid dying gruesomely in front of his mother, it felt unnecessary to stay any longer. All that was being discussed in the courtroom did not benefit Schindler or his family. It only was to reiterate how Hevley murdered Schindler.

## May 27, 1993

Three days later, Helvey was back in court for his sentencing. He was given a life sentence for unpremeditated murder with hard labor at the Fort Leavenworth Disciplinary Barracks serving his term at the Federal Correctional Institution in Greenville, Illinois, Register number: 13867-045 before being eligible for parole each year. He serves with other famous inmates such as James J. "Whitey" Bulger (famous mobster), Thomas Silverstein (Former gang leader for the Aryan Brotherhood) and John "Sonny" Franzese (the Underboss of the Colombo crime family and the oldest living American gangster in the world). Fort Leavenworth had also housed famous inmates such as Machine gun Kelly and James Earl Ray (who assassinated Martin Luther King Jr.).

Dorothy, Allen Schindler's mother, did not want Helvey to be executed as she wanted Helvey to think for the rest of his life of what he had done to her son. She also did not want Helvey's mother to endure the pain which Dorothy had of her son being dead. Maybe the power of a mother is stronger than any level of court as Dorothy got what she hoped for Helvey. And Dorothy has said through her raising her son Allen Schindler, "I don't care if you're my husband, you don't mess with my children".

Charles Vins, the so-called, "co-conspirator" was only given a 78-day prison sentence (in exchange for his testifying against Helvey), reduce rank to E-1 (the lowest), forfeiture of all and future pay and given a "Bad Conduct Discharge" for his testimony against Terry Helvey. He was mostly prosecuted for not reporting a serious crime which is not clearly defined in the Uniform Code of Military Justice (seeing a murder or seeing someone steal a piece of candy are not clearly defined).

The days following, reporters from all over the world (especially from the United States) gathered in front of the Yokosuka Naval Base gate. Where once curious Japanese girls hope to get a glimpse of

American life behind the gates are now the international center point for homosexuals being harassed and equal rights advocates ensuring that in the years to come, homosexuals can equally serve alongside other military personnel in an equal right employment.

By the end of the week, everything about the murder trial faded just as relationships between sailors and local women around the base. No other information was relayed to me by the attorneys. The case was closed. Helvey was then sent to Fort Leavenworth to begin his life sentence with hard labor. Vins returned to Illinois just as Dorothy and everyone carried on with their lives.

## September 14, 1993

Weeks after the United States versus Helvey trial ended, I continued my night watches, securing doors and perimeters. Once my watch was ended, I'd go out to drink at the bars in "The Honch" just right outside and across the street from the main gate. It was repetitive, but I found myself affixing my habit in doing nothing and then drinking alcohol the rest of the time. And a lot of it.

Alcohol began to take over my life. The medication which the psychiatrist prescribed worked against me so I stopped taking them. By achieving a certain level of drunkenness was enough to rid the feeling and pain that had consumed my mind, heart and perspective in life. No one had answers. Though meeting the psychiatrist and a counselor only helped me understand the few of the PTSD symptoms. We all agreed that we caught it way too late. At the age of 18, it would forever be present in my mind and uncontrollable

The symptoms a part of my response to future experiences. Day after day and week after week, we would meet together to learn how to respond naturally without any intrusions of the PTSD symptoms getting in the way.

What I really wanted was to go back to my original ship, the USS Belleau Wood and return to the fun life and adventures that I had with my shipmates. The Navy is all that I knew and loved before the fateful night of the murder. Besides my PTSD symptoms, there wasn't anything wrong with me. Heck, a large portion of active military personnel had PTSD and still served. Why not me?

A request for my presence in the administrative building was given to me on one of the weekdays that I had off.

"Finally!", I said to myself, excited to get my orders out of the JAG's witness protection and back onto my ship in Sasebo. I was so excited that I packed my gear ahead of going to the admin building. I walked happily and confidently from the dormitory building to the admin building, which was located close to the main entrance of the main gate of the base. Being a bit nervous, I stopped for a drink at the water fountain, walked over and sat on the brown bench. With my sailor cap in my hand, I waited anxiously until my name was called by the Yeoman (clerk).

"Witte, please sign here", the Yeoman says.

"What is this?", I asked. What the yeoman handed me was not official orders, a lot larger actually and had more pages than general orders.

"Your request for honorable discharge was approved", the yeoman replies.

It was a shocking moment as this was something which I had not expected.

"What is this?!", I exclaimed. My 4-year term was cut short because of Helvey murdering Schindler!? It wasn't fair at all. I was not signing for this and it was clearly marked on my expression and in my eyes as if I were going to jump over the counter and beat the yeoman. The yeoman matched my expression as if we were ready to brawl in the office.

The Yeoman leveled with me not as a clerk, but as a shipmate or brother, "Dude, you're very lucky to have this. Do you know how many sailors would love to have this opportunity?"

"I ain't sign'n", I stubbornly concluded.

Still, I wasn't signing. There was no reason for not having me back with my ship and brothers aboard the USS Belleau Wood. Having refused signing and not knowing what my next actions were, I returned to the brown bench and sat down.

The yeoman returns to his desk and about ten minutes later, I am greeted by two men in civilian clothing who bring the documents that the yeoman asked me to sign. They were military but were not wearing their uniforms. One was wearing a yellow Polo shirt and khakis while the other one wore a blue, buttoned-up shirt and jeans, tucked into his jeans. They both were white, blond and brown hair. I first assumed that they were officers.

Both the men introduced themselves by their first name (which I have forgotten), not their rank and last name which was un-military-like. It was really confusing to know who they worked for but they seemed important.

Neither one of them smiled. The gentleman in the yellow Polo sat to my left on the bench and the other with the blue, buttoned-up shirt sat to my right. This man spoke the majority of the time and told me that there were still people in the fleets and Naval installations that didn't like homosexuals. There was change happening in the military (Army, Air Force, Marine, Navy, Coast Guard) but during this change, they thought it would be in my best interest and safety to leave the military.

I felt guilty for no reason. I wasn't gay, I didn't kill anyone and I upheld the Uniform Code of Military Justice. I was very mad.

"Why do I have to resign!?", I yelled at them.

The man in the blue, buttoned-up shirt said, "You don't have to sign and you can go back but not to your ship."

He also explained that my name was known and some people in the military who hated or disliked homosexuals could seek revenge. I couldn't believe that this was valid information but in his tone, he sounded concerned.

I felt that I had gotten the short end of the stick. Trying to persuade the two men to allow me to remain hidden on the Yokosuka Naval Base until things quiet down from the murder trial, they still couldn't guarantee my safety.

"When will this so-called transition be finalized?", I asked in a whimpering voice.

"It's hard to say now, but our president's administration (Former President Bill Clinton) is working on this and changing the military's position in regards to homosexuals in the military.", the man in the blue, buttoned-up shirt says. What was for certain was that they couldn't let me back to my home on the USS Belleau Wood.

He continued to explain that our ship the USS Belleau Wood known in the fleet as being one of the roughest ships in the Pacific, was also going through some type of "cleansing" of those who disliked homosexuals, interviewing sailors on their character and opinions about homosexuals serving and living closely together.

As the murder that happened only seven months ago, the feelings of fear and anxiety was still fresh. In some way, I felt that I could be prone to harassment by those who disliked homosexuals and those who defended homosexuals openly serving in the military. I personally have no opinion either way as such sexual practices (either straight or gay) are left in the bedroom and in privacy. Just as anyone who loves their country and gives their lives protecting our country, I wanted to do the same. I did not however, want to be pushed to either side's agendas. That was where I was forced to be. When I explained this to the two men who sat with me on the wooden bench, they understood however, they could not protect me.

Not knowing the real reasons for Schindler's death at that time nor knowing who else was in the military that would find out about my testifying and possibly do harm to me, I signed the document allowing me to Honorably Discharge from the United States Navy.

I remained hidden and my location unknown until I was officially and honorably discharged from the Navy at Treasure Island which closed in 1997.

# CHAPTER 17

# PTSD AND ME ARE FRENEMIES

## 1993-1995

"What do you think about gays?", the new crew of officers who were assigned to the USS Belleau Wood asked many of the ship's sailors. "I f**king hate them", some sailors answered and is soon met with administrative discharges. The majority answers, "They don't bother me. As long as they keep to themselves, no big deal".

This new sweep or "cleaning of the ship" to get rid of sailors who discriminated against gays was an initiative by the new captain who replaced Captain Bradt. The Navy wanted each and every sailor vetted to reflect the values of the United States Navy and the Uniform Code of Military Justice. To cleanse the ship and its culture from top to bottom, they had to force Captain Bradt into retirement and assign him to shore duty in Florida. Harassment was never allowed in the military nor will it ever!

From my shipmates who remained on the ship told me that this captain was quite an a**hole which frightened many of the sailors. They had no idea why Captain Bradt had left the ship and why they were serving underneath d*ck of a captain. As far as they knew, the killers, the Fabulous Five, Captain Bradt and I simply disappeared. The new captain was focusing on changing, what was known as the "roughest ship in the pacific" to a more progressive one. He was very strict, tight, and did not accept any type of harassment what-so-ever. Any mention of homosexuality or teasing was met by a force of officer who would either sternly scold and belittle the sailor for harassment or discharge them.

Many of my shipmates I left behind on the ship endured this tight-ship culture that was unlike no other ship until they were assigned to another ship, shore duty, retirement or kicked out for behavior, unbecoming to a soldier. I'm quite certain that if I had remained on the ship and would have most likely fully transitioned into a Master-at-Arms like Szerlag. But I had already signed the documents to leave the military early. If I hadn't coincidently witnessed Allen Schindler's murder, I would have made a career out of the Navy. It was a wonderful opportunity that was disrupted by one of the biggest conspiracies in the military and regretted signing the Honorable Discharge documents...or would I have been killed instead?

After arriving back in Texas as a civilian with just an Honorable Discharge, I stayed with my family to figure out what my next steps were. I decided to cook at a local restaurant in the meantime to save up for my first car (my second car if we include my first girlfriend, Yukiko). It was a piece of s**t, 1987 Golf Volkswagen. Every time I would stop at a stoplight, the steering wheel would come out. I'd have to jimmy it back into the steering column as fast as I could before the signal turned green. My pay was s**t, my car was s**t, my life was s**t and I was still living with my parents. I took this as a blessing however as I could have been dead. I simply pulled up my big boy pants and worked hard every day trying to save up money.

This continued on for a few years and was finishing up my college in 1997. By then, I met another Japanese girl named Mayumi who was studying English as a second language at Rice University, close to where I worked as a sous chef at an Italian restaurant called "Baci". It was a famous restaurant where I cooked for celebrities such as Jeff Goldblum, Ron Howard, Billy Gibbs, Ted Danson and others who were well-known in the 1990s. I had the honor to work with a waiter who only waited tables for a few weeks named Jim Parsons before he became famous. Some may know who this fellow is but those who don't, he was an actor on the "Big Bang Theory" that played the part as Sheldon. He was attending the University of Houston a few miles away and was working part-time with us at the restaurant.

Jim was obviously gay in his appearance and character. He was happy, humble and very open about it by his feminine tone and his body movements. Several workers and cooks would tease him however, Jim didn't mind at all. He already accepted who he was and simply didn't care.

At the end of the night, after the cooks cleaned up from dinner and the waiters set the tables for tomorrow, we would raid the bar and drink a few beers. Jim, as we know now, was hilarious! He was very kind, thoughtful, smart, quick and very, very funny. In one of the Big Bang Theory episodes, Season 6, episode 4, Sheldon competes with his friends eating a blueberry pie. He subsequently gets one in his nose and shouts, "Blueberry in my nose, Blueberry in my nose!" This same situation happened on one of the nights at the Baci restaurant when we were drinking. Instead of a blueberry, it was a cannellini bean.

"It's in my nose, it's in my nose!", Jim shouts as he runs off into the bathroom to blow it out. Till this day, I have no idea why he would do that, but it was absolutely hilarious! I cannot remember every laughing that hard in my life to the point where I almost pissed my pants! Not only Jim getting a bean stuck in his nose was hilarious, but his reply and stories were very entertaining. He was very likeable and difficult to dislike.

There was some harassment towards Jim from other workers, unfortunately. Some of the cooks didn't like him cause he was too openly gay. I remained reserved. I never had a good influence on gays growing up, hearing how dysfunctional they were and their flamboyant lifestyle. Strangely, Jim Parsons and Allen Schindler were the only two gay people I have met in personally, that I am aware of. And they were both really kind, friendly, fun, honest people. I couldn't speak ill about either of them. During that time in my life, I didn't know what to say or how to react when someone tells me that they are gay or is known for being gay. Regardless, Jim made us laugh and seemed like a great guy to end a work shift with.

"Let's go to Bingo-Bango bar!", Jim exclaims. I forgot the name of the bar but it was well-known as a gay hangout which was located off of Montrose Blvd and West Alabama street just south of downtown Houston. Since my last experience drinking with someone who was gay didn't end to well, I was extremely hesitant to go drink with Jim and the other waiters to the point where I began to smell blood again. My heart started racing and I became angry inside myself.

Trying to validate my feelings, I asked Jim, "I don't want to go to a gay bar". Jim smirks at me as you see him in the Big Bang Theory and replies, "We don't go to the bar to f**k people, we go there to dance… you should come! You'll have fun, trust me". I had no experience on how to reply to Jim's suggestion so I stumbled on my words. I simply just watch Jim and the waiters and waitresses leave for the gay bar excited and happy. I simply went home. I regret not going out with the others and with Jim. It would have been a great time...

Two weeks later, Jim quit and as others who we briefly met on the way of our journey, he disappeared into his own.

## The Conspiracy Continuation

Mayumi and I were now in a more serious relationship. I completed my college and was working every day at Baci Restaurant. The restaurant was preparing to close due to the owners getting arrested for secretly dealing cocaine in large quantities while using the restaurant as a front (simply what I heard). I had no future so I felt that it would be a great opportunity to move back to Japan with Mayumi and start a life as an English teacher teaching Japanese, American English.

It was quite easy to find work as an English teacher in Japan during the 1990s as the only qualifications were that you were American and had a degree. They pay was pretty good and the hours were just about at 35 hours a week – just enough for English language companies to get out of paying teachers' social insurances. This ended up being a very, very bad idea since that allowed me plenty of time to think and feel which resulted in my heavy drinking and writing short stories and poetry...emotions which I laid on paper.

During these years, the internet became part of the world's furniture – a commodity. For answers to the 'whys' of Allen Schindler's murder, I did my search.

Basically, the only information which I found turned out to be repeats of the news about Schindler's murder. Some were exaggerated by saying that five people killed him to Helvey and Schindler were lovers. All were false. But that's the internet.

Searching further, I was shocked to come across something which some of us sailors aboard the USS Belleau Wood suspected: "Schindler was hunted, selected by our superiors to be the next one thrown off the ship. He was a distraction from the USS Belleau Wood becoming a flag ship, the best ship in the pacific fleet."

It was a rumor that perhaps, rang true.

The night of the murder, the ship's XO, with Captain Bradt behind him smoking a cigar, threatened that "If I told anyone about what happened that night, that something similar would happen to me".

I read this letter a billion times written by the Deputy Director, at Appellate Defense Division, Navy-Marine corps, Appellate Review Activity to the Secretary of the Navy which was published in 1999.

JAG/045
31 Mar 99

Honorable Richard Danzig
Secretary of the Navy
1000 Navy Pentagon
Washington, D.C. 20350-1000

Dear Secretary Danzig:

Mr. Bruce Tyler Wick, an attorney from Westlake, Ohio, has been retained by Terry M. Helvey, a sailor currently serving a sentence to confinement at the United States Disciplinary Barracks, Ft. Leavenworth, KS. Mr. Wick contacted me during fall, 1998, when I was then Deputy Director, Appellate Defense Division, Navy-Marine Corps Appellate Review Activity.

Terry Helvey's case has been reviewed and affirmed on appeal before military courts. Terry Helvey wrote your predecessor in 1997, asserting that his participation in the death of Allen Schindler was part of a larger conspiracy by Navy leaders to eliminate undesirables from the ship on which Helvey served. After this letter, Terry Helvey was visited at the Disciplinary Barracks by one of the Naval Criminal Investigative Service agents who had investigated his case, who advised Terry Helvey that he was suspected of conspiracy to commit murder. Terry Helvey, after advice of Miranda rights, chose to say nothing further.

Mr. Wick was then retained, and has become familiar with the facts of the Helvey case. Through a series of letters and telephone calls, he has made a great effort to gain an audience with Naval officials with the authority to direct a serious, open-minded investigation into allegations by Terry Helvey that Allen Schindler died as a result of the specific instructions of superiors who had recruited him as a ship-board enforcer – revelations he chose not to make at trial out of a misguided sense of loyalty to the very superiors who directed his actions.

Mr. Wick's repeated efforts were met by repeated refusals by those in authority to actually consider the possibility Terry Helvey was, in fact, following orders. His efforts were also met by a Navy position that Terry Helvey was the property and problem of the Army, not the Navy, since he is confined at Fort Leavenworth and his discharge from the Navy has been executed.

*Though hard to read, this was the exact letter sent to the Secretary of the Navy in 1999 hinting that Helvey was elected to murder Allen Schindler because he was gay.*

It reads:

*31 March, 1999*

*"Mr Bruce Tyler Wick, an attorney from Westlake, Ohio has been retained by Terry M. Helvey, a sailor currently serving a sentence to confinement at the United States Disciplinary Barracks, Ft Leavenworth, KS. Mr. Wick contacted me in Fall 1998, when I was then a Deputy Director, at Appellate Defense Division, Navy-Marine corps, Appellate Review Activity.*

*Terry Helvey's case has been reviewed and affirmed on appeal before military courts. Terry Helvey wrote your predecessor in 1997, asserting that his participation in the death of Allen Schindler was part of a larger conspiracy by Navy leaders to eliminate undesirables from the ship on which Helvey served. After this letter, Terry Helvey was visited at the Disciplinary Barracks by one of the Navy Criminal Investigative Service agents who had investigated his case, who advised Terry Helvey that he was suspected of conspiracy to commit murder. Terry Helvey, after advice of Miranda rights, chose to say nothing further.*

*Mr. Wick was then retained and has become familiar with the facts of the Helvey case. Through a series of letters and telephone calls, he has made a great effort to gain an audience with Naval officials with the authority to direct a serious, open minded investigation into the allegations by Terry Helvey that Allen Schindler died as a result of the specific instructions of superiors who had recruited him as a ship-board enforcer*

*- revelations he chose not to make at trial out of misguided sense of loyalty to the very superior who directed his actions.*

*Mr. Wick's repeated efforts were met by repeated refusals by those in authority to actually consider the possibility Terry Helvey was in fact, following orders. His efforts were also met by a Navy position that Terry Helvey was the property and problem of the Army, not the Navy, since he is confined at Fort Leavenworth and his discharge from the Navy has been executed.*

The prosecutors asked for the death penalty for Helvey. Allen Schindler's mother pleaded for 'life imprisonment'. The media reported that Helvey received just that: life imprisonment and eligible for parole in 20 years.

Here's where it gets a bit interesting. An NCIS report (via FOIA) confirms this conversation with Helvey on October 7, 1997 two years before this letter (to the Secretary of the Navy on March 31, 1999) stating that Hevley was getting "Jacked around" by one of the prosecutors and that if Helvey disclosed details and names of those who instructed him to carry out harm to "rough Allen Schindler up" that Helvey would remain in prison for his entire life. If Helvey kept his mouth shut, then the prosecutor would make sure that Helvey's sentence would be reduced to thirty years. No one can determine if this was what the prosecutor said but we can find this coincidental as Helvey is being released in June 2020, minus 3 years for good behavior while serving in prison...this adds up to the year 2023.

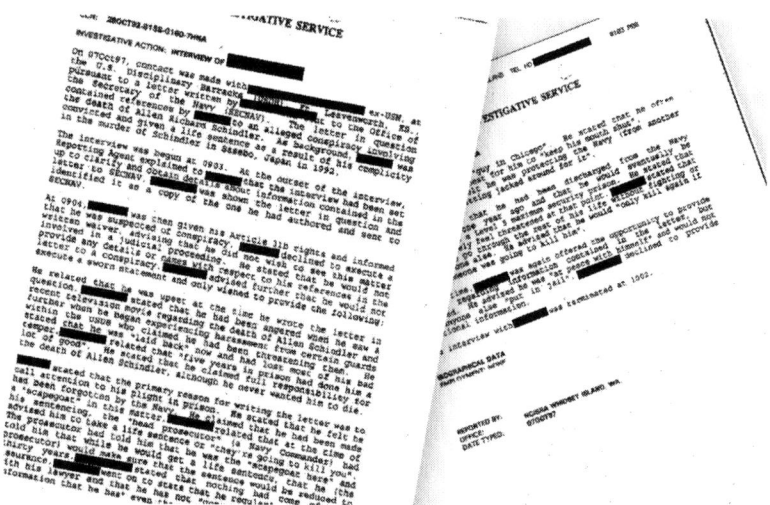

"Released under the FOIA (Freedom Of Information Act), NCIS interview with Helvey where he states that he was told by certain individuals, who he would not name, instructed him to "rough Allen Schindler up".

Captain Bradt and XO Franklin already knew that Allen Schindler was homosexual. Allen Schindler was supposed to report to Yokosuka for administrative discharge for admitting his homosexuality however, they made Allen Schindler remain aboard the USS Belleau Wood. But why would any senior officers not proceed with the administrative discharge? Were they unaware of the protocols? Or was there another reason?

Further researching, I happened to stumble upon the "New Port Sex Scandal" in 1919 regarding the Navy's witch-hunt in finding and imprisoning those who engaged in homosexuality. An event which President Franklin Roosevelt oversaw during his term as the Assistant Secretary of the United States Navy. He was never confronted in congress as he began to fall ill from an influenza outbreak on a ship which he visited and the news of his health deterred from the investigation as well as his democratic candidacy for President of the United States. In total, 17 sailors were charged with sodomy in a matter of three weeks. Some of the 17 sailors were held in prison for months without trial in hopes of pressuring those accused to inform Navy investigators of others who were known for being homosexual.

https://en.wikipedia.org/wiki/Newport_sex_scandal

As homosexuality was considered immoral in 1993, anyone who practiced or supported homosexuality in the Navy was considered an "undesirable". To maintain the Navy's reputation and much like hazing for initiations, it became an unspoken rule to not be a homosexual and those who were gay, were rumored to be potentially and physically 'thrown off of the ship" – especially on the USS Belleau Wood.

Without todays social media and internet in the early 1990s educating the society of homosexuality, it was thought if you shared a toilet seat with one who had aids, you too would be infected. The distance between homosexuality and heterosexuality made someone being gay as 'infected' or unsanitary. The Navy loves and supports sanitation so if anyone was to be found out being gay, they would have been arrested and dishonorably discharged.

This information about the Navy getting rid of homosexuals in combination with the letter which Terry Helvey submitted to the Secretary of the Navy made me believe that it could have been possible that the XO and Captain Bradt were ensuring that their ship was not run by gays. It could have been possible that the letter was indeed true and that the XO and Captain Bradt did request Terry Helvey to "rough Allen Schindler up to make him straight again".

Everything began to add up:

1. The captain and XO were knowledgeable with the ongoing harassment on the USS Belleau Wood.

2. Two days before the murder, Allen Schindler opened up to me and explained his situation with the captain. Schindler was supposed to be sent to the 7ᵗʰ Pacific Fleet headquarters for dishonorable discharge however, the captain kept him on the ship exposing Schindler to continuous harassment.

3. When sailors fight or reported (reporting was very rare), all sailors are punished by restricting all sailors ranked E6 and below from leaving the ship or base. After Eastman was hit in the berthing area, the ship did not restrict us.

4. On the night of the murder, the captain threatened Martinez and I to keep our mouths shut about our involvement.

5. The clandestine, four-member team taking me off the ship and to the 7ᵗʰ Pacific Fleet headquarters in Yokosuka without the knowledge of anyone on the USS Belleau Wood.

6. A few months after the trial, Captain Bradt was demoted transferred to shore duty in Florida.

7. In 1919, a special team was recruited to find homosexuals and dishonorably discharge them (known as the 'Newport Sex Scandal').

8. In 1999, Helvey's attorney informs that he was hired to be a 'ship-board enforcer' to 'eliminate undesirables'.

It was more likely a murder conspiracy and not coincidental. But who would believe us enlisted personnel? Could they still be after me though I've been out of the military for less than a decade? If I talked will they come hunt me down and kill me, too?

Churning this possible conspiracy in my head after I had gone through a lot of hell was bringing back the memories which I had tried control for years. It all came flooding back to me again. Hallucinations of skin peeling off of people's faces who were simply walking on the street, the smell of blood again became quite apparent, I was more aggressive, pushing people, kicking over parked bicycles, punching trees, car windows while drivers were stopped at a stop light, buildings and fights were becoming a norm for me in Japan.

At my apartment in Tokyo while brushing my teeth, I could see my face melt, my eyes popping out and the peeling of my skin to where I could see the muscles. It was very real to me back then. It was extremely hard to sleep so in the addition to my 4-6 beer and 2 rum and coke, and Nyquil, I would take another dose of Nyquil until I passed out on the floor or on the sofa. I'd wake up in a cold sweat and sore muscles. Every waking day would seem like a dream and my nightmares during my sleep would be the reality. I literally became a zombie.

There was no help available back then. Even during my panic attacks, which I thought were heart attacks, was met by a laughing doctor who performed a heart examination. His reply, "nothing is wrong with you. Go home". Psychiatrists didn't really exist in the 1990s in Japan so if you were different, they would tell you, "don't be different".

Fine… I just continued on being as I was… a violent, walking time bomb zombie.

The memories and feelings of Allen Schindler's murder, the letter about the possible conspiracy and all the questions which I had about "why he was murdered" played so many scenarios. I felt that I had lost my mind again. And to find my sanity and after my violent and aggressive bouts, I would trespass into buildings to reach the roof and sit on the ledge. I could accomplish my own death to end the continuous thoughts and feelings by getting drunk enough that I'd fall to my death. I'd end up sitting on the ledge of a seven-story building until I got hungry or had to pee which would take me away from my pending thoughts of suicide.

Many times during stressful events, I would smell blood and would purposely shove people or yell "what the f**k are you looking at" at them. I also took on many secret girlfriends and was quite rough with them. All of these feelings and thoughts bottled up with nowhere and no how to let them out with a hint of sanity was not known. I was basically pissed off at humans in general. After I had exerted my feelings and thoughts, the smell of blood would go away. It was a textbook Classical Conditioning that helped my return to civility and sanity.

The aggressiveness, suicidal attempts and infidelity with my then girlfriend would happen many, many times during the many years that I was in Japan. I did not care if I got hurt or if I hurt others both physically and emotionally. I'd intentionally seek out the innocent and twist their worlds into the things that haunted me internally so that I wouldn't feel lonely. It would go to the extremes of hunting wives, dull in their stable relationships and tearing their marriages apart.

One of these wives would frequently return home to her husband with my bite marks on her thighs, neck and breasts explaining to him that she could be pregnant by me – several times. On our on-going affairs, she would tell me how much her husband would cry helplessly. This gave me so much control over pain, though it was someone else's pain I controlled. It made me very happy and further away from my internal pain. This feeling motivated me to use his wife more until it all fell apart when he left her. Then she meant nothing to me and I would move on to another innocent soul to twist and bully. I became the devil himself and I was satisfied happily.

I wanted everyone who was happy, to become unhappy to the extreme without caring about their own hurt and repercussions. In hindsight, I f**king hate myself for doing those things to those poor, innocent souls. There were so many other bad things which I had done that I regret. They were victims of my angst; the results of what Terry Helvey created. But I could not tell good from bad except that bad was more gratifying, exciting and it made me happy to know that there were unhappy people around me. There was response. Evil answered. God didn't do s**t. He just sat back and rolled his eyes at me. I was going down this path of evil, I might as well be good at it. I wasn't good at anything else. It was a distraction from my memories of Allen's murder and the smell of his blood that was always in my nose.

Wash, rinse, repeat. From one innocent soul to the next. It became so frequent and regular that I became bored of it all. I could have sworn that I practically and simply ran out of sperm. Sex in general, just became boring. I destroyed marriages, hurt people to the best of my abilities, I just simply felt that I had already climbed the tallest mountain. Why climb it again? In some self-realization, I needed to do something more creative. Something that would impact the world and not just a marriage or a woman. I wanted to impact the world.

Since the murder of Allen Schindler, I had been writing, well, scribbling down poems that made absolutely no sense (unless you were drunk as I was when I wrote them). It was the only thing that kept me close to the earth. It kept my brain intact. All the emotions and feelings I had all went to the paper.

"I'll tape all 450 poems to my body and jump off the Tokyo Tower", I drunkenly exclaimed on my sixth beer and third rum and coke. It seemed like the perfect idea at the time but I wouldn't be able to see the affect from this action.

## God Sent Angels

As I was in my repetitive cycle of drinking heavily (4-6 beers plus 2 rum and cokes combined with a shot of Nyquil) and numerous affairs, I met a wonderful woman named Ruzelle who would soon become my wife. She was one of the transcribers who I hired that would transcribe my 450 poems and digitize them on digital media. I had planned on publishing them before I was soon to die from all the hell I was living.

She invited me to a Novena which she partly facilitated with her Filipino coworkers in Japan. They were honestly happy. She was happy. I hadn't seen so many happy people all together having fun without drinking.

'Happy' is an understatement. It's just a word which we have over-used, but the way that Ruzelle interacted, reacted with situations, my reactions, words, the world, food, drink, television…she was genuinely happy. She was the definition of happy. She defined the song written by the UK music group "Pet Shop Boys" – "Miracles". Every word written in that song precisely defined how she moved my perspective in the world.

I hadn't met anyone quite like Ruzelle in my life. She had taken the beatings in life and simply moved on. She was confident in herself and saw the world much differently than any other human I met. She was very religious, attended Sunday Catholic mass, prayed before going to sleep and before each of her meals. She was thankful for just the smallest things in life. Things were simple to her. I was jealous of her systematic and simple life. I tested her as I did with every other woman I had before but she didn't react as they did. The type of evilness I gave her meant nothing to her.

She herself already suffered, but she had her own share of pain growing up in the Philippines; drinking rice water after it was used to wash rice instead of baby formula when she was little, sleeping on the ground in a basement while cockroaches and rats ran amuck around her body, no toys for Christmas as her family was living in poverty and skipping meals simply because there was no money to pay for it. She wasn't mad at life for giving her those struggles – she thanked God for giving her life.

When I would get mad at something such as being jealous of others for having a luxurious life, she would simply reply differently by saying, "more money, more problems". I could not react nor reply to her perspective cause she was right. If I saw her getting screwed over by her coworkers, she would simply turn the other cheek and move on whereas, I would find some opportunity to seek revenge.

Her reply was simple and true – why spend time getting angry when you can just be blessed for having a job.

All of her reactions were taught by attending church and she wanted to spend more time with my horrible self that she invited me to go. And so I did every Sunday.

Week-by-week, I felt my life improve. I felt my perspective had changed quite a bit and I was less angry at strangers. I honestly looked up to her for advice and suggestions. When I thanked her, she never took credit. She would simply say, "I am blessed to be alive with the things I have now". She ultimately became the first human who I could trust (outside of my family) with my life!

After a several, fun and happy Novena parties together, Ruzelle and I began to date. A few months later, we were to expect news from two pregnancy test sticks that I was to become a father. It was then that I realized that I needed to become more mature and responsible in preparations for the most wonderful gift God gives – a new life! It became the best opportunity to rid all the horrific events in my experience and make the only possible change in a world which I saw as an evil one.

About a year later, my wife, newborn son Ian and I moved back to the United States and began our life as a family. Six years afterwards, God blessed us with another son, Johan. From these new and wonderful, life-changing events, I was again able to see God's hand. It had been a turbulent, troublesome, dark path that I had been living without God's hand…the hand which I shoved away. He had always been there the whole time however; the darkness overpowered me. I wasn't strong enough to find God alone. The love which my wife and children showed me each and every day gave me the strength to take God's hand. Without them, I would not be alive today.

## The Crusade For It To Be Okay To Be Gay

Allen Schindler's mother Dorothy was picking up the pieces of her broken one. She wonders the reasons for her son's death. She stalks Terry Helvey's petition for release to ensure that he stays in prison although he would be up for parole every year after 2003.

It took almost 20 years after Helvey was convicted of murder before I got the courage to call Allen Schindler's mother, Dorothy.

"Hello?", a warm, fragile voice answers the phone.

"Dorothy? This is Jonathan Witte. Do you remember me?", I asked.

"Of course.", she replied. I couldn't figure out what words I would say next so the line was silent for a bit. But we both knew what we wanted to talk about.

We caught up on all the things we knew about Allen Schindler. When she talked about how wonderful of a person he was, I could hear her voice crack and cry. She was very proud of him. Having met and talked and got to know Schindler two days before his murder, I agreed. If I were to be his coworker at the company I was working at that time, he would have been a wonderful man and a fun person to hang out with.

Dorothy updated me on Terry Helvey by telling me that he had changed his religion to become a Jew so that he could enjoy better tasting food at the Fort Leavenworth prison. Other inmates finding out that he converted to the Jewish religion, they beat him up...the Irony!!!

She was quite disappointed in learning that Terry Helvey was up for parole every year after his initial 20-year sentence though he was to be in prison for life.

"How is that possible!? He killed my son! He should never been given the opportunity to get parole!", she said in her breaking voice.

I agreed with her. It wasn't fair. I continued to tell her the details (besides the grotesque parts) which she never knew about. Honestly, no one ever knew until I wrote this book. It took a lot of bravery for me to call her and was the reason why I hadn't called her in the two decades after his murder. But she needed to know.

Dorothy then explained further that she had been the center-most person in trying to repeal the "Don't Ask, Don't Tell" policy. Though I disagreed with her position, I remained silent. It is a personal perspective but from mine, I never wanted anyone to witness or experience the hell that Schindler and I went through. Life in the military is far abstract and distant from the civilian life which civilians wouldn't understand if they had never been in the military.

Schindler was her son, taken away from her for a very stupid reason and she had every right to exert her emotions and mind productively. And she did a great job articulating her position ensuring that the policy would be repealed.

Michael Petrelis, who is an LGBTQ activist, has dedicated the majority of his life to fight gay hate and who had been heavily involved with the Allen Schindler murder trial by pressuring the Navy for Allen's death. He and Dorothy joined forces to inform the world that it isn't right or human to commit violence towards gays. For decades, they both have been raising awareness of hate crime in the United

States. Still to this day, they are fighting for the rights of homosexuals to be able to openly serve in the US military.

"Witte!", a stale voice calls out to me at the Seattle Veterans Hospital. I was guided into a room with now the fifth psychologist I had seen for my PTSD symptoms. All were simply probing for my experience so that the Veterans Administration would compile in their database. I continually ask for help for my condition but they would all fail.

"You should join a counseling group to share your experience of PTSD with other veterans.", the VA psychologist suggests.

Though it sounds like a good suggestion, it would not work. I never joined the group but already speculated that bullets flying above my head, a shipmate getting shot and dying next to me or a bomb going off around me did not simulate to what I went through.

PTSD affects people differently. I had no stories about being shot at, but I could share how I was hunted and killed by others who I didn't recognize. Schindler wasn't shot, he was practically mutilated with passion. Sure they could share their stories, but I felt I was still being watched if I ever leaked the story. The bullets stopped flying over my fellow veterans' heads but I still had a target on me. I always thought that if Terry Helvey ever got parole, he would be after me or the senior officers would be out to hunt me or lock me up in prison for sharing my story to the world. Perhaps those who still hate gays would be out to get me for siding with homosexuals. Or perhaps, everything has calmed down.

The murder incident still affects me to this day. Sometimes, I cannot tell what is reality, a foggy sight, dream, nightmare or if I'm alive or dead simply walking around the earth. At times, I give up hope and ambition. The world somehow makes me feel horrible, guilty and not worth living. I admit, I still frequently think that my non-stop roller coaster feeling in my stomach which I have every day could easily be resolved with a bullet to my head or a leap from a building...But if I think about how my children would react to my death and how they would deal with their lives afterwards, I give up preparing for my suicide. When I have these suicidal tendencies, I look at my children and watch how innocent they play and smile, I again see purpose to live another day further.

The Veterans hospital provided me with Sertraline, Trazodone, Prochlorperazine Maleate, Hydroxyzine Pamoate, Propranolol and Citalopram. These medications do absolutely nothing to cure me but it does knock me out. I have tried medical marijuana, but that too doesn't work. Playing with my children does cure me but at times, I need time to escape from too much happiness.

## Everyone Is Still The Same

In the later years in early 2000, homosexuality became to be known as simply being different than heterosexuality – not a contagious, unhuman, unsanitary or just a lifestyle. The effects of Allen Schindler's murder, more and more people became vocal to be against gay-bashing and for homosexuality to be acceptable. Gay marriage first became legal in Amsterdam in 2001. Then in 2015, gay marriage became legal in the United States on June 26, 2015. No one died from knowing or shaking the hands of homosexuals in fact, more and more people became happy and to publically admit to yourself and others that you were gay was encouraged.

In 2001, The US Army published a comic book to educate its personnel the protocols to enact when someone "heard" or "Suspected" someone to be homosexual or bisexual either by seeing or hearing comments relating to homosexual acts. Such depictions of these situations would be considered sexually discriminatory. And the consequences for those being considered homosexual were automatically required to start the process for separating from the military.

"*Dignity & Respect*" comic book provided by the Assistant Secretary of the Army for Manpower and Reserve Affairs, Department of the Army. To see the whole comic book, visit http://ep.tc/problems/38/

*"Dignity & Respect"* comic book provided by the Assistant Secretary of the Army for Manpower and Reserve Affairs, Department of the Army. To see the whole comic book, visit http://ep.tc/problems/38/

*"Dignity & Respect"* comic book provided by the Assistant Secretary of the Army for Manpower and Reserve Affairs, Department of the Army. To see the whole comic book, visit http://ep.tc/problems/38/

Success in the Army depends on teamwork. Teamwork flows from trust and confidence between soldiers, leaders and subordinates, and within units. Without trust, cohesion and morale in your unit will suffer.

Each soldier deserves and should expect fair treatment with dignity and respect. Soldiers should expect a safe and secure environment and the support of their chain of command. Harassment of, or threats to, soldiers for any reason has no place in the Army. Such acts are inconsistent with the Army's core values. In exchange, the Army expects soldiers to meet established standards of conduct and performance. The execution of the Army's Homosexual Conduct Policy is based on fulfilling the requirements of public law and sustaining the trust between soldiers, leaders and units.

The purpose of this magazine is to help soldiers and leaders understand the "Don't Ask; Don't Tell" policy. Such understanding is essential to unit cohesion and high performance.

*Our mission is to comply with the law that prohibits homosexual conduct while at the same time*

This magazine is designed to help you understand the Army's Homosexual Conduct Policy and the rights of soldiers and actions of the commander under this policy. It provides examples of the policy in action and includes frequently asked questions and answers.

The sponsor for this publication is the Assistant Secretary of the Army for Manpower and Reserve Affairs, Department of the Army.

*"Dignity & Respect" comic book provided by the Assistant Secretary of the Army for Manpower and Reserve Affairs, Department of the Army. To see the whole comic book, visit http://ep.tc/problems/38/*

This oddly strange comic book not only helped educate the military personnel about harassment and what to do with those who were suspected being homosexual but it also largely angered the LGBTQ community. This further exacerbated the need to change the military's mentality and beliefs about homosexuality. Protests, anger, confusion and concerns were on the minds of Americans as homosexuals were considered equals in the workplace however not fit enough to protect the country that they love. It made no sense.

## My Final Thoughts And Concerns

Here I sit writing this book about the details around my life growing up just as anyone else in the 80s and 90s and the possible murder conspiracy of Allen Schindler, I think that without Allen Schindler sacrificing his life to become honest with himself and others that it's okay to be yourself, gay or straight, our culture would not be where it is today. It shed the light on sexual harassment and hate crime and how deadly the effects had become. People began taking a stand and holding those accountable regardless of individuals or a powerful institution such as the military.

At times we hear those complaining on television or social media on how homosexuals claim that they are discriminated against because they're simply gay, I want to shake them silly and say, "Do you know what happened to Allen Schindler and what he sacrificed!? You have no idea what he gave up to give you the freedom what you have today – both as an American and as a homosexual. Allen Schindler gave his life for both." It is a horrible experience to endure harassment or a joke for being gay and I'm not saying that homosexuals endure nothing, I'm saying that a few have made deadly sacrifices and never had a chance to complain or experience far more outcomes than the majority.

People are quick to judge, especially in the United States. We are however, fortunate to have the right to free express ourselves in any way to tell others who we are. Black or white. Straight or gay. Democrat or Republican. Catholic or Atheist. Unsure how we all became unique and different since we all were born exactly the same. Our mothers loved us with all their hearts. And we loved them. Though we do not agree with how others grew up to be does not give anyone the right to harass, harm or murder them. We all have a purpose in life and that purpose is to live free and happy without prosecution or harm. And as Allen Schindler said; "If you cannot be yourself, then who are you?"

As our culture has changed since 1992 and accepted gay marriage and equal opportunity, this allowed me to open up a bit to others by writing this book. I simply was at the wrong place at the wrong time. I was however, fortunate to have spent time getting to know Allen Schindler and be able to talk with him and share his conversation, the truth and details of his murder so that everyone would know how awesome he was and how he shouldn't have been brutally murdered for simply being gay. If you got to know him as I did, you too would be asking the question; "Why was Allen Schindler murdered if he was such a nice guy who loved to honorably serve his country?"

# EPILOGUE

On July 6, 1993 (only two months after the sentencing of Terry Helvey's murdering of Allen Schindler), Captain Bradt was removed from the USS Belleau Wood, demoted and transferred to shore duty in Florida until his retirement in 1994. Though it is not written anywhere, I was told by a few high-ranking officers versed with the case that he was forced to retire due to his involvement in the Allen Schindler murder for not handling the harassment correctly. He is currently a Docent volunteering on the USS Midway Museum in San Diego, California...ironically, the same ship which Allen Schindler's first happily and proudly served in the Navy before he was transferred to the USS Belleau Wood.

On December 21, 1993, Former President Bill Clinton, along with the Chiefs of Staff conducted a research of homosexuals serving in the military to see if it was safe for homosexuals to serve openly. It was not. Then on February 28, 1994, the "Don't Ask, Don't Tell" policy which required all military personnel to "Not say if you were homosexual or not" and for any other military personnel to "Not ask if another military personnel was homosexual or not". This policy was part of the intake procedure of new recruits and through their whole journey in the U.S. Military.

There were a lot of people who were unhappy when they found out that this policy had been put in place but I thought it would be a great buffer from not allowing homosexuals to serve to allowing them to openly serve. If homosexuals were allowed to serve openly without educating the military of inclusivity and diversity, there would have been a tremendous number of harassments and assaults.

Do note that this incident could have happened outside of the military. I still love the Navy and firmly believe that anyone who wants to serve their country should do so. A lot of young men such as myself during that time either had no money for college, was running out of options after finishing high school or wanted to see the world and adventure! You can still do this and enjoy living in the military. Unfortunately, this incident had to happen to change our American culture to become more acceptable of others who were born differently.

My time in the Navy was an enjoyable one and you can enjoy it as well. Just respect each other. Serve proud. Enjoy the world. Through any adventure through life, you will meet many different types of people. Some you can relate with and others you cannot…But in the end, we all the same.

•••

On May 29, 1994, the first enlisted woman was assigned to the USS Belleau Wood.
https://www.history.navy.mil/research/histories/ship-histories/danfs/b/belleau-wood-lha-3-ii.html

On September 20, 2011, homosexuals were allowed to serve openly in the military.

According to the Family Research Council, there are over 48,000 gay, lesbian and bisexual personnel that serve in our great military force. Since the end of the "Don't Ask, Don't Tell" policy, there has been over 1,600 reports of sexual assaults in the military which 8.2 percent were homosexual in nature.

https://downloads.frc.org/EF/EF10E118.pdf

https://williamsinstitute.law.ucla.edu/wp-content/uploads/Gates-GLBmilitaryUpdate-May-20101.pdf

Since the repeal of "Don't Ask, Don't Tell" policy on September 20, 2011, reports of sexual assaults have doubled

http://www.sapr.mil/public/docs/reports/FY17_Annual/DoD_FY17_Annual_Report_on_Sexual_Assault_in_the_Military.pdf

http://www.sapr.mil/index.php/reports

According to the current Uniform Code of Military Justice article 125 (2018) states that sodomy is still punishable upon acting parties of the same or opposite sex.

http://www.sapr.mil/public/docs/ucmj/UCMJ_Article125_Sodomy.pdf,

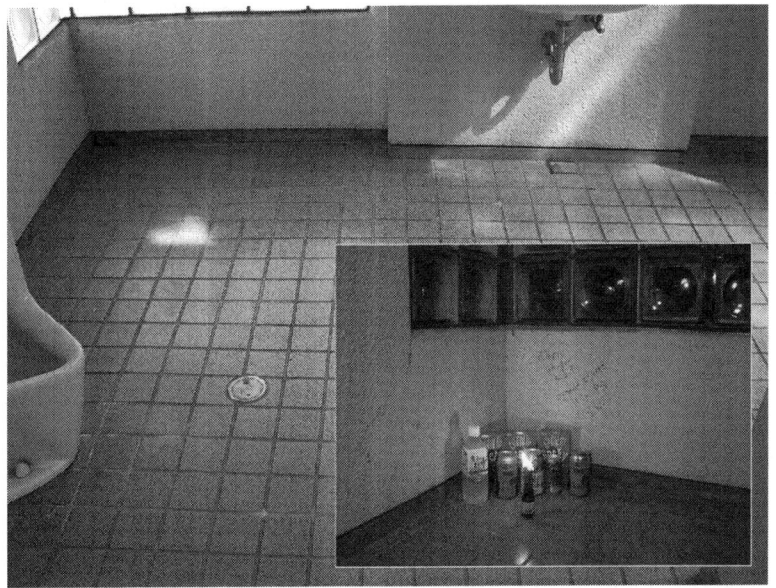

*Schindler left a heart-shaped reflection above where his head once laid.. I made a shrine and got drunk with Allen Schindler's ghost in the bathroom. Picture taken in 2009.*

On July 13, 1993, **Richard Eastman** was accused of obstruction of justice for fabricating the facts (that he was there during the murder, according to his testimony), false swearing, sodomy, rate reduction to E1 and was given 4-months confinement. He received a bad-conduct discharge and released from the Navy.

**Keith Sims** was honorably discharged from the Navy on June 29, 1993

**Richard Eastman**, **Keith Sims** and **Charles Malcolm** ( The "Fabulous Five"), Kurt Parsons, Michael Johnson and NCIS Agent W's locations and occupations are not known.

**Knight** (name is changed to conceal his identity) is still proudly serving in the United States Navy. His rank, rate and location are unknown.

**Szerlag** has since retired as a Master-at-Arms, Chief Petty Officer, USN, happily living in Guam with his wife and family.

**Helvey's** Defense Attorney Lieutenant Jacques Smith, moved into a civilian occupation as a successful private attorney in Washington DC

**Captain Douglas Bradt** is currently a Docent volunteering on the USS Midway Museum in San Diego, California.

**XO R. Franklin's** location is unknown. His name was changed as by exposing his identity could cause serious moral disruption to sailors serving beneath him which could result in security risks.

Allen Schindler's prosecuting attorneys **Major Wilson** and **Captain Maggio's** current locations and occupations are unknown.

Due to the age and reputation of the ship, The **USS Belleau Wood LHA3**, Amphibious Assault Ship was purposely sunk during a RIMPAC exercise on July 13, 2006 and lays at the bottom of the ocean off the coast of Hawaii. Once coined as the "Roughest Ship in the Pacific", the USS Belleau Wood made its way to the bottom of pacific ocean floor, as well as the memories of those who proudly served and lived aboard it.

*(image provided by Ste Elmore from Flicker of the USS Belleau Wood's Sinking)*

**Terry Helvey** became eligible for parole in 2013. He is set for release on June 6, 2022.

**Charles Vins**, for his involvement for "not reporting a serious crime" until after the fact, is free as a civilian after serving only 78 days in a military jail. On February 9, 1993, he was released, given a reduction of rate to E1, forfeited all pay and was given a Bad Conduct Discharge from the Navy in his exchange for testifying against Helvey for the murder of Allen Schindler. Vins is living somewhere in the state of Illinois. He was accused of no other crime.

As for myself, **Jonathan Witte,** am a Senior Product Designer (when working) living in Seattle, Austin and Tokyo with my wife and two children. I am able to handle my PTSD symptoms however I appear to be different, donning my thousand-yard stare. With my PTSD symptoms including hyper-vigilance (the frequent attempting of predicting outcomes of scenarios) has helped me accomplish my career as a Senior Product Designer.

**Dorothy Hajdys-Clausen,** still consumed with pride and love for her son, continues to pursue the truth on why her son was murdered and see that those responsible (for covering up or hiding facts) for his death be held responsible. If you are on her good side, she is a kind and wonderful mother to know.

**Allen Schindler** lays peacefully at the Evergreen Hill Memory Gardens in Steger, Illinois. His happy, passionate, ghost is still in us all.

*"If you can't be yourself, then who are you?"*

—Allen R Schindler (1969 - 1992)

# ABOUT THE AUTHOR

Jonathan Witte is a US Navy Veteran who was stationed in Sasebo, Japan in the early 1990's aboard the USS Belleau Wood LHA-3 Amphibious Assault Ship in the US Navy's 7th Pacific Fleet.

Upon receiving his Honorable Discharge soon after the murder, Jonathan Witte had lived his story and life in silence about the murder and its cover up. Since then, he has found many forms of creative outputs such as writing short stories, poems, producing music. He has shared his story about the murder on the Investigation Discovery Channel's "Deadliest Decades 1990s" Don't Ask, Don't Tell, providing his side of the Allen Schindler story that he may finally close the book for many who had wondered "Why was Allen Schindler murdered?"

in 2004, he found his profession where he could combine creative arts with technologies working as a Senior Product Designer with some of the largest fortune 500 companies.

Such creative expressional outputs have helped him work through his PTSD symptoms as traditional therapy hasn't.

He has resided in Tokyo, Seattle and Austin with his family yet unsure where to call home. When he isn't designing digital products, he spends time with his loving wife and two boys, Ian and Johan.

http://www.JonathanWitte.com/